DATE		

Cambridge Studies in Historical Geography 14

PEASANTS, POLITICIANS AND PRODUCERS

Cambridge Studies in Historical Geography

Series editors
ALAN R. H. BAKER   J. B. HARLEY   DAVID WARD

The series Cambridge Studies in Historical Geography encourages exploration of the philosophies, methodologies and techniques of historical geography and publishes the results of new research within all branches of the subject. It endeavours to secure the marriage of traditional scholarship with innovative approaches to problems and to sources, aiming in this way to provide a focus for the discipline and to contribute towards its development. The series is an international forum for publication in historical geography which also promotes contact with workers in cognate disciplines.

PEASANTS, POLITICIANS AND PRODUCERS

The organisation of agriculture
in France since 1918

M. C. CLEARY

Department of Geography, University of Exeter

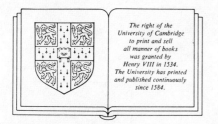

The right of the
University of Cambridge
to print and sell
all manner of books
was granted by
Henry VIII in 1534.
The University has printed
and published continuously
since 1584.

CAMBRIDGE UNIVERSITY PRESS

CAMBRIDGE
NEW YORK   NEW ROCHELLE   MELBOURNE   SYDNEY

Published by the Press Syndicate of the University of Cambridge
The Pitt Building, Trumpington Street, Cambridge CB2 1RP
32 East 57th Street, New York, NY 10022, USA
10 Stamford Road, Oakleigh, Melbourne 3166, Australia

First published 1989

Printed in Great Britain at Redwood Burn Limited, Trowbridge, Wiltshire

British Library cataloguing in publication data

Cleary, M. C.
Peasants, politicians and producers:
the organisation of agriculture in France
since 1918. (Cambridge studies in historical
geography; 14)
1. France. Agricultural industries.
Organisations, 1918–1988.
I. Title   II. Series.
338.1′06′044

Library of Congress cataloguing in publication data

Cleary, M. C.
Peasants, politicians, and producers: the organisation of
agriculture in France since 1918 / M. C. Cleary.
    p.   cm. – (Cambridge studies in historical geography: 14)
Bibliography.
Includes index.
ISBN 0 521 33347 4
1. Agriculture – France – Societies, etc. – History – 20th century.
2. Agriculture, Cooperative – France – History – 20th century.
3. Peasantry – France – History – 20th century.   4. Agriculture and
state – France – History – 20th century.   I. Title.   II. Series.
HD 1945.C58 1989
306.34 – dc 19   88 – 39764

ISBN 0 521 33347 4

RB

Contents

Figures

Tables

Preface

The transformation of rural France since the beginning of this century has been most clearly expressed through the effects of depopulation and the technical modernisation of farming on the landscape. Perhaps less visible, but no less important changes have taken place in the social fabric of farming, in the associations – the syndicates, cooperatives and mutualist groups – of the agricultural community. It is these associations that are the subject of this book. Their history provides an insight into the ways in which peasant and farmer alike sought, through association and cooperation, to influence the character and direction of economic change. In the changing relationships between members of the farming community, their associations and the state, the relationships between peasant, politician and producer, lie the real fascination of the changes that have affected the French countryside this century.

I am grateful to many institutions and individuals for their support and encouragement in facilitating the research for this book. Departmental archivists were always helpful and accommodating during my searches for material in the often labyrinthine Series M. The financial assistance of the University of Exeter and the British Academy is gratefully acknowledged and thanks are extended to Terry Bacon who drew the figures. I owe a particular debt to Alan Baker and Roger Béteille for all their help. Final thanks must go to my mother for all her encouragement and to Marie for her constant support.

Abbreviations

ACJF	Association catholique de la jeunesse française
AGPB	Association générale des producteurs de blé
APCA	Assemblée permanente des chambres d'agriculture
CGA	Confédération générale de l'agriculture
CGT	Confédération générale du travail
CNJA	Centre national des jeunes agriculteurs
CUMA	Coopérative d'utilisation du matériel agricole
FDSEA	Fédération départementale des syndicats d'exploitants agricoles
FNSEA	Fédération nationale des syndicats d'exploitants agricoles
JAC	Jeunesse agricole catholique
JACF	Jeunesse agricole catholique féminine
MODEF	Mouvement de défense des exploitants familiaux
SAFER	Société d'aménagement foncier et d'établissement rural
UNSA	Union nationale des syndicats agricoles

Base map of the départements of France

Introduction

The study of agricultural associations in France is based on both the richness and diversity of their history, and their continued place in contemporary society. The power of the farm lobby in France is testimony to the historical importance of agricultural syndicates, cooperatives and mutual movements; equally, the loud, lively and usually good-natured demonstrations that periodically enliven the streets of Paris or Brussels show that, despite the fall in the size of the agricultural population, its political and economic power remains considerable.

Few, if any, farmers now remain untouched by an increasingly complex network of associations which shape the character and direction of agricultural change. The syndicate, cooperative, Chamber of agriculture and Crédit agricole are integral parts of the administrative, economic and political structures of contemporary rural France. Their views are courted by government, their policies the subject of fierce internal and external debate, and their role as representatives of the economic and social interests of farmers has always been a subject of dispute and controversy amongst farmers themselves. It is the prime task of this book to consider the origins and development of these associations since the end of the First World War. When and where did the agricultural syndicate first develop? What political and economic forces shaped its evolution and underpinned its policies? And how have such policies – towards rural depopulation or the small family farmer or the organisation of the agricultural market – changed over time? How has the cooperative movement developed? What links tied that movement to the syndicates on one hand or the food-processing firms on the other? And when were the chambers of agriculture or the Crédit agricole, such potent forces in the reshaping of the French countryside, first established? How has their role altered over time?

Answers to such questions can best be sought through an examination of the history and geography of these groups. Indeed it is argued that without an appreciation of how such groups have evolved, without a sensitive and

1

contextual examination of their roots and preoccupations, an understanding of their contemporary role and importance is greatly impoverished. This book therefore seeks to provide both a history of agricultural groups and some indications of their contemporary character and policies; it attempts to show how the history of these movements is of interest, not only for the light it can shed on the transformation of rural France this century, but also because understanding that history deepens our appreciation of their contemporary importance.

A further element structuring the book is the attempt, wherever possible, to situate national developments in a regional and local context. Divorced from that context, national accounts of syndicalism, mutuality or cooperation run the risk of becoming reduced to administrative histories of presidents, executive committees and changes in minute-book regulations. As Samuel has argued, 'the General Secretary walks in and out, a familiar figure; the rank and file, on the other hand, remain anonymous, a dark outsider, and appear in the record only as troublemakers . . . or members in arrears'.[1] Such problems, intrinsic to the nature of historical evidence, can never be wholly overcome. It is possible, however, through the use of archival records, newspapers and personal interviews, to try to correct the centralist, administrative bias of some organisational histories. Detailed work on agricultural associations has been undertaken in a number of departmental archives in the hope that such material, seemingly parochial and obscure, can greatly illuminate their origins, development and current character. This work – in Aisne, Aveyron, Charente, Côtes-du-Nord and Landes – does not pretend to provide histories which are 'typical' of the movements. But their different economic and political contexts do, it is hoped, reinforce the importance of local and regional work in examining the development of these varied groups.

In order to situate the emergence and evolution of agricultural associations in their economic context, chapter 1 provides a summary account of the main facets of rural change this century. It does not seek to provide a fully comprehensive account – other works more than adequately cater for that need – but rather it highlights three aspects of those changes: demographic change, the evolution of landholding and the technical modernisation of farming. In the transformation of peasants into producers these three elements were of central importance. Chapter 2 reviews the relationship between individual and group in rural France. To what extent was the image of the individualistic, land-grabbing peasant of the late nineteenth century a true reflection of the extent of association in the agricultural community? The major associations active in the community, their legal framework and their specific roles are also considered briefly in this chapter.

The history of the more important of these associations prior to 1914 is considered in chapter 3. In the years from about 1880 to 1914 some of the most powerful regional syndicates were established as the conflict between church and state in the early years of the century sharpened external concern with the political loyalties, religious fervour and economic interests of the peasantry.

Chapters 4 to 8 examine, within a chronological framework, the development of agricultural associations from the end of the First World War. The massive agricultural restructuring of the nation had its foundation in the state intervention during the war years and, since 1918, the pace of change in the rural community has accelerated as improved communications, advances in farming techniques and the rural exodus have taken hold. Chapter 4 considers what may be termed the 'golden age' of agrarian syndicalism between 1918 and 1930, when the power and influence of regional syndicates brought in its train a major expansion in the numbers and activity of allied groups such as cooperatives, mutual insurance groups and the agricultural credit movement. In chapter 5 the effects of the Depression on agricultural organisations are considered. The rise of the corporatist philosophy as a means of regulating the profession, and the creation of the Office du Blé, presaging an upsurge in state intervention in farming, were important developments in this period. In chapter 6, the triumph and ultimate demise of the edifice created by corporatists, the Corporation paysanne, are examined. Some of the more durable features of those years of turmoil are highlighted.

The theme of chapter 7, the rural revolution, draws on the term used by Gordon Wright in 1964 to describe the changes in the organisation and leadership of agricultural cooperatives and syndicates in the late 1950s. These changes are critically examined here, for, as research on the period has deepened, some of the hopes and aspirations of those years, a period of heady optimism and expansion, appear increasingly illusory. In chapter 8 this sense of pessimism is considered further. With the huge advances in agricultural production and productivity achieved since the 1950s, policy preoccupations have changed. Overproduction, the reduction of public expenditure, the expanding role of the Common Market, have led to continued debate and dissent within farming organisations as all of them – syndicates, cooperatives, the chambers of agriculture, the Crédit agricole – have been drawn into the policy arena.

Chapter 9 considers agricultural organisations from the standpoint of those two groups often considered as marginal: the salaried workers and women. How have these groups been recognised by the associations of the rural world which make such great play of their ability to represent and defend agricultural interests? How far have the divisions between capital and labour or between male and female been reinforced by the rhetoric, policies and interests of the major associations? The subject remains complex and under-researched but central to understanding the debates and dialogues which animate farming organisations today.

The book therefore seeks to provide both an evocation of the social history of agricultural groups and a backcloth to the contemporary debates about the rate, direction and influences upon agricultural policy. If, as recent debates have suggested, studies of agriculture must shift from an emphasis on the location, regionalisation and internal decision-making of farm production to a focus on the political economy of agriculture, its place in capitalism and its relationship with the state, then an examination of the history and contemporary character of French agricultural associations may go some way towards that end.

1

The transformation of rural France

On the eve of the First World War France was dominated by a rural and agricultural ethos. The strength of its agricultural traditions, the powerful and often contradictory images that surrounded its peasant population, and the force of its agricultural lobby, continued to exert an influence at odds with the newly urbanising and industrialising nation.[1] And, whilst the conquest and colonisation of peasant by urban France was accelerating to an ineluctable and, to some contemporaries, alarming degree, the dominance of the agricultural ethos remained. The myth of the peasant as the cornerstone of the nation, strong in 1914, was reinforced by the horrors of the war, in whose trenches so many peasants died.

If peasant culture in France has had perhaps one of the longest of all death-knells, with a periodic *tocsin* heralding its demise since at least the early nineteenth century, the changes in agricultural life since 1918 have nonetheless been profound and deep-seated. Social transformations accentuated by the rural exodus, revolutions in farming techniques and productivity, and changes in the mentalities and *genre de vie* of peasants have irrevocably altered the structures and geography of rural France. Farms are now larger in size and smaller in number. Technical changes and the expansion of the market have changed peasant into producer. New forms of sociability have replaced the older fabric of fair and *veillée*. Distances between farms are now measured in hours, not days.

The literature of change

These themes of change and assimilation, of decay and reconstruction have elicited a varied and growing body of descriptive and analytical work from many disciplines. The theme of landscape change, not as powerful in the French as in the Anglo-Saxon tradition, has nevertheless produced a literature which, building on the traditions established by Bloch, has sought to situate twentieth-century changes within the themes and models of

European landscape change.[2] The detailed and revealing cross-sectional analyses of the French rural scene in the 1830s and on the eve of the First World War carried out by Clout have served to elucidate both the diversity of the rural landscape and the potential of such geographic analyses.[3]

Foremost in the literature on the transformation of peasant France has been the work of historians. Two major multi-authored works, the *Histoire de la France rurale* and the *Histoire économique et sociale de la France* have been published in the last decade.[4] The former has provided a sometimes controversial interpretation of the course of recent rural history with a combination of description, analysis and theoretical speculation. The contemporary sections of the latter constitute a cogent and balanced review of rural developments since the late nineteenth century.

Alongside these general overviews, a growing number of theses have dealt with the themes of socio-economic and political change in the countryside since the agricultural depression of the late nineteenth century. The classic works of Bois, Agulhon and Corbin have been complemented by major works looking at rural change in areas such as the Var, the Beauce, the Lyonnais, Calvados, Roussillon or the Nord.[5] For Hubscher the 1970s were a period of expansion in work by historians on regional and rural themes and, whilst each work emphasises a different balance between the economic, social and political, an increasing recognition of the intermeshing of the rural, urban, agricultural and industrial has been evident.[6] Certainly, the earlier emphasis on the autonomy and specificity of the rural environment lessened as these studies began to move beyond the psychological divide of the First World War.

Increasing attention has also been given to the ways in which the countryside has been opened out: geographically, through the development of communications; mentally, through education and military service. Weber's *Peasants into Frenchmen* has been influential in emphasising both the character of these processes and their impact in the late nineteenth and early twentieth centuries.[7] If the precise chronology and model of change employed by Weber has been subject to scrutiny and criticism, the influence of his work has been considerable. Themes such as the suppression of regional cultures, the impact of the market economy and the place of politics in peasant culture are now firmly at the core of historical debate on twentieth-century rural France.

Within this broad suite of changes a more specific focus has been evident in the work of British historians. Clout's work, in focusing on the question of agricultural techniques which, in the late nineteenth century, presaged 'the quickening transition from subsistence to commercial farming and from polyculture to specialisation' has stressed the theme of regionalisation within the rural economy.[8] The effects of communication improvements, primarily the railway, have been seen by Price as underpinning the widening of economic and cultural horizons from the middle of the nineteenth century onwards with improved access to markets increasing the commercial opportunities of many communities and ending the fear of dearth.[9]

Sections in the work of Magraw and Zeldin on the character of French society have equally emphasised the significance of rural and agricultural changes from the late nineteenth century onwards. Studies by Jones in the southern Massif and Judt in Provence have sought to determine the character and meaning of politics in rural communities.[10]

In examining rural and agricultural change after the First World War, historical work has yet to fully blossom and the major contributions have come from other disciplines. The increasing number of regional monographs moving beyond 1914 will alter this position. Some of the most perceptive analyses of the pattern of economic and social change have come from the economist Dumont, from geographers such as Klatzmann, Kayser, Béteille and Chapuis, or from the *doyen* of rural sociology, Mendras.[11] The latter, in emphasising the theme of the erosion of the peasant community in his *La fin des paysans* (1967), provided both a general framework for analysing change, as well as particular case studies with which to enrich the general economic histories of the period.

The strength of rural sociology and political science has produced a diverse body of work on change in rural France since 1945. The period of the *Trente glorieuses* (1945–73/4), a phase of unprecedented growth in agricultural production due to massive restructuring, has stimulated work on both the economic components of these changes and their social and political dimensions. The description and analysis of the process of change, the evolution of the *politique agricole*, the effects of the national and international expansion of markets on farming structures and mentalities have been central to work in cognate disciplines. If the statistics, spatial patterns and flows of capital and goods can be described in an objective manner, their meanings and consequences are inextricably bound up with a number of themes. The theme of the vanishing peasantry sits uneasily with the continued dominance of the family farm. The increased capitalisation of French farming and massive indebtedness of many farmers form the backdrop to the huge strides in productivity and techniques of farming made since 1945. The process of change in rural France has been inextricably bound up with such contradictions and juxtapositions.

Patterns of change

In the first decade of this century rural France resembled a patchwork quilt of *pays* divided by economic structure, degree of isolation, access to the unifying culture of Paris, religion and education. Between the large farmers of the Paris Basin, employing twenty or thirty workers on a monocultural

Table 1.1. *Size of landholdings, 1892*

Size (hectares)	No. (millions)	No. (%)	Area (%)
Below 1	2.235	39	2.7
1–5	1.829	32	11
6–10	0.788	14	11.3
11–40	0.711	12.5	29
Over 40	0.138	2.5	46

Source: Barral (1968)

cereal farm, well-educated and attuned to market fluctuations, and the polycultural peasant of the Massif Central, farming a few hectares and sunk in the obscurity of his isolated country lanes, lay a world of differences. Rural France was neither as unified nor monolithic as bourgeois myth or economic generalisation would suggest. It rather exhibited huge spatial and social contrasts which, wide at the onset of the First World War, were widened further by the changes which were to follow.

It was Jules Ferry who had argued in 1884 that 'the Republic will be a peasants' Republic or it will cease to exist', but such fine rhetoric concealed the fact that rural society, far from being built on the equitable property democracy suggested by politicians, was sharply divided.[12] Property, still the prime source of agricultural wealth and social standing, was distributed in a highly uneven manner. In the 1892 census some 20 per cent of all landowners were recorded as holding 46 per cent of all the nation's land.[13] As Table 1.1 indicates, whilst the numerical importance of small landowners was clear, a reflection of the land-hunger prompted by demographic expansion in the nineteenth century, the overall amount of land they held was small. These social differences between the tiny *minifundia*, the small family farm and the large landowner were further reflected in distinct geographical patterns, with the latter concentrated in the *pays de grande culture* of the Paris Basin and the north, the former groups in the west, south and south-west.

Economic differences reflected, in part at least, these basic divisions in *patrimoine*. As Clout has emphasised, the transformation from *ancien régime* to modern France, a transformation underpinned by transport improvements, population growth and the emergent market economy, encompassed a myriad of changes in farming techniques, land-use and attitudes which widened the gap between the peasantry, anchored to a polycultural routine, and the producer, catering for the expanding national and international market.[14] If, for Weber, the last quarter of the nineteenth century saw the quickening of a move to a single nation, in economic terms the peasant economies of the south and west stubbornly resisted such shifts. The generally impressive growth rates of many northern departments contrasted with the stagnation of peasant France – outside the specialist producers of wine and fruit, 'the great majority of farmers . . . were still only loosely adapted to meeting the fluctuating requirements of the market'.[15]

This pattern of capitalist and peasant farming produced four broad regions (Figure 1.1). In the north-east were the regions of capitalist farming; characterised by larger property units, often tenanted rather than owned, they increasingly specialised in cereal and sugar-beet production with advanced farming techniques and the employment of salaried labour. A second, intermediate zone, in a broad belt around Paris, included areas specialising in dairy and vegetable produce (Normandy) or the more advanced cereal farms of parts of the Loire valley, bordering on the Beauce. A third category of small peasant holdings specialising in products for the market was characteristic of regions such as the Charente (dairy products), the Bordelais (wine) and Languedoc-Roussillon (wine), though in the latter two regions, larger capitalist farms were important. Outside of these groups were the characteristic polycultural family farms of peasant France, anchored to family needs and often physically isolated, though far from monolithic in their property structures or economic base.[16]

Work by anthropologists and sociologists has emphasised the peasant characteristics of many parts of France at the turn of the century. Many such communities were intermeshed within distinctive social and geographic territories – *terroirs* that embraced both physical and mental space. The exchange of labour and goods, legal and religious dealings and what little marketing of produce there was, took place within horizons that were limited by physical environment and codified by custom and tradition. Hierarchies within these communities, the positions of labourer and landowner, peasant and priest, were rigid and strictly enforced with the family, whether nuclear or, as in the southern *oustal*, extended, at the centre of economic and social life. Little wonder that Mendras has argued that a strong ideological cohesion structured the daily lives and contacts of countless peasant communities.[17] If education had, according to Weber, 'brought a suggestion of alternative values and hierarchies and of commitments to bodies other than the local group', the dominant themes of isolation and autarchy remained powerful in 1914.[18]

Socially, one of the features of both peasant and capitalist parts of France was the dominance of the mediator. In Catholic areas – Brittany, much of the Massif Central, the Alps and Pyrenees, eastern France – the priest was a crucial figure in organising the community, structuring contacts with the outside world, and enforcing a particular world vision within the group.[19] Others – the schoolteacher, doctor, veterinary surgeon, large landowner – also fulfilled this role through exploiting the transitional position they occupied between village and *préfecture,* region and capital.

Diversity was thus a central feature of rural France on the eve of the First

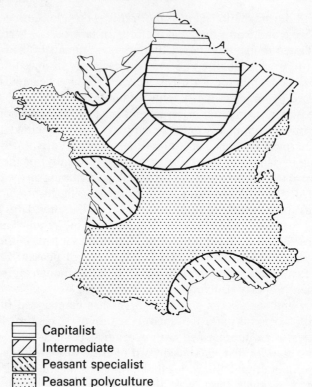

Capitalist
Intermediate
Peasant specialist
Peasant polyculture

Figure 1.1 Farming Regions *c.* 1914

World War. Habitat (the nucleated settlement pattern of the north and east, the dispersion of the west and south), economic structures, degree of contact with urban culture, access to communications and the degree of control exercised by the *notabilité* influenced the shape and character of rural communities. But change was inevitably in the wind. The progress of agricultural techniques was beginning to penetrate even the most obscure and isolated agricultural community and the implantation of national schooling, the developing network of roads and railways, the melting-pot of military service were influencing both capitalist and peasant France alike. By 1914, notes Price, 'the rural world had lost its independence and had become economically and culturally far more dependent upon the towns and cities'.[20] The effects of these changes in population, property, agricultural methods and *genre de vie* were far-reaching.

It is perhaps not without significance that over one-third of Ephraim Grenadou's biography of his life as a farmer on the Beauce was devoted to his experiences in the First World War. The contrast he draws between the drama and excitement of those four years and the banality of everyday

Table 1.2. *Active agricultural population, 1911–1981*

Date	Population (millions)	Annual decrease (%)
1911	10.27	
1936	7.24	0.8
1955	6.14	3.1
1970	3.85	4.3
1975	3.10	2.9
1981	2.55	2.5

Source: Barral (1968); INSEE

farming life is striking.[21] Such an emphasis is hardly surprising, for the war had a catalytic effect on the attitudes and experiences of countless peasants thrown into a world they knew little of, with townsmen whose lives appeared foreign. In other, sadder, ways the impact of the war was deep, for the bloodletting hit the countryside especially hard as countless *monuments aux morts* in village and hamlet show. It is a reminder that at the heart of the rural transformations of this century lies a profound shift in demographic vitality.

Since the middle of the ninteenth century a chronic rural exodus had been reshaping the social structure of the country and, by the 1860s, all but the most isolated rural areas were beginning to experience population declines; by 1900 this population fall had become something of a national obsession, helping to create powerful pronatalist movements. Between 1851 and 1961 the proportion of the population classed as rural (i.e., those living in communes in which the *chef lieu* had a population below 2,000) fell from 74 per cent to 38 per cent. In 1982 the figure stood at only 27 per cent.

Over the same period the proportion of the population dependent on agriculture for a living fell from 54 per cent to 17 per cent and in 1982 was only 7 per cent. As Table 1.2 indicates, the size of the active agricultural population has fallen throughout this century. This rural depopulation was, at least until the 1950s, regarded as an economic and social scourge, sapping the nation of that supposed peasant fortitude, fertility and stoicism. Ideologically, the decline of the rural and agricultural population deprived conservatives of their habitual power base (though, of course, by no means can the peasantry be considered innately conservative); economically these changes were, as Ogden notes, 'a reflection of deep-rooted economic change; the shift from a peasant-subsistent to a centralising urban-capitalist economy'.[23]

In a century, then, rural France has lost close to ten million of its rural inhabitants and the emptiness of parts of the countryside is now a structural feature of *la France du vide*.[24] Three phases of migration can be identified. Between about 1850 and 1918 massive emigration took place – earlier in parts of the Paris Basin, Lorraine, the Alps, later in central and south-central regions. The war, killing 675,000 rural inhabitants and injuring close on half a million more, further accentuated the decline. Between 1918 and 1946 the rate of exodus slowed somewhat and became more regionally differentiated. A steady decline in rural birth-rates as a consequence of the out-migration of younger people also influenced overall population levels. Between 1946 and 1975 some 3 million more rural inhabitants have disappeared, a diminution of some 20 per cent. The steady extension of an empty France where large swathes of the country (notably the centre and south-west, parts of the east and the mountain regions) are underpopulated threatens the provision of services and the maintenance of some semblance of community life. If the rural population actually increased between 1975 and 1982 by almost 1 per cent per year for the first time in over a century, the geographically restricted impact of such growth (primarily the Île de France, Provence, the Lyonnais) seems unlikely to alter the progressive desertification of the marginal zones of rural France.[25]

Within this structure of a declining rural population the place of agriculture has altered significantly. If traditional peasant society was occupationally and socially diverse, with artisanal and industrial activity forming an integral part of the *collectivité*, the onset of large-scale industrialisation, in undermining the competitiveness of rural industry, dealt a severe blow to that diversity. Many rural communities had, by the inter-war years, become almost entirely agricultural in character, turned in on the land and lacking the balance of earlier, occupationally diverse societies. As Béteille has argued, many areas are increasingly condemned to a purely agricultural role, accentuating still further the problems of service provision in the countryside. The rapidity of these changes during the period of major agricultural restructuring after 1945 has therefore had much wider consequences for both the rural community and the local and national state as the population of many rural areas has become increasingly agricultural and predominantly elderly.[26]

Geographically, farming is still the employment mainstay of those areas considered peasant regions in about 1900. The Massif Central, Brittany and lower Normandy, and parts of the Loire valley remain dominated by agriculture. West of a line from Le Havre to Marseille, farmers form at least a quarter of the active employed population compared to a national average in 1981 of around 8 per cent. This pattern, the outcome of a century of demographic change coupled with economic restructuring, continues to shape the formulation of agricultural policy by both government and agricultural organisations alike.

At the heart of agricultural systems, and integral to their transformation,

Table 1.3. *Size of landholdings, 1929–1983*

Size	1929		1955		1963		1983	
(hectares)	No. (millions)	%	No. (millions)	%	No. (millions)	%	No. (millions)	%
Below 5	2.16	55	0.80	35	0.55	29	0.29	26
5–19	1.31	33	1.01	44	0.85	45	0.34	31
20–49	0.38	9	0.37	16	0.39	21	0.33	29
50–100	0.08	2	0.07	3	0.08	4	0.12	11
Over 100	0.03	1	0.02	2	0.02	1	0.03	3

Source: INSEE (1986)

is the question of the size and system of tenure of landholdings. For Bloch, the nineteenth century, with its seemingly insatiable land-hunger, saw the acceleration of agrarian individualism as communal ownership and practices were cast aside for the much-vaunted benefits of private ownership and use.[27] 'The magic of property', noted Arthur Young, 'turns sand into gold'. The French took this maxim to heart. Soboul, writing of the long-term effects of the Revolution, argued that it 'liberated the productive forces from their feudal shackles, unchaining economic individualism in the village'.[28] This yearning for property meant that in 1892 three-quarters of all farm units were classed as owner-occupied. Tenant-farming remained restricted to Brittany and parts of the north-east, whilst share-cropping was widespread in Landes and Allier. The social importance of landownership was crucial. Barral has argued that property was the key element differentiating between 'rural democracies' where small property units were most important and 'hierarchical' societies characterised *inter alia* by the economic and social dominance of large landowners.[29]

Since the turn of the century three trends in property evolution stand out (Table 1.3). First, the tiny *minifundia* have rapidly disappeared – the labourer with a small farm plot was amongst the earliest groups in the community to seek betterment in the town. Secondly, and most remarkable, has been the steady reinforcement of the importance of the medium-sized farm. Thus farms between five and fifty hectares, some 42 per cent of the total in 1929, had risen to 60 per cent in 1955 and remained a majority at 60 per cent in 1983. If, in the late nineteenth century, the epithet, 'peasant Republic' belonged to the realm of rhetoric rather than reality, by the inter-war period observers have rightly noted the triumph of the family farm as inflation and rising prices helped in the repayment of farm debts. Since 1945, despite massive changes in production techniques and productivity, the numerical importance of the single family farm of between about ten and fifty hectares has remained undiminished.

A third associated feature has been the slow rate of growth of large property units. Geographically concentrated in the north and parts of the south-west, their relative importance has been notably stable. The proportion of holdings over a hundred hectares, 1 per cent of the total in 1929, had, by 1983, risen to only 3 per cent. Despite the predictions of Marxian economics, the family farm has stubbornly resisted the incursion of the very large capitalist unit. The failure of the large unit to submerge the family farm has been one of the more puzzling and paradoxical features of rural change. For some observers, its survival has reflected a deliberate strategy on the part of both politicians, anxious to ensure a stable (and often conservative) force in the countryside, and capitalist food-processing firms who see the potential for maintaining a family labour force (labour which is usually uncosted) as useful for supplying products unsuited to the larger capital-intensive units. The development of vertical integration whereby farmers are tied to using both the raw materials (feedstuffs; seeds) provided by multi-nationals, and delivering the final product to the same company for a fixed price, represents another explanation for the maintenance of this sector.[30]

Family ownership of the medium-sized units has continued to be the dominant form of tenure; sharecropping systems were transferred into the tenant sector by legislation passed in 1946. Tenant farming has, however, expanded as farmers have sought to lessen the weight of fixed capital investments in order to release working capital for technical innovations. The association of both rented and owned land on the same unit and the development of co-ownership schemes are formulae which have been increasingly applied to overcome rising land prices in the 1960s and 1970s.

Alongside these changes in demography and landownership has been the most visible aspect of change in the countryside – the technical modernisation of farming. On the eve of the First World War farming techniques were exceptionally diverse. If, in the course of the nineteenth century, the advance of the better cereals (especially wheat), the steady decline in the fallow, the expansion of artificial meadows and improvements in farming tools had laid the foundations for an agricultural revolution, such changes were geographically restricted. The highly capitalised farms of the northeast contrasted sharply with the often rudimentary farming methods of the south or the Massif Central. In relation to machinery, agronomic methods or attitudes, the north–south contrast between progressive and traditional rural areas continued to be evident in 1914. High fallow, low productivity, the persistence of oats and rye in the diet and the predominance of tiny farms continued to characterise large swathes of the national territory. The task of winning the daily bread varied enormously in its complexity and efficiency.[31]

Since then two general categories of change may be identified – technical and infrastructural. In the first category it is useful to distinguish between

Table 1.4. *Indices of agricultural change, 1905–1984*

Machines (000s)

	1929	1950	1959	1967	1974	1984
Tractors	20	137	628	1106	1327	1528
Combine harvesters	–	5	43	117	140	149

Productivity (quintaux/hectare)

	1949	1959	1967	1984
Wheat	19	26	37	65
Sugar beet	240	200	382	553
Maize	6	26	45	60
Milk (litres per cow per year)	1940	2268	2902	3879

National self-sufficiency (%)

	1905–14	1935–8	1956–60	1966–70	1983–4
Cereals	90	93	109	140	178
Potatoes	100	99	100	101	98
Butter/cheese	101	100	102	112	131
Oils	15	4	8	19	38

Source: INSEE (1987)

agronomic and mechanical changes. Agronomic changes were led by the steady suppression of fallow-farming in the poorer regions (its disappearance had already heralded agricultural modernisation in the north and north-east) and, as a corollary, the widespread application of chemical fertilisers. Consumption of these increased fourfold between 1900 and 1950; between then and 1980 it rose from 1.4 million tons to over 5 million tons.[32] The development of better livestock breeds through herd books and artificial insemination, new hormone techniques to improve meat production, the development of new seeds, and improvements in soil testing and modification have resulted in much greater yields especially since 1950. The role of government, especially through the Ministry of Agriculture and the Institut national de la recherche agronomique, has been of fundamental importance.[33] These production improvements, especially in the years of unprecedented growth after 1945, have made France a massive exporter of agricultural products. Agriculture has become, in popular parlance, the 'green petrol' of the nation (Table 1.4).

Mechanical changes in farming have been equally spectacular. The adop-

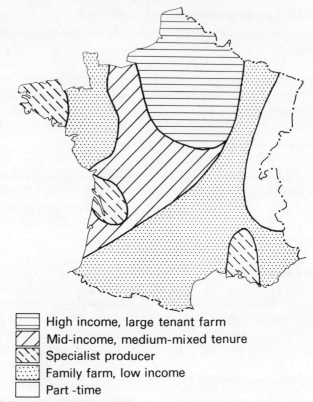

High income, large tenant farm
Mid-income, medium-mixed tenure
Specialist producer
Family farm, low income
Part -time

Figure 1.2 Farming regions *c.* 1980

tion of agricultural machinery in the late nineteenth century had been partially restricted by the labour surpluses present in many rural areas – despite the exodus, adequate and cheap labour inhibited the adoption of labour-saving innovations. The exodus of the inter-war years prompted the adoption of machines, especially on the large cereal farms of the north-east. The really dramatic upsurge in adoption came in the early 1950s with the onset of a veritable 'tractor revolution' sweeping not only the modernised enterprises of the north, but also the family farms of the south and west. There, even the smallest farms were caught up in the fashion for tractors (whether the latest model or a modified US Army jeep). For many farmers, unable to keep up the interest payments on their purchases, this first incursion into the market economy with its costings of labour, efficiency and debt repayments, proved to be their last. The adoption of tractors, noted Chombart de Lauwe, 'implied for the farmer profound changes in systems of production and in the management of the farm'.[34] Such innovations increased farm indebtedness from some 16.5 per cent of added value in agriculture in the late 1930s to 140 per cent in 1983.[35]

Infrastructural change has been equally important to the process of agricultural modernisation. Just as the coming of the railways marked the first piercing of the peasant strongholds in the middle of the nineteenth century, so the motor-car and lorry, coupled with the road improvements of the inter-war years, when so many of the small *chemins vicinaux* were built, transformed agricultural patterns and practices. Rural electrification in the inter-war period paved the way for improvements in both living conditions and production methods. These changes then, have influenced all sectors of the economy although their effects have been far from even.

As Figure 1.2 indicates, marked geographical differences in farm structures existed in the early 1980s. Four very broad groups can be distinguished. In much of the north and north-east is a sector of large farms, often in the rented sector, with a high degree of technical modernisation, largely producing cereals and sugar-beet, and with some of the highest incomes in farming. A zone of medium-sized, medium-revenue farms to the south and west of Paris can also be distinguished. Specialist producers of fruit, vegetables and wine constitute a third category with varied property structures. Finally, the family farms of the south and south-west have some of the lowest revenues and are frequently polycultural in character. Geographical and social differences in farming structures have thus remained an important feature of the economy, compounding the problems of policy formulation and exacerbating the difficulties of organising the profession itself.[36]

Government intervention in agriculture has been of major importance in the process of agricultural change. The origins of this intervention lay, at least in part, in the organisation of the war-time economy. If direct intervention in production decisions declined after 1920, the general role of the state in fostering agricultural change remained. Legislation on agricultural credit, farm reorganisation, new forms of property rights, agricultural education and the provision of technical and advisory services have marked this role. With the expansion of the Ministry of Agriculture, national and departmental advisory services have become an important cog in the machinery of agricultural improvement.

This increased intervention has marked both the development of the farm economy and the relationship between the profession and the state. It is possible to identify a series of different phases in these policies: At the end of the nineteenth century, the countries of Europe reacted in a number of different ways to the crisis provoked by agricultural imports from the granaries of North America. In France that reaction was primarily defensive. The Méline tariffs of 1892 marked the establishment of a system of protectionism designed to slow down imports (notably of wheat) in order to allow the economy to adjust to increased competition. The effects of these customs barriers has been a subject of considerable debate. For some, they provided an umbrella beneath which French agriculture could continue its somnambulent progress. For others it provided vital breathing space for restructuring and reorganisation. In France the well-being of agriculture and the economic health of the nation were generally regarded as one and the same.[37]

. Government intervention, however, was focused primarily on pricing rather than structural reform and, for Augé-Laribé, this lack of structural reform in the inter-war years was a crucial failing. If lip-service was paid to the need for restructuring, little encouragement in the form of coherent structural policies was provided.[38] High profits during the period of food shortages in the early 1920s disguised the poor structural condition of agriculture – it was not until 1926 that overall agricultural production returned to its 1910 levels.[39]

The crisis of the 1930s marked an important turning-point in agricultural policy. A twofold framework centred on, first, the return of severe protectionist measures and, secondly, increased intervention in the domestic market had emerged by the middle of the decade. If market reform was a novelty, with the Office du Blé at the heart of these reforms, intervention in other sectors was limited. It was not until the food crises of the Occupation that, for reasons of necessity rather than interest, sustained intervention in all sectors of agriculture through price control, quota systems, centralised marketing and structural reform, took place.

These changes were greatly accelerated from 1945. The Monnet Plan emphasised the need for a viable, competitive agricultural economy and, once the material privations of the early post-war years were over, agriculture, nurtured by a centralised, modernising and increasingly technocratic state, embarked on a period of phenomenal growth. These years, between the late 1940s and early 1970s, were a period of expansion, optimism, investment and change. By the middle of the 1970s the ever-increasing scale and cost of agricultural policy were beginning to be questioned. The oil crisis, increased demands on the public purse, the frailty of industrial growth and, paradoxically, the very success of the agricultural sector in creating new surpluses, created a changed political environment within which agricultural demands were formulated.[40]

The evolution of agricultural structures since 1914 has thus reflected this trilogy of factors. Demographic changes have made many areas even more dependent upon agriculture than was the case in the nineteenth century. Farm populations are much older as the exodus has drained away younger people to the industrial and service sectors. And, whilst recent statistics show a return of population to rural areas, agriculture seems unlikely to benefit from this new dynamism. Coupled with these demographic shifts has been a series of changes in landholding structures and technical capacity of agriculture. The medium-sized holding, the classic family farm employing two people (the *deux unités de travail d'un homme par an* – 2 UTH – enshrined in the Orientation Laws of 1960 and 1962) remains numerically preponderant but its national and international competitive power remains open to question. Regional contrasts in agricultural structures and technical capacity are as strong today as at the turn of the century.

Peasant, politician and producer

The inter-relationships between a capitalist agricultural sector and the peasant economy has been a persistent theme in the literature of agricultural change. Central to those inter-relationships must be a consideration of the role of the state in the political economy of agriculture and, arising from that, the place of those professional associations seeking to represent farming interests.[41]

In France, changes in farming structure, organisation, social context and techniques can only be fully explained by reference to the political economy of agriculture. To the historian, perhaps, a focus on the ideological character of farming groups and their varied relationship with the state and political parties is a natural outcome of situating such groups in their regional and social context. Discussions of agricultural change without reference to such contexts run the risk of ignoring a central part of the transformation of rural France.

The uneven penetration of capital into agriculture has, it can be argued, had the effect of increasing the social and geographic disparities between the specialist and polycultural producer in different regions. Similarly the development of systems of vertical integration of farms into the food-processing sector diversifies the interest groups within the farming profession. Analysis of the role of agricultural associations, their origins, history and contemporary character reflect, at times clearly, at other times, in a vaguer fashion, these changing relations between producer and peasant.

Debate continues over the question of the family farm. Its survival poses problems for Marxist analysis, predicated on the assumption of continuing scale economies and the widening division of capital and labour.[42] But the survival of family farming, and its central place in the discourse of farming associations, should not be allowed to conceal the real differences in the form of such farms. Vertical integration, new forms of sharing fixed capital investments in land, and new market relationships have continually re-shaped the form of farming and the process of capital accumulation.

What then of the place of associations in such changes? Their historical importance in structuring the character and pace of agricultural change, in shaping the attitudes and mentalities of farmers, in negotiating with an increasingly interventionist state is considerable. Syndicates have sought, with greater or lesser degrees of success, to influence agricultural policy.

Such efforts are central to an understanding of the nature of national farm policy in the past, and its character in the present. The syndicates, cooperatives, banks and mutuals that cover rural France conceal a history that is richly revealing of the aspirations and illusions of a powerful and diverse section of French society.

The social and cultural changes that have taken place in rural France – the decline of the *notable*, the emergence of a new rural élite, the colonisation of agricultural France by the representatives of the technocratic state – have continually reshaped and reformulated the relationship between farmers themselves and between their organisations and government. The process of agricultural change cannot be separated from both the organisation and character of farming organisations themselves, and the political underpinnings of policy formulation. To describe such changes, recourse to the statistics, case studies and government agencies is possible. To understand how and why these changes have come about is impossible without a knowledge of the formation, development and character of professional bodies themselves.

It is for that reason that the focus now shifts from the broad patterns of landownership, demography and technical change to the central issue of how and why such changes were brought about. Such a shift can only come from the immersion of the broader characteristics of change into a particular context in which the politics of change are considered. Economic and social transformation, with its spurts and hiccups, its leading and laggard sectors, its diffusion curves and capital inputs, remains abstract and unclothed until centred on those groups and institutions that sought to guide or restrict particular changes. The importance of such groups in structuring the links between peasant, producer and politician remains to be sustained in the chapters that follow. In their history lies the real fascination of the changes that have transformed rural France this century.

2
Individuals and associations in the farming community

It is something of a paradox that French farmers, often caricatured as highly individualistic and independent, have nurtured one of the most complex and fertile networks of cooperative institutions in western Europe. Agricultural syndicates, credit and cooperative organisations, Chambers of agriculture and mutual-aid societies abound in rural France and few farmers remain outside this nexus of groups. The history of such groups reflects the tension between individual and community in the countryside – between the desire for independence and self-reliance common to many peasant societies and the necessity for cooperation in order to ensure economic survival. Out of that tension a range of such institutions has emerged – some with a longer history than others – and their general characteristics and inter-relationships are examined in this chapter.

The individual and the community

The relationship between individual and community has been an important theme in studies of the peasantry in many different parts of the world. The literature on the economics of peasant farming, especially that centred on the model of the peasant economy developed by the Chayanov school, has frequently emphasised the primacy of the peasant family as the central unit of production and consumption. Changes in family size and structure have been seen as central to production decisions in the peasant economy whose objectives, noted Franklin, were genealogical rather than strictly economic. But, as an array of anthropological and sociological literature has shown, the peasant family meant little outside of its social or community context. Group values and decisions, communal pressures and the sheer weight of tradition meant that checks and balances between the individual family and the community were always important.[1]

More than fifty years ago Marc Bloch focused on this relationship between individual and community in examining economic and social change in rural

France in the nineteenth century. He argued that the triumph of individualism and the disappearance of communal practices was one of the hallmarks of the agricultural revolution of the nineteenth century, which saw the emergence of a capitalist agriculture based on the profit motive.[2] New property rights and the relentless struggle for land typified this new agriculture. Zeldin, too, has argued that peasant individualism, expressed in this hunger for property, was the central motif of rural life in the nineteenth century.[3]

This agrarian individualism, anchored to the emergence of individual ownership, use and profit of property and seeking to dissolve 'traditional' bonds between individual and group, between family and village community, was not, of course, particular to more recent periods but reflected long-term pressures for the abolition of such customs as common pasturing and communal farming practices. Pressures to replace these with individual ownership and use dated back to at least the fourteenth and fifteenth centuries in some parts of France – Picardy and the Île de France for example. But the pace of change accelerated in the nineteenth century both organically, as in the steady nibbling away of traditions of communal farming, and through legislation, as in the abolition of remaining common pasturing rights in the late 1880s, or the selling off of communal village lands to individuals.[4]

This apparent trend towards individualism is reflected in the statistics on both the size and tenure of land holding. The farming system was numerically (though not economically) dominated by family farming from the middle of the nineteenth century onwards. Older systems of communal organisation of farming fell into decline and family labour provided the key labour source, particularly as the exodus began to drain the countryside of its salaried labour force. The change was accelerated by the manpower losses of the First World War, which reinforced the family-farming character of the countryside.[5]

But to argue that these trends towards family farming automatically resulted in a much more atomistic and individualistic rural community from the late nineteenth century ignores the continued reality of communal systems and controls in many regions of France. The middle of the nineteenth century, with its relentless struggle for land, a struggle central to Zola's bleak portrayal of peasant life in *La Terre*, marked a lull in communal life, but not its disappearance. In many upland areas cooperatives continued to thrive. In the Jura, for example, the late nineteenth century saw the reemergence of older cooperative traditions, not their disappearance, as a fall in cheese prices necessitated a more rational and profitable organisation of commercial circuits through cooperation.[6] The exploitation of upland pastures, whether by transhumant or indigenous animals was, from the Pyrenees to the Jura, governed by traditional negotiations elaborated by the village communities of both upland and lowland areas.[7]

Baker has also stressed the importance and power of community pressures, even in a period usually considered as marked by individualism. His studies of associations in the Loir-et-Cher have emphasised the deep-rooted commitment of agricultural communities to communal organisation of social and economic life.[8] A typology of such groups would include those serving aspects of agricultural life such as threshing associations and livestock insurance societies, or social and cultural life such as the organisation of brass bands or other popular musical fraternities. The practice of association was an important and, it can be argued, an under-estimated part of peasant culture and society.

Rural life was thus marked by strong networks of formal and informal cooperation or *entraide*. The impetus for such association came from a number of directions. Undoubtedly, cooperative work in agriculture constituted a central aspect of community organisation in order that the *grands travaux* of the agricultural calendar, especially harvesting tasks, could be carried through. Such cooperation required no formal institutions but was rather organised through the mechanisms of tradition and neighbourliness. Early efforts at the creation of mutual-aid societies and cooperatives can also be detected in the middle of the nineteenth century. The example of the German mutualist F. Raiffeisen, and the Rochdale pioneers in Britain were followed with interest in French agricultural circles.

The church was also a powerful force in many parts of rural France exerting an influence on the communal organisation of village life, and underpinning the fabric of material and spiritual life in countless peasant communities. In much of rural France (though religious sociologists have rightly stressed that parts of rural France were resolutely hostile to the church – the anticlerical Limousin, the indifferent Midi), faith, *patois* and *paysan* were inextricably bound together. Such an influence was important in shaping the collective *sociabilité* of rural France.[9] As Mendras has emphasised, religious rituals and traditions served to reinforce the collective cultural and social cohesion of peasant groups who shared 'an ideological accord . . . the same vision of the world, the same values and identical means of intellectual expression'.[10] As Jones has also noted in his work on the southern Massif, the church was able to exercise a near-monopoly over the means and nature of community self-expression, for the community was the parish and the pulpit its mouthpiece.[11] To argue for the predominance of individualism in late-nineteenth-century rural France is to ignore the powerful role played by the church in the organisation of community life. In some parts of rural France, other social and political forces helped shape community life – the old forms of Provençal sociability, based on habits of collective activity, continued to manifest themselves in distinctive patterns of cooperation, which helped, for example, to underpin the emergence of socialist groups.[12]

Type	Example	Period of activity
Individuals	Gentleman farmer *Notable* Agricultural representatives Government technicians	19th century 19th/early 20th century 1945 → 1945 →
Voluntary associations	Peasant parties Church organisations	1930 s/1950 s Throughout
Voluntary state-aided associations	*Comices/Sociétés d'agriculture* Syndicates Cooperatives Mutual-aid groups Agricultural credit	19th century 1884 → Throughout 1900 → 1900 →
State-funded agencies	Chambers of Agriculture State marketing bodies Advisory services	1924 → 1936 → 1945 →

Figure 2.1 Individuals and associations in rural France

Individual and group in rural France

It can therefore be argued that the range of agricultural associations – syndicates, cooperatives, mutualist organisations – that are the subject of this book were not planted *de novo* in the social and economic landscape of rural France. Alongside such associations the role of particular individuals is also important in the articulation and representation of agricultural interests or the provision of particular goods and services to the farming community. Figure 2.1 indicates some of the more important of such individuals and groups. Four categories are considered – individuals, voluntary associations, voluntary associations set up with state aid and, finally, state agencies.

At the base of this typology, then, are the enlightened individuals active in stimulating small-scale, localised agricultural innovation. France, no less than England, had its innovative squires and gentlemen farmers keen to test out new crops, rotations, machines and animal breeds. Many were active in the agricultural, literary and scientific associations that began to flourish, particularly under the Second Empire. If their most striking role as catalysts for agricultural change was perhaps in the nineteenth century, when their economic power and political influence was greatest, one should not lose sight of the importance of individual innovation in the process of agricultural change in later periods. As Bodiguel has shown for the Côtes-du-Nord, the importance of enlightened individuals adopting particular innovations (the tractor, for example) in the 1950s cannot be overemphasised.[13]

Other individuals – government technicians and the representatives of agricultural firms, for example – were also important catalysts of change. The latter, in particular, were significant in the tractor revolution of the 1950s when fashion and prestige, encouraged by the advertising skills of the machinery manufacturers, frequently overcame economics in the decision to adopt particular innovations. The history of such agents would constitute an important chapter in the literature on rural change in France which remains to be written.

The second category, voluntary groups, is an enormously diverse one. Political parties with a specifically peasant clientele and set of policies are, not surprisingly, hard to disentangle from the general appeal of the major political groups. But, at certain times, distinctive peasant parties were created. The Défence Paysanne and Front Paysan of the 1930s, or the Poujadist wave of the 1950s, were examples of alliances between particular political groups and the agricultural population. As a group, however, the peasantry cannot be said to have lent themselves to straightforward political alignments.

The role of the Catholic church as an agent for mobilisation and organisation is particularly important, for its clergy and lay institutions impinged on the rural *collectivité* in countless ways. Priests played an important role in the creation of many mutualist and syndical organisations in rural France – as the better-educated and more articulate members of the community their role as catalysts remained important through to the 1980s. Such action was not confined solely to individuals – it was also articulated through a range of church organisations. Two groups in particular have made an enormous contribution to the development of rural France – their history and that of the peasantry generally are inseparable. The Association catholique de la jeunesse française (ACJF) was especially active in the first two decades of this century in founding agricultural associations, whilst the Jeunesse agricole catholique (JAC) played an equally formative part in transforming the structures and attitudes of rural France between about 1940 and 1960. The action of these groups forms an integral part of the history of French agricultural associations.

The third category, voluntary state-aided associations, includes most of the organisations that are the subject of this book. In the early nineteenth century, societies of agriculture were important, if isolated agents of technical progress in agriculture. In 1819 a national advisory body, the Conseil d'agriculture, with ten nominated members was created and, ten years later, department conseils were established. These groups, whose activity was highly varied and variable, were formed from three or four eminent gentlemen-farmers in each arrondissement. These were formalised into the *comices agricoles* in March 1851, whose role included the organisation of agricultural shows and competitions and the testing of new crops and animal breeds.[14] Much, however, depended on the inclinations and temperament of its members but, for Désert and Specklin, they played the role of 'catalysts in diffusing the ideas of modern agriculture'.[15]

In Aveyron, for example, the departmental Society of Agriculture was founded as early as 1792 by a local aristocrat, Rodat d'Olemps.[16] Its records through the nineteenth century show a group of landowners, rarely more than thirty or forty, preoccupied with improving the quality of pastoral production on which the future of this upland area depended. In the latter part of the century a concern with rising labour costs, a consequence of the accelerating rural exodus, led the society, together with local *comices*, to try and introduce labour-saving machinery into the department.[17] The society was later to be instrumental in the creation of other ancillary agricultural groups. As Jarriot noted, 'many members of the society of agriculture were subsequently very active in developing other groups in the rural world: cooperatives, mutuals, and syndicates'.[18] Not that agricultural innovation was the sole preoccupation of such groups – Flaubert and Maupassant have provided evocative and often amusing vignettes of the social pretensions and style of these gatherings of the great and good at annual meetings and fairs.

Whilst the agricultural population had to wait until 1881 for its first Minister of Agriculture, the broad task of representing agricultural interests had fallen since 1798 to the Société nationale d'agriculture and, since 1867, to the much more influential Société des agriculteurs de France. What this society lacked in numbers (under 2,500 in 1878 and around 11,000 in 1894) was more than compensated for in terms of the prestige of its membership.[19] The largest landowners and aristocrats, members of the élite Jockey Club and ardent Royalists, combined to create an important, conservative and influential grouping. It was an organisation anxious both to propagate agricultural modernisation and to ensure the loyalty of the peasant population, 'their' peasants, to its traditional, long-ordained leaders. It is hardly surprising that in 1880 Republican worthies set up a rival Société nationale d'encouragement à l'agriculture with similar aims.

The key legislation governing the establishment of syndicates, mutual-insurance groups and cooperatives was passed towards the end of the nineteenth century. The Waldeck–Rousseau legislation of March 1884 established the right of industrial workers, merchants and (as an afterthought on the part of the legislators) the agricultural population to form syndicates to defend their interests. If the law was intended primarily for the industrial sector, the legislators were quickly surprised by the speed with which syndicalism developed in the countryside. The central importance of the syndicate was that it provided the catalyst around which a range of other organisations – cooperatives, mutuals, rural banks – could coalesce. In the panoply of agricultural organisations the agricultural syndicate was to occupy a central and pivotal place.

The development of the mutualist movement in rural France reflected different legislative frameworks. Mutuals, local organisations through which peasants pooled resources to help cover the costs of damage to property or animals, had existed since at least the 1850s rooted in the old communal bonds which led to a variety of customs and groups with varying degrees of formality. Many such mutuals established complex systems of subscriptions (based on property value or the number of animals) which allowed back-up funds to be established. By the end of the century they were widespread. The Vigier legislation of 1900 regularised the status and functioning of these mutuals and, in particular, required the reassurance of local risks through regional and national mutual insurance companies to prevent fraud or collapse. The creation of these regional and national groups, usually under the umbrella of syndical organisations, provided the ideal opportunity for groups such as the Société des agriculteurs to create the symbiotic networks that were to link syndicates and mutuals at local level with the powerful regional and national associations.

The third element in this organisational nexus, the agricultural association for the provision of goods and credit, also appeared in this period. The first syndicates quickly established cooperatives which could buy and sell agricultural goods and produce under their general remit of defending agricultural interests. The association of pecuniary gain with syndical membership was not unattractive to a peasant membership. Such cooperatives were, however, in a difficult legal position because if they sold to non-members, or sold non-agricultural produce, they would be abusing their original statutes. A 1908 court judgement threatened the position of these cooperatives and it was not until 1920 that their position was legalised. Finally, the provision of credit for agricultural purposes was fostered by legislation passed in 1894 and 1900 which allowed syndicates to create their own credit organisations. The relationships between syndicates, cooperatives and credit groups remained legally and constitutionally close in many areas until legislation in 1945 clarified the distinctions between them.

The final category, state agencies, was a late arrival. As has been noted, it was not until 1881 that a government department of agriculture was created; a response in part to an impending agricultural crisis and to rural discontent with the Gambetta government. But, as Barral noted, the budget of the department was limited – only some 1 per cent of total government spending in 1890.[20] The real expansion of government intervention has come only since the early 1950s. Expenditure by the Ministry of Agriculture rose tenfold in real terms between 1950 and 1979 with massive expenditure on structural and social programmes in the countryside.[21] Legislation establishing the Chambers of agriculture in 1920 marked an attempt by government to provide representative bodies in rural areas. In their early years the chambers fulfilled an essentially advisory and consultative role. Since the early 1950s they have become the prime agencies of state intervention in

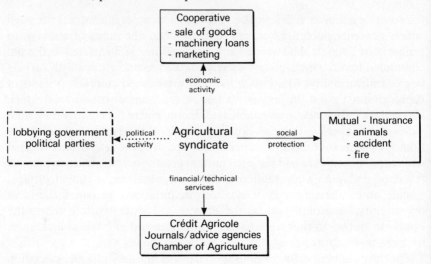

Figure 2.2 The activities of agricultural syndicates

agriculture, acting as coordinating bodies for structural reform programmes.

The aims and contradictions of the syndicate

The task of defining the functions of many of the organisations noted above
is relatively straightforward. Thus the mutuals, cooperatives and govern-
ment-sponsored technical agencies had clear and unambiguous economic
and social aims – agricultural improvement, marketing reform, or the provision of insurance for agricultural goods. As Figure 2.2 shows, the syndicate, a pivotal organisation in that it actively created and sponsored so
many other groups in the early part of this century and continues to influence
their policies today, had rather less clear-cut aims.

   Its activity impinges upon numerous aspects of social and economic life,
its political influence has always been considerable and some of its aims
contradictory and confused. Because of this it is hardly surprising that its
history is neither self-evident nor without controversy. It is important,
therefore, to recognise that the syndicate and, by extension, many of its
allied institutions, developed within a particular ideological climate. The
creation, development and continued role of the syndicate and, moreover,
its role as a catalyst for organisational growth in many agricultural spheres,
has always taken on much wider dimensions than the simple pragmatism
which its economic activity might suggest. Syndicates were, and have
remained, organisations intermeshed with a variety of economic, social and
political currents; indeed, shorn of this broader context, their role and

influence cannot be fully appreciated. Three particular interpretations of the development and role of syndicates can be identified: the agrarian thesis, the class-based interpretation and work emphasising their emerging corporatist relationship with the state.

Barral has argued that the syndical movement in France was of a part with similar movements elsewhere in Europe that he has termed agrarian.[22] These diverse movements developed largely as a response to the increased urbanisation and industrialisation in western Europe which threatened the power and influence of agricultural interests. These somewhat intangible influences, coupled with an agricultural depression in the late nineteenth century, created the need for powerful farming organisations. The growth of syndicates in France, the Boerenbond in Belgium, the Peasant Union in Switzerland and the Bund der Landwirte in Germany were linked, Barral argues, to this agrarian upsurge. The imposition of tariffs on imported cereals and the beginnings of a protectionist policy towards agriculture in Germany (1885, 1887), France (1885, 1887, 1892) and Italy (1887) reflected, it has been argued, the growing power of this agrarian lobby.

Such associations were predicated on the supposed unity of all country-dwellers in the face of a perceived 'threat' from the town. The rural community – landowner and labourer, doctor and priest – had, it was argued, a unity of interest which overrode class interests. This unity, as Barral rightly notes, was largely mythical but it nonetheless constituted a 'widespread and powerful myth which helped to determine the collective behaviour of the village community'.[23] Set against this background the particular characteristics and aims of syndicalism become clearer. Its expressed desire to embrace all members of the community in a single body sets the agricultural syndicate apart from the industrial union where the interests of capital and labour were usually clearly and explicitly distinguished. A strong opposition to supposedly corrupting urban values reflected the growing effects of rural depopulation with its corrosive effects on the power base of the rural *notables* and bourgeoisie. Whether this loss was real or perceived is largely irrelevant – it formed part of the agrarian myth which underpinned many of these organisations and which has continued to be influential in the movement.

This particular interpretation of the origins and role of the syndicate has been challenged by Gratton.[24] His work has emphasised the importance of class conflict in the countryside, conflict which, he argued, the agrarian interpretation of peasant protest tends to ignore or underestimate. Gratton's analysis of such conflict brings into sharp focus the diversity of socio-economic conditions in the countryside, and argues that a supposed global opposition to the town was little more than a device employed by those holding power to disguise the real inequalities that thousands of peasants and salaried workers were fleeing from. This diversity inevitably makes a global interpretation of peasant protest open to dispute. Barral, however, does fully recognise the seductive deceptions of the agrarian view and emphasises that it reflected myth as much as reality. It did, however, explain the way certain social groups perceived events in the late nineteenth century rather than constituting an objective analysis of those events themselves. To argue that urban and industrial growth inevitably undermined rural society or that all members of the rural community shared common interests would be untenable; what Barral does is to marshal sufficient evidence to suggest that these myths were a major force in shaping the development of countless farming organisations at the end of the nineteenth century in France and elsewhere in Europe.

A third theme to emerge from recent work on syndicalism is the developing relationship between these groups and the state. If, at their inception, most organisations sought to remain independent from the state, the pace of change in the post Second World War period, and the increasing involvement of the state in agriculture has meant that syndicates have inevitably been drawn inside the apparatus of state intervention and management. What this has meant is that government policy on such issues as land reform, price support, the development of new markets, the installation of young farmers has increasingly been mediated through and implemented by farming groups. The profession, through the syndicate, has increasingly taken on the role of a client of the state – retaining some input into policy formulation in exchange for agreeing to implement and service that policy either directly or through such bodies as the chambers of agriculture. Such corporatism, 'whereby representative interest groups assume some responsibility for the self-regulation and disciplining of their own constituency in return for the privileges afforded by their relatively close relationship with government', has become an increasingly important feature of the syndical movement in France.[25]

Whilst it is certainly true that the growth of the syndical movement was closely linked with the tangible practical benefits the organisation could offer – cheap seeds and fertilisers, access to cooperative marketing facilities, technical advice or special insurance facilities – the history of the movement cannot be understood without reference to its broader political and ideological context. Policy towards the rural exodus, on the issue of family farms as against larger, capitalist units, on national and European farm policy inevitably involve broader political considerations.

If, from the outset, the leaders of the movement, whether allied with the Republican or Conservative wings, professed complete political neutrality, in practice their actions were imbued with political overtones. The concept of 'defending the profession', a leitmotif of the movement, inevitably required, and continues to require, such choices and alignments. As Augé-Laribé, one of the most distinguished activists and historians of the movement noted, 'to suggest that agricultural associations have succeeded in maintaining their supposed political neutrality would be to grossly misunderstand the history of agricultural syndicalism in France'.[26] The agricultural syndicate was more than a simple professional organisation – whether in the village cooperative or government offices in Paris, they constituted a veritable crossroads of social, ideological and political debate. Politicians and parties of right and left have continued to vie for control and influence in the movement, perceiving the syndicate to be a powerful force in shaping the attitudes and loyalties of the agricultural population. As Mendras has noted, 'the history of agricultural organisations has sometimes seemed to be little other than a struggle and rivalry between the local squire and the radical-socialist deputy'.[27]

The question of unity

One of the fundamental features of the syndical movement has been its aim of representing all members of the agricultural community. Whilst, as later chapters will show, there have been many rival organisations seeking support, almost all have at least the expressed aim of representing all interest groups. Only one exception can be noted here. If, in the period prior to 1945, most syndicates sought membership from both landowner and agricultural labourer, since 1945 the distinctive and separate interests of the labourer have been recognised and the FNSEA, the dominant syndicate today, makes no attempt to attract the membership of the salaried agricultural worker.

It can be argued that this question of unity has been a fundamental feature underpinning the history of syndicalism since the end of the nineteenth century. Farming interests are diverse spatially, socially and sexually and this diversity has frequently created tensions and contradictions within a unitary syndical movement. Spatial conflicts of interest are a reflection of the diversity of French agriculture, a diversity which, as was noted in chapter 1, has tended to increase with the modernisation of agricultural structures. The process of technical change in agriculture has accentuated contrasts both between and within regions. A large-scale capitalist agriculture in the north and Paris Basin regions, centred on the production of cereals, contrasts with intensive, vertically integrated poultry production in Brittany and poorer pastoral farming in the uplands of the Massif Central. A diversity of economic conditions requires economic policies which often conflict. Should syndical action be centred on the provision of high prices for key products (notably cereals) or should structural reform policies to help the small upland farmer be developed instead? Such conflicts of interest have been chronic within the movement and have helped shape both the policies and types of institutions that have developed around the syndicate.

Within regions, interests also conflict. Variations in landholding structures and technical advancement can make the elaboration of agreed policies very difficult. The conflicting interests of large and small farmer are often further compounded by differences between farming generations. Geographical differences are further reflected in syndical policies towards particular products – the changing emphasis between cereal (generally well supported) and animal products is indicative of the difficulties a unitary syndicalism faces. Equally important are differences between male and female interests. Throughout its history, the syndical movement and the multitude of associations it has fostered have been the preserve of the middle-aged male. The role of women in agriculture has been transformed with the onset of technical modernisation; there can be little doubt that the place of women in the syndical movement is changing as they have demanded equal status in the eyes of the family and the law. Such contradictions have been inherent in many agricultural associations since the turn of the century and have proved a source of conflict which has played an important role in the history of the movement. The relations between peasant, producer and the state have been structured and shaped by these conflicts.

The study of agricultural associations is therefore of particular importance, for their development and role highlights the theme of association and cooperation in rural society. Their aims have been diverse, even contradictory, but their history represents an important part of the fabric of social life. Through these ideas of association and mutual aid, put into practice in the syndicates, cooperatives, banks and mutuals of the rural community, peasant and farmer could seek to influence the direction and nature of economic change. Their success was variable as subsequent chapters will show; the history of their efforts, and the continuance of those traditions remain a central part of the social history of twentieth-century France.

3

Agricultural associations before 1914

In late-nineteenth-century France, the representation and organisation of the peasant mass of the population lay largely in the hands of a small élite of landowners and nobility. In their local *comices agricoles* and departmental societies of agriculture, they sought both an amelioration of the often restricted social life of the country gentry and an improvement in the quality of local farming. The agricultural fair, monthly exchanges of ideas and information, and the occasional attempt at agricultural experimentation constituted the sum total of most of their activity. The impact of such groups on the mass of the farming population is hard to judge – it was likely to have been minimal. Membership was small and the resources of such groups equally limited and, whilst some regions were better endowed with such groups than others, their role as catalysts for economic change remained restricted.[1]

The origins of syndicalism

When the Waldeck–Rousseau legislation of March 1884 was passed, the response of the most important national farming body, the Société des agriculteurs de France, was swift. Its committee members quickly endorsed the need to encourage the creation and expansion of a movement capable of focusing the diverse interests of the peasantry into locally based groups with a clear economic potential. The society itself was financially strong and, with its membership of influential landowners and *notables* such as the Marquis de la Vogue, de la Tour du Pin and Emile Duport, it had a strong regional base to support the national policies of the organisation. Its activity prior to 1884 had been to act as a pressure group on issues such as trade tariffs and social questions. A strongly conservative organisation – relations with republican governments since the late 1870s had not been smooth – the legislation on syndicates seemed to offer an opportunity for the society to consolidate its influence in the countryside. As Barral has noted, the influence of the society was crucial in giving the syndicate a pivotal role in the organisation of agriculture: 'it was only due to the efforts of this powerful, conservative organisation that the syndicate was to become so widespread in France'.[2]

The precise shape and character of these new organisations was not immediately apparent to society activists. The primary intention of the legislation had been to legitimise the formation of industrial trade unions, but the model of a class-based syndicalism, designed to negotiate between the interests of capital and labour, was not one that appealed to the aristocratic and bourgeois interests of the society. Their image of a tranquil, unified countryside required the elaboration of a different model of social organisation – the mixed syndicate – whose wide membership of landowner, peasant, tenant farmer, sharecropper and labourer would render visible the organic unity and harmony of all rural interests.[3]

Such doctrines were attractive to the conservative membership of the society as well as to other social and political forces in France. In particular the Catholic church was not slow to seize on the expansion of syndicates as a means of consolidating its already considerable influence in the countryside. Whilst church involvement in lay movements was a matter of some delicacy at the time, the separation of church and state in 1906, the culmination of chronic friction between the Republican administration and the hierarchy, made church involvement more likely. The development of social catholicism in France, encouraged by Pope Leo XIII's encyclical *Rerum Novarum* in 1891, was a further stimulus to the early syndical movement.[4]

One of the most active catholic groups, the Association catholique de la jeunesse française, founded in 1886 by Albert de Mun, sought, through the application of Christian principles to the concrete problems of everyday life, to widen and deepen church influence. From the early 1900s, its leaders expressed their concern with rural social problems, especially the growing rural exodus, and sought, through the creation of syndicates, to improve daily life in rural communities and thereby render less attractive the urban way of life.[5] As one militant noted, the syndicate provided 'a marvellous instrument to maintain the religious fervour of our peasants, to improve their living conditions and to prevent the iniquitous spread of socialism into our tranquil villages'.[6]

Not surprisingly, republican groups, equally anxious to ensure a measure of support in rural areas, were no less enthusiastic supporters of syndicates. The republican Société nationale d'encouragement à l'agriculture, set up as a rival to the Société des agriculteurs in 1880, also tried to develop a syndical movement together with cooperatives and mutual-aid groups. The establishment of the Fédération nationale de la mutualité et de la coopération agricole in 1910 consolidated the rivalry between the conservative society, located on the rue d'Athènes, and the republican federation on the boulevard St Germain, a rivalry which continued until 1940.[7] It was to underpin

Table 3.1. *Expansion of agricultural syndicalism,*
1885–1914

Date	Syndicates	Membership
1885	39	No data available
1890	648	234,000
1895	1118	403,000
1900	2069	512,000
1905	3116	659,000
1910	4948	813,000
1914	6647	1,029,000

Source: Faure (1966)

the expansion of syndicalism into the countryside, an expansion which surprised both the legislators and the two main agricultural societies. As Table 3.1 indicates, the numbers and membership of syndicates grew steadily until, by 1914, at least one in six of all communes in France had an agricultural syndicate.

The *maison sociale* of agriculture

The development, at the turn of the century, of a range of other social and economic institutions linked to the syndicate was to be a potent force in widening the influence of local and national syndical movements. The Vigier law in July 1900, establishing special conditions for the development of mutual insurance groups, was an important stimulus to both syndicate and mutual groups alike. The existence of mutualist groups in the countryside dated back to at least the start of the nineteenth century, especially in traditional pastoral regions where schemes covering animal losses had been established.[8] In general, however, the bulk of the business (the insurance of animal loss, hail damage, fire loss or personal accident) had remained in the hands of the private companies. Agricultural syndicates had largely limited their involvement in this important sphere to grouping insurance policies in order to negotiate favourable tariffs with the private companies.

The legislation, however, allowed syndical activists to create their own mutual insurance groups. It was, not surprisingly, strongly opposed by the commercial companies who saw an important, and profitable, sector of their market threatened. What was especially significant about this legislation was the impulse it gave to a tighter administrative organisation of agricultural groups. The rue d'Athènes and boulevard St Germain soon created their own national *caisses* to organise the reassurance of the risks underwritten by local and regional groups. The expansion of regional syndicates – the Sud-est in the Lyonnais or the Plateau central in the Massif Central – was both encouraged and facilitated by this expanding mutualist business.[9]

Alongside this mutualist role the development of agricultural cooperatives within the syndicalist framework was a second building-block. From the outset, the sale of fertilisers which were both reliable in terms of their content and cheaper than that sold by merchants, was an important aspect of syndical activity. For the larger local syndicates and regional unions, business activity soon widened and a range of products – seeds, machinery, clothing, animal feedstuffs – found their way onto the shelves and helped to make syndical membership more attractive.[10] But the 1884 legislation strictly limited the commercial activity a syndicate could engage in, and the legislators and fiscal authorities viewed the increasing scale of involvement in commerce with some hostility. The Ruau project of 1908 sought to distinguish 'economic' and 'social' agricultural syndicates, a project opposed by the rue d'Athènes whose support rested on a convenient confusion between the two. The project was never fully implemented but, had the legislators succeeded in limiting the commercial activity of syndicates in these early years, a limitation keenly sought by merchants, the growth of the movement would undoubtedly have been compromised.[11]

The development of agricultural credit was the final element of the emerging *maison sociale*. As Gueslin has shown, the systems of agricultural credit in France had their origins in the crisis of the late nineteenth century.[12] The creation of rural *caisses* had been legalised in 1867 but the expansion of the credit movement in Germany on the Raiffeisen model found few imitators in France. In the middle of the 1880s there were a number of attempts by the rue d'Athènes to create viable agricultural credit groups, but the real development of these groups was the work of republican rather than conservative activists. The Caisse mutuelle de crédit was established in 1894 and fully funded from 1899; it facilitated the creation of local and regional banks, able to collect deposits widely but permitted to loan only to the agricultural sector. Such groups were to be strictly professional, mutualist and decentralised; as Table 3.2 shows the foundations for the expansion of credit for agricultural modernisation were laid in this period.

Alongside this system, nurtured and sustained by a republican government anxious to increase its support in the countryside, a system which came to be called the *crédit libre* developed on the rue d'Athènes. The powerful Union du sud-est was at the forefront of this movement, similar in structure to the state credit organisations, but integrated instead into the paternalistic regional organisations of the period.[13]

Regional and local associations

The implantation of local and regional agricultural associations was both geographically and socially diverse. With national control of the syndical

Table 3.2. *Development of agricultural credit 'caisses' 1902–1910*

Year	Caisses		Members	Government advances
	regional	local		(million francs)
1902	37	456	22,400	6.87
1904	54	963	42,783	14.10
1906	74	1,638	76,188	22.98
1908	94	2,636	116,866	35.78
1910	97	3,150	142,000	55.40

Source: Institut international d'agriculture (1911)

movement divided between a republican 'left' and conservative 'right', and with the identity and character of syndicates and their allied associations highly varied, it is difficult to generalise about the movement in these early years.

The most striking feature was the expansion of a number of powerful regional associations, generally linked to the conservative paternalism of the rue d'Athènes. With the syndicate as the local pivot, mutual insurance and credit organisations, together with powerful cooperatives, constituted an umbrella of organisations to enhance local solidarity and improve village life. In south-eastern France, the Union du sud-est was one of the most powerful of these early groups.[14] Its founder, Emile Duport, was steeped in the social catholicism of the period which provided a philosophy of Christian self-help and cooperation ideally suited to underpin the practical policies of the developing movement. Founded in the late 1880s, it had grown by 1914 into the most powerful and influential regional union in the national Union centrale (Table 3.3).

Its real success, however, resided less in the syndicates themselves than in the range of allied associations the union sought to create. Emile Duport was active in creating a regional bank in 1899 which had some 130 local branches by 1912. Initiatives to develop agricultural education in the region, and the widespread diffusion of insurance mutuals to cover the risks of fire and animal loss, formed part of the range of services to improve the quality and security of village life. Such practical, pragmatic policies were wedded to a paternalistic, social catholic ideology well expressed in the writings of Duport. Refusing the tutelage of the state, it was the profession itself, he argued, which must take charge of its affairs. Though its links with religious groups such as the Association catholique de la jeunesse française were never blatant, its leaders were the catholic *notabilité* and bourgeoisie and its ideology, noted Garrier, 'deliberately conservative, Catholic and corporatist'.[15]

Table 3.3.   *Expansion of Union du sud-est, 1895–1912*

Date	Syndicates	Membership
1895	100	26,000
1900	275	60,000
1905	325	88,000
1912	450	112,000

Départements in order of importance: Isère; Savoie; Drôme; Ain; Loire; Saône-et-Loire; Rhône; Ardèche.
Source: Garrier (1969)

A similar pattern of practical policies characterised some of the first syndicates to emerge in northern France. Much of that expansion was, according to Hubscher, the work of rural *notables*, already active in local and departmental agricultural societies. The creation of syndicates, the grouping of the peasantry, constituted, for them, one possible response to the agricultural crisis of the late nineteenth century. Initially organised at the *arrondissement* scale, by the late 1890s local, communal syndicates began to emerge. The Union des syndicates agricoles du nord, created in 1891, was close to the conservative ideology of the rue d'Athènes. But its power was challenged at the turn of the century by the republican Union des syndicats agricoles du Pas-de-Calais. Created under the auspices of the departmental professor of agriculture, it rapidly established both credit- and fire-insurance mutuals.[16]

It was not until 1902 that a strongly conservative rival was created, the Fédération agricole du Nord de la France. The initiative for its creation had come from social Catholic circles: the Archbishop of Cambrai had specifically asked two of his priests to act as 'working missionaries in the countryside'. Through collaboration with the ACJF a considerable number of syndicates were founded: 'the support of the local clergy', notes Hubscher, 'was decisive in the expansion of the organisation'.[17]

The importance of this Catholic, conservative local élite in shaping the policies and character of the movement is also evident from Berger's study of syndicalism in Britanny. Whilst occurring somewhat later than in other regions, by the end of the first decade of this century, a powerful and original syndicalism had emerged here. The creation of the Office central des oeuvres mutuelles agricoles du Finistère at Landernau in 1911 was a response to the kind of demographic and economic pressure present in other regions. 'The beginnings of peasant organisation', noted Berger, 'are riveted to this moment when the rural élite began to recognise, in the disturbances provoked by commercial contacts, the structural weaknesses of the countryside in confronting the city and the state, and to fear that peasant society would lose its autonomy'.[18]

Autonomy, independence, structural weakness – these themes recur in so many other organisations founded at this time. They are a reminder of the dual character of syndicates and their allied groups. Practical, pragmatic, ordinary even in the policies and advantages they offered to their members – veritable *syndicats-boutiques* to some of their critics – they equally reflected deep-seated uncertainties amongst their founders about the economic and social conjuncture. Thus the programme of the Office central embraced a range of mutuals (fire, personal accident, loss of animals), an agricultural cooperative, banks and a campaigning syndicate whose journal, *Ar vro goz*, advocated a *politique agricole* which would support the peasantry without compromising its independence. Alongside such practicalities was an ideology emphasising the integrity of *la profession agricole* (which, at least in theory, embraced landlord, tenant farmer, peasant and labourer) and the maintenance of *la paix sociale*. The conjunction of social catholicism, a crusading rural élite and a sense of Breton regionalism was a potent force in the expansion of the movement.

In the southern department of Var, Rinaudo has also noted the importance of social and political ideals in the development of syndicalism in this period. The syndicate, he has argued, 'represented a sure and solid way of maintaining political influence in the countryside which, at that time, was the main source of voting strength'.[19] By 1910, more than one-half of all communes had their own syndicate. The overproduction crisis in wine in 1907/8 had been a powerful stimulus to the creation of syndicates, especially in the Brignoles region: 'in the Var, as in Languedoc generally, the link between syndicates and the vine was a powerful one'.[20]

Rinaudo is, however, careful to make clear the gap between ideals and reality in the movement. The syndicate at Saint-Maximin, he notes, remained primarily a drinking and card-playing association, whilst a number of other local groups existed largely on paper alone with a highly ephemeral life. But some of the general characteristics of the movement are interesting. First is the preponderance of non-peasants at the head of the syndicates – it was the *notable* who created and led the bulk of these groups. Secondly, the creative role of the syndicate in establishing credit, insurance and cooperative organisations is emphasised. Finally, the considerable involvement of other professions in the syndicate is noted – the diverse occupational structure of the southern countryside was reflected in membership – between 20 per cent and 40 per cent of all members before 1914 were employed in the non-agricultural sector.[21]

The national rivalry between the rue d'Athènes and the boulevard St Germain became increasingly mirrored at regional and local level. But the practical differences between such groups on the ground should not be exaggerated. If the origins of syndicates in different regions were often linked to particular political traditions, the form the organisations took, their mixture of fertilisers, finance and moral exhortation, was often remarkably similar.

Many of the 'republican' syndicates owed their creation to departmental professors of agriculture who were encouraged by the administration to play an active role in encouraging these new institutions in the countryside. Jules Tanivray, the first professor in the Loir-et-Cher, played a formative role in creating some of the earliest syndicates in France, initially as a measure to counteract the phylloxera epidemic, but later to be transformed into a major syndical movement, the Syndicat des agriculteurs de Loir-et-Cher. Created in 1883 (almost a year before legislation officially sanctioning syndicates was passed), by 1892 it had a membership of almost 4,000 which had increased to 17,000 by 1914. A steady increase in business through the syndical cooperative reinforced the power of the syndicate but, unlike numerous other regional syndicates, it did not venture into the sphere of mutuality. It had, by the turn of the century, created important initiatives in rural banking designed to help small peasants to cope with the increasingly capitalist nature of their enterprises.[22]

In the Beauce, the granary of France, the syndicate at Chartres, created in 1885, owed its development to the role of the professor of agriculture, M. Garola. At the heart of the syndicate was a group of radical republicans who, in the course of some fifteen years, established a network of syndicates and cooperatives in the region. The policies and action of the syndicate were, according to Leveau, vital in helping to transform the economic and social milieu of the region. The local depots of the syndicate (15 in 1914), a network of some 24 banks in 1912 and a widely distributed journal, *La Défense agricole*, were designed both to transform the economy of the region and cement the influence of its republican *notabilité*. Whilst some votes did result from the services rendered by the syndicate to the farmers of the Beauce and Perche, the general technical advancement of the farmers of the region led them, argues Leveau, to naturally identify with bourgeois republican values without the need for heavy-handed pressure from the syndicate. Perhaps the most important characteristic of the syndicate was less its attitude to politicians than its policy of cooperation with the public administration.[23]

The peasantry – class or community?

One of the central tenets of so many of these syndicates – whether of the republican 'left' or conservative 'right' – was that their membership was open to anyone 'with an interest in agriculture'. The wish to include all members of the rural community, without regard to economic status or social position, was founded on the belief that landowner and peasant, sharecropper and labourer, blacksmith and teacher shared a common interest in the economic and social well-being of the countryside. By uniting the interests of capital and labour, of landowner and worker, the apparent dangers of industrial syndicalism, with its division of factory-owner and worker along class lines, could be avoided. As Barral has argued, such a vision subsumed internal division in the community into a global myth of opposition to the corrupting influence of the factory and city.[24]

Just how realistic such claims to represent all members of the rural community were is difficult to judge in the national context. There is evidence to suggest that some groups in rural society, especially the poorer agricultural labourers and small farmers, did not enrol in these groups in anything like their proportionate numbers. Augé-Laribé argued that, in 1912, no more than 5 per cent of the members of the syndicates of the rue d'Athènes were agricultural labourers at a time when some 35 per cent of the active agricultural population fell into this category. The view, propounded by the essentially *notable* founders of the movement, that all classes freely mixed in the syndicate was, he argued, 'absolutely contradicted by the facts'.[25] Gratton has similarly argued that whilst some 41 per cent of all family farmers were enrolled in syndicates in 1914, the figure for agricultural labourers was a derisory 1.5 per cent.[26] What organisations existed, then, to cater for such groups?

The numerical and geographical extent of class-based syndicates was limited and most were confined to areas with two particular features, firstly, distinctive socio-economic structures and, secondly, left-wing political traditions. Whilst the argument that the peasantry was incapable of advocating class-based organisations and policies cannot be sustained, the evidence of their involvement in class syndicates is slim.[27] Other groups in the countryside – salaried workers, woodcutters and sharecroppers – were much more likely to form such groups. Geographically, areas where these social groups were numerous – the vineyards of Languedoc, the market-garden enterprises of the Paris region, the forests of Cher, Nièvre, Yonne and the Landes or the sharecropping regions of the Bourbonnais – were the locations for such syndicates.

Their objectives were different from the traditional syndicates which were spreading so rapidly at the turn of the century. Whilst not eschewing the range of practical policies (mutualist associations for example) common to other syndicates, their aim was an improvement in wages and conditions of tenure through the arm common to industrial unions, the strike. Thus the *bûcherons* of central France, sustained by the Bourse du travail, formed a national federation at the turn of the century, with members in both the centre and the Landes. Strike action, political agitation and a tradition of left-wing voting coalesced to create a syndicalism which was very different from the image of harmony and social peace central to traditional syndical circles in rural France.[28]

A radical, class-based syndicalism, the Fédération des travailleurs agricoles du Midi, had been founded in lower Languedoc in 1903. As a bastion of left-wing voting throughout this period, the region, with its increasingly industrialised viticultural enterprises producing *vin de table* for the Parisian market, had a reservoir of salaried workers whose conditions and pay prompted chronic disaffection. Early strike action in 1903 and 1904 gave the federation some fleeting success, but the activity of the movement became submerged in the general malaise which precipitated the overproduction crisis in Languedoc in 1907.[29] In other parts of France, most notably the Paris Basin, syndicates for the salaried agricultural worker were also important – the Fédération ouvrière horticole, founded in 1904, sought to improve pay and conditions largely through strike action. As Barral has stressed, the life of such syndicates was often haphazard and ephemeral. The ambiguity of socialist propaganda in the countryside towards the question of property – most notably in the years between 1899 and 1905 when the debate over the unification of French socialist parties was fiercest – further reduced the organisational capacities of the left-wing political parties in the countryside.[30]

One of the most notable class-based syndicates at the turn of the century was that of the sharecroppers of the Allier. In the writings of one of the animators of the movement, Emile Guillaumin, the historian has access to a sensitive and moving evocation of the hardships and struggles of the sharecropper in the Bourbonnais.[31] Contracts were often very harsh in the range of services and costs required and the position of the sharecropper – one foot in the landholding peasantry, one foot in the labouring class – was socially and politically ambivalent. Halévy, in his *Visites aux paysans du centre*, quoted some of the correspondence of Bernard and Guillaumin, the founders in 1904 of a sharecroppers' syndicate: 'some four years ago, I saw clearly that, in order to achieve emancipation from the yoke which oppressed us, only one means sufficed – to unite, acting together in a syndicate . . . and, helped by a few other young people, and in secret in case my family found out, we set about founding a syndicate'.[32]

Guillaumin, who had achieved recognition in literary circles with his *La Vie d'un simple*, edited the syndical newspaper and, by 1905, a Fédération des travailleurs de la terre with 1,800 members had developed. After having obtained some improvements in sharecropping contracts the movement stagnated in the latter part of the decade, although the debate engendered on the form and economic rationale of sharecropping remained strong within left-wing circles.[33] The sharecropping syndicates in the Landes, unlike their counterparts in the Bourbonnais, developed and retained strong links with the industrial unions of the Bocau region which animated their activity and ideology. Their history is treated more fully in chapter 4.

Table 3.4. *Property holdings of Plateau central members, 1908–1914*

Property (hectares)	No.	%
No land	83	23
Under 5	27	7
6–10	117	31
11–15	51	14
16–20	12	3
21–30	26	7
31–50	30	8
Over 50	24	7

Source: A.D. (Aveyron) 7 M 43–44

If the extent of class-based syndicalism, whilst important, was much less widespread than community-based movements, it is appropriate to consider the extent to which this majority syndicalism actually included all members of the rural community within its ranks. It is only through the detailed analysis of local syndicate membership records that such information can be obtained. Such material is available for a number of syndicates and mutualist organisations though source problems do pose two sets of difficulties. First, the records themselves are often incomplete. The 1884 legislation required only that syndicates register their headquarters, number of members and executive members – the names and addresses of all members appear only rarely on the registration documents. To overcome this difficulty the use of mutual insurance records, which are usually much more complete, as a surrogate for syndical membership, is a possibility. Such records, however, may well omit the poorest members of the community whose goods were not worth insuring. Secondly, the use of the *cadastre* to ascertain the status and extent of property owned by members is complex and time-consuming in that information is given solely on land ownership, not on whether that land is farmed by the owner. The problem of individuals owning land in several communes further complicates attempts to estimate the economic status of members.

Notwithstanding these difficulties, local studies have served to test the claim that the syndicates embraced all members of the community. In Aveyron, the development of the mutuals and syndicates of the Plateau central had been remarkable. From one village syndicate in 1905 and a group of six syndicates in 1909, a flourishing group of syndicates and mutuals had been established to form the Union du plateau central in 1914, with 32 syndicates, 106 fire and animal loss mutuals and 32 banks in the department. The union, heavily imbued with the doctrine of social catholicism, sought to unite all country-dwellers against the pernicious wickedness of the factory and town. The coexistence in the same organisation of large landowner and

Table 3.5.   *Membership of Union du sud-est in 1899*

Département	Syndicates	Landlords (%)	Owner/ farmers (%)	Labourers (%)
Isère	69	8.6	80.2	11.2
Savoie	41	16.8	63.1	15.1
Drôme	34	8.0	73.7	18.3
Ain	32	4.5	40.5	51.2
Loire	23	28.5	52.6	18.9

Note: Only *départements* with a sizeable membership are listed.
Source: Garrier (1969)

landless labourer, peasant and *domestique* was central to the social philosophy of the organisation. Examination of the detailed membership lists of 31
mutuals in the period 1908–14 was carried out to test the spread of membership between different social groups. As Table 3.4 shows, the range of
membership was wide, with a large membership drawn from the smaller
landowners and labouring groups.

An examination of insurance evaluations, however, shows that the leaders of syndicates and mutuals were consistently drawn from the richer
groups in rural society. It was the large landowner, the solicitor and the
veterinary surgeon, rather than the small peasant or labourer, who exercised
control over the activities and direction of both local syndicates and the
departmental organisations.[34]

Information from other regions can also shed further light on the claims to
representativeness advanced by the advocates of community-based syndicates. Garrier, in his study of the Union du sud-est, perhaps the most
powerful regional syndicate at this time, has used the syndical sources to
provide a breakdown between landlords, owner–farmers and workers for
1899 (Table 3.5).

The relatively large numbers of salaried workers in the syndicate contrasts
with the data for the Plateau central but a particular feature of the Sud-est
was that a large mass of subscriptions were paid by the employers and that,
for many agricultural workers, membership was, to all intents and purposes,
compulsory. The dominance of the owner–farmer was striking and, for
Garrier, unsurprising in this 'rural democracy' of small and medium-sized
farmers. It is unfortunate, however, that the category cannot be further
broken down to examine the actual size of holdings, which has an important
bearing on social and economic status. The difference between an owner–
farmer with one hectare of land, and the salaried worker was, in reality, only
theoretical. A further feature brought out by Garrier's analysis, supported
by work in Aveyron, is the importance of other rural professions in the

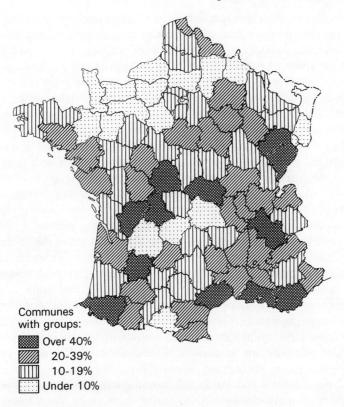

Communes
with groups:

▨ Over 40%
▧ 20-39%
▥ 10-19%
⬚ Under 10%

Figure 3.1 Geography of agricultural associations in 1911

organisation – the doctor, solicitor, and teacher all played their part in the movement.[35]

Agricultural organisation on the eve of the First World War

By 1914, then, the network of organisations in the countryside was well-established. Syndicalism, stronger in some regions than others, was nonetheless present in most areas with two powerful, rival bodies at national level vying for membership. With over a million members in late 1914, the attractions of syndicalism to the rural and agricultural populations was evident. As Figure 3.1 shows, the density of associations was highest in the south and south-east; a reflection of the powerful Sud-est organisation and of the developing network of cooperatives and mutuals in the wine-producing regions of the south. An emerging network in the peasant regions of the Massif and its flanks can also be noted – syndicalism was to put down deep roots in such areas.

Mutualist and cooperative organisations were the practical arms of the syndical movement. The expansion of the Crédit agricole from the beginning of the century paved the way for an increase in government funding to set up agricultural cooperatives for a range of products. In 1911 government support for some 53 milk and cheese cooperatives and 31 wine *caves* was noted. Overall over 2,500 cooperatives of various kinds were reported, the majority in the dairy sector.[36] The development of mutual groups following the 1900 legislation was one of the most remarkable features of the organisation of community life in rural France. The degree of practical solidarity implied by such organisations must make assertions about the innate individualism and isolation of the peasant difficult to sustain with over half a million agricultural members of these diverse groups on the eve of the war.

By 1914, the fundamental features of many agricultural organisations were already well-defined. That the creation and development of syndicates was imbued with political and ideological connotations is clear. The flowering of syndicates and their allied groups around the turn of the century was closely allied with the republican–conservative conflict for which the separation laws acted as a catalyst. The development of powerful 'social Catholic' organisations (the Sud-est; the Plateau central; the Office central at Landernau) mirrored the central role played by the religious issue in the political life of the nation. The syndicate can be seen as a focus for ideological conflict and the forum for exercising political and social influence. At the same time, however, the exercise of direct political influence through the syndicate was anathema to many activists, republican or conservative alike. Political neutrality, a constantly reiterated axiom of the movement, was rarely more strongly expressed than during these years, years when, paradoxically, the very growth of the movement was imbued with political overtones. For an activist such as Hyacinthe de Gailhard-Bancel it was through the syndicate that the path from plough to parliament could best be trod.[37]

The ideological division within the movement between the conservative rue d'Athènes and radical-republican boulevard St Germain was a product of this period and was to remain a characteristic of the movement for at least two further decades. It can be argued that this competition may indeed have stimulated the early growth of the movement as old ideological rivalries became reflected in the competition for the pockets and support of the peasant through the syndicate, mutual group or cooperative.

If such conflicts, the very stuff of prefectoral correspondence, police reports and newspaper comment, are undoubtedly seductive to the historian, the more prosaic and practical aspects of the movement were equally important in the longer term. The economic impact of the sales of fertiliser, seeds and machinery coupled with the modernising ideals of many syndicates was of fundamental importance. The spread of mutualism in these years was an important agent of change, diffusing the idea of solidarity and community, ensuring greater economic and social security in the rural milieu and creating a nexus of links between the locality, the region and the national group. Credit provision, emerging for the first time in this period and soon to flourish in the post-war years, constituted a fundamental factor in the evolution of techniques, structures and, perhaps most of all, mentalities in rural France. By the outbreak of the war, the foundations for the emergence of a powerful organisational network in the French countryside had been laid. The structure and varied styles of this new edifice remained to be built.

4
The heyday of the regional unions, 1918–1930

It was in the 1920s that the family structure of French farming was firmly established.[1] At the same time external pressures from consumers fearful of rising prices, and from politicians more concerned for the peace and harmony of the industrial workforce, the consumer of agricultural products, than for their producers, the peasantry, meant that the defence of the profession, through the agricultural syndicate, and the improvement of farm production and marketing, through cooperatives and mutuals, was to become ever more important.

It was in this decade that the syndical movement built on the mutualist and cooperative basis laid in the political and religious turmoil of the pre-war years, to establish a widespread, thriving and influential set of institutions. Not, it should be added, that the period was unmarked by struggle between rival movements: as Augé-Laribé was to remark in referring to the syndical history of this period, 'the war having ended, Frenchmen could now get on with the serious business of arguing with each other'.[2] But, more positively, the period saw the consolidation of a deep-rooted network of local and, more especially, regional unions together with the expansion of the mutualist and cooperative framework of these associations. Government intervention through the creation of the chambers of agriculture and the consolidation of the Crédit agricole were further important developments in this period.

From conflict to unity? – the CNAA and the agrarian right

One of the paradoxes of pre-war agricultural associations had been the extent to which political influences were important in their development; this at a time when protagonists of both left and right sought to keep their associations distant from politics. The mosaic of groups, some communist, some socialist, the majority either 'Catholic-reactionary' or 'lay-republican', that had developed pre-war had led to a duplication of services and functions and the wasting of energy in internecine struggles. The dramatic effect of the war on mentalities and attitudes was no less evident in the lives of those agricultural associations which emerged from the conflict. Frequently depleted of members, kept going in many cases by the support of the women and older men left behind and imbued with a sense of unity engendered by the sacred union of the trenches, the early post-war period was characterised by an optimism that the conflicts of previous years were to be forgotten. A new sense of unity prevailed.

That sense of optimism led to the creation of the Confédération nationale des associations agricoles (CNAA) in 1919, which sought to unite in a single body, representatives of the syndicates, mutuals and cooperatives of the rue d'Athènes and boulevard St Germain. A council with members drawn equally from both factions sought to put forward common views on the problems of agricultural regeneration, market organisation and pricing policy. Its success was limited. Few financial and organisational powers were ceded to the confédération by the powerful national rivals. In particular, the influential regional unions of the rue d'Athènes were jealous guardians of their independence and financial strength and, in 1925, they effectively withdrew from the CNAA, reducing the group to little more than a consultative body. For Augé-Laribé, its first secretary-general, the failure of the CNAA to unite these diverse agricultural associations was felt as a severe blow – he remained as secretary-general until the body disappeared in 1940.[3]

Perhaps the main reason for the failure of the CNAA is to be found in the increasingly powerful regional unions that developed in these years. It was in the regions that the real financial and organisational power base of syndicalism and its associated arms of cooperation and mutuality lay; important though the national bodies were, their role was little more than a coordinating and supporting one. If pre-war years had seen the emergence of one or two powerful unions, the twenties saw their numbers blossom with active and influential regional unions in most parts of rural France. National membership of syndicates grew from about one million in 1914 to one and a half million in 1926 and just under two million in 1930.[4] But national figures mean very little when divorced from the context of the regions.

Many regional unions were, first and foremost, powerful financial bodies. After all, one of the earliest rationales for creating these regional groups had been to provide secure organisations for reassuring the risks of local mutuals. The bond tying local, regional and national groups was, first and foremost, a financial one. Thus in Aveyron and Lozère, the Plateau central, created in 1914 and subject to massive expansion in the twenties, was initially established to group local insurance mutuals and banks and to reassure their risks through a regional *caisse* and subsequently through the rue d'Athènes.[5] The tightness of these links at different scales was therefore a reflection, not of the importance of a unified, centrally controlled syndical

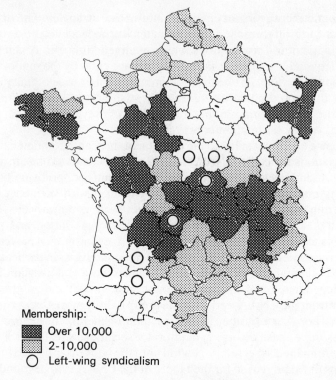

Membership:

█ Over 10,000
░ 2-10,000
○ Left-wing syndicalism

Figure 4.1 Geography of agricultural syndicates in 1926

grouping, but rather of financial and accounting necessity. The ability of the regional unions to embrace the agricultural syndicate and to incorporate those groups within a powerful financial and administrative machine was almost incidental. Once again, it should be stressed, without the mutualist and cooperative 'wings', the development of the agricultural syndicate would have been greatly hampered.

Similarly in the Côtes-du-Nord, the expansion of the Office central at Landernau in the 1920s was based, not on the drawing together of a range of local syndicates, but rather on the development of popular insurance policies. The legislation requiring compulsory accident insurance in the agricultural sector (passed in 1924) provided that organisation with a good opportunity to expand from its base in Finistère into the neighbouring Côtes-du-Nord, through the encouragement it gave to local accident mutuals. As one local syndical group in the Côtes-du-Nord noted, few syndicates in the region were sufficiently well implanted to be able to create their own accident insurance groups – the solution offered by affiliation to the neighbouring department was both timely and convenient.[6]

In those regions devastated by the war, the syndicates were able to play a part in agricultural recovery. In the Nord, the Fédération agricole was important in facilitating the supply of agricultural goods to the devastated region. In the recovered regions of Alsace-Lorraine a rich and powerful syndicalism developed after 1921 when two pre-existing groups, both with powerful cooperatives, united. As Barral notes, the maintenance of German legislation in the region meant that credit banks, modelled on the powerful Raiffeisen formula, were successfully developed.[7]

The powerful regional groupings of the pre-war period continued to consolidate and expand. The most influential, the Sud-est continued to play a leading role in the rue d'Athènes whilst newer unions in Provence, Alsace-Lorraine, the Massif and Brittany emerged into the forefront of union activity through the development of important regional cooperatives and mutualist groups. By the end of the decade a wide geographical spread of agricultural associations had been created (Figure 4.1). The strength of the movement in the peasant regions of the Massif and the south-west testifies to the success of the rural élite in reinforcing their influence in traditional rural society. Class-based syndicates remained limited both numerically and geographically. Powerful national groups with influential parliamentarians as allies gave the agrarian movement a moral and political power which coexisted with a clear practical vision of the importance of credit, insurance and cooperative facilities to a predominantly peasant membership.[8]

Specialist groups and the state

It was during the 1920s that the first attempts at creating complementary specialist agricultural organisations were made and this impetus came from two directions: first, the state, and secondly, the producers of the more heavily commercialised agricultural commodities.

The question of state intervention in the agricultural sector had frequently posed difficulties, particularly for the more conservative syndical leaders, for whom state intervention was viewed as the harbinger of socialism in the countryside. For the theorists of the rue d'Athènes, anticipating the corporatism of later years, it was to the profession itself that the task of regulation and control should fall. Whether the matter was accident insurance for agricultural workers, or the creation of large-scale cooperatives to smooth out market irregularities, traditional syndicates sought their own solution rather than having recourse to government. A view which was an integral part of the social Catholic philosophy which had underlain the creation of most of the powerful regional syndicates was underlined when one observer wrote that the task of the syndicates should be to 'hold on to the traditional methods of the countryside, traditions expressive of the wisdom of centuries, and to prevent the legislator from intruding brutally into the profession through ill-conceived measures and projects'.[9]

Since the creation of the *comices agricoles* and the departmental societies of agriculture in the early nineteenth century, the state had sought to establish at least a toehold in the functioning of the profession. Indeed, a project to create chambers of agriculture had been mooted under the Second Republic only to be abolished with the *coup d'état* of December 1851. On the eve of, and, more especially, during the First World War the government was forced to take an increased interest in the technical state and general productivity of the agricultural sector, resulting in an important role for the newly created *Offices agricoles* at departmental level. Legislation in October 1919, creating the chambers of agriculture as elected representative bodies to coordinate technical progress in agriculture, and to help mediate between the state and the agricultural community, was enacted to continue the work of the offices. For four years however, the legislation remained virtually a dead letter, largely because of uncertainty over the role of the chambers and because of the hostility of the syndicates of the rue d'Athènes.[10]

In their 1920 congress, their president, Toussaint, expressed the fear that the new chambers would lead to 'political' (by which was meant republican) intervention in agricultural affairs. In particular, the fact that the new bodies were to be elected by the profession raised fears that they might come to be perceived as more representative than the syndicates and hence dilute the power and influence of the latter. Thus one of the solutions advanced by Toussaint advocated the election of representatives on a professional rather than an agricultural suffrage – if the representatives came from the syndicates, cooperatives and mutuals of the rural world, the continued influence of those organisations could be assured. For the rue d'Athènes, in a stance which prefigured the corporatism of the Vichy period, the chambers would solely concern themselves with technical and educational matters under the firm tutelage of the syndicates.[11]

In the event it was not until January 1924 that the legislation was finally implemented, largely through the action of Joseph Faure, senator of the Corrèze, who later became the first president of the national organisation representing the chambers.[12] A crucial advantage that the chambers received was secure funding in the form of a property tax which was to help both with the administrative costs of the new groups and with the costs their technical role in agriculture would incur. The first elections to the departmental chambers took place in 1927 with, estimates Mora, about 50 per cent of the agricultural profession taking part. Suffrage was limited – only those over 25, agricultural labourers resident in the same place for two years, women farming alone and the traditional owner-occupier were eligible – but the involvement was at least as great as in the agricultural syndicate. In practice, however, the role and influence of the traditional syndicates and cooperatives were not compromised for they were able to elect representatives to the chambers in two ways. First, most departmental syndicates proposed lists for election which, with few exceptions, were unopposed. Secondly, departmental groups (syndicates, cooperatives, mutuals) were able to elect members to a set number of seats on the new chambers, thereby ensuring the maintenance of the 'traditional' rural élite in the new organis-ation.[13] The same cadres were once more in positions of influence – the chambers did not provide the occasion to create a new rural élite.

In this early period the role of the chambers was limited. Their degree of representativeness gave them the authority to pronounce on government legislation in agriculture but, in practice, their national role, through the creation of the Permanent Assembly of Presidents of Chambers of Agricul-ture in 1927, was limited by a lack of legal authority which was not remedied until 1935.[14] At the departmental and regional scale their role was hesitant – initiatives in agricultural education and the development of technical advice for example – the real expansion of their action was not to come until the 1950s.

Alongside the general 'social' syndicalism which had proved so successful in rural France, a second wing of syndicalism, geared more towards the technical infrastructure of specific products, developed in this period. The most striking example of this had been the development of the Confédéra-tion générale des vignerons du Midi, created in 1907 at the height of the overproduction crisis in the wine industry of Languedoc. Although con-cerned largely with organising the protest movement in Languedoc, the confédération played a part in encouraging the creation of producer cooper-atives and in expanding and improving marketing conditions for the region's wines.[15]

In the 1920s, particularly in areas where monoculture was dominant, similar specialist groups multiplied. Their creation raised the longstanding question of the suitability of general purpose agricultural syndicates for an industry becoming ever more specialised. In this period, the question was posed only in one or two regions. The north and north-east was the home for the two most important producer organisations. The Confédération géné-rale des planteurs de betteraves (1921) and the Association générale des producteurs de blé (1924) were able to command the support of the large producers of departments such as the Somme, Aisne, Pas-de-Calais and Nord. With the help of an affluent membership they were to develop into powerful lobbyists for their members, seeking to ensure adequate prices for their products or to foster the creation of more rational marketing or distilling schemes to cope with the dangers of over-production.[16]

Attempts were also made to create similar specialist organisations for other products. Thus, groups were created for producers of meat (1928), potatoes (1929) and milk (1924). Given the very different structures of production in these sectors, generally characterised by small, often poly-cultural farms, they were, not surprisingly, not as successful as their progen-itors.[17] The development of such groups was important, however, in

Table 4.1. *Changing area of vines in the Charentais, 1858–1922*

Arrondissement	Vines (1858)	Vines (1922)	% change
Saintes	24,470	17,753	−27
Jonzac	16,920	17,509	+ 3
Marennes	9,954	8,086	−18
St Jean d'Angely	29,275	5,773	−80
La Rochelle	17,927	3,660	−79
Rochefort	12,457	1,818	−85

Source: Reverseau (1925)

reflecting an attempt to introduce a more technocratic, less ideological approach to the organisation of the agricultural sector. As Houée notes, 'these groups brought a new style to the old organisations through their dynamism and technical competence unencumbered by doctrinal consider-ations or obsessions'.[18] Their experiences were to prove formative in the economic crises of the 1930s.

Alongside these producer syndicates, the agricultural cooperative con-tinued to be an important component of the organisational structure of farming. It is certain that the roots of cooperation in agriculture were long-standing in many areas, with cooperatives ranging from informal neighbourhood networks to strictly controlled producer cooperatives. One of the most striking and earliest examples of cooperative development was in the Charente region of western France. In the late nineteenth century the departments of Charente, Charente-Inférieure (now Charente-Maritime) and Deux-Sèvres had based much of their agricultural prosperity on the vine. Vines from the region were marketed either as *vin de table* or sold to the distilling companies of the region for cognac or *eau de vie*. The arrival of phylloxera in the 1870s decimated the vineyards of the region – the 130,000 hectares of vine in Charente-Inférieure in 1866 had fallen to only 32,000 hectares in 1892 and around 23,000 ten years later. Similar collapses took place in the other two departments.[19]

The recovery from the disease was both slow and spatially differentiated. Whilst in some *arrondissements*, especially those in proximity to the regional distilleries, some sort of recovery of viticulture had taken place by the middle of the 1920s, in others the collapse was almost total (Table 4.1). It was in the regions hardest hit by the collapse of viticulture, especially the northern Charente-Inférieure and southern Deux-Sèvres, that an agricul-tural recovery, based on dairying and linked to an expansion of cooper-atives, took place. In these regions a marked increase in forage crops led to dairy specialisation. In Charente-Inférieure, for example, the number of dairy cattle increased from 30,440 in 1852 to 41,990 in 1882 and 60,205 in 1892. By 1929 they stood at over 134,000.[20]

Coincident with, and at least partially responsible for this expansion of dairying, was the development of a network of powerful cooperatives. The origins of cooperatives in the region are generally ascribed to Eugène Biraud who founded a first cooperative at Chaillé, near Surgères, to collect milk and produce butter, largely for the Paris market. By 1889 six more cooperatives had been founded around Surgères. By 1923 there were 127 dairy cooperatives with a total membership of over 81,000.[21] Their geography closely reflected the pattern of viticultural recovery. Where the vine survived, largely on the basis of contracts for distillation with the cognac houses of the region, dairy farming had little impact. Outside the limited zones of the better quality cognacs, dairying, and with it, the cooperative, was widespread (Figure 4.2).

The role of the cooperative was twofold – to safeguard standards of milk quality and to ensure adequate markets for the butter that left the gates of the cooperatives. As the statutes of one typical cooperative, the Laitérie coopérative de Montjean in the Charente, stated, 'we seek to stimulate the manufacture and sale on a cooperative basis of butter in order to both develop a better product and ensure higher prices'. Rules were strictly enforced. Thus the council of the cooperative was empowered to exclude cattle deemed to be of poor quality (a rule designed to exclude the more rustic cattle breeds) or milk which fell below prescribed levels of buttermilk. The council could also inspect the farms of members to check conditions of hygiene and was able to refuse milk 'which had a disagreeable taste or smell'. A high degree of discipline and a commitment to better farming methods were the consequences of this new cooperative spirit.[22]

It is clear that the number of cooperatives advanced by Reverseau underestimates the total of active groups. In Charente, for example, the total number was much higher than the four given by Reverseau. The origins of the movement in that department dated from the late 1880s when a M. Boutelleau founded a cooperative at Barbezieux in the south of the Charente. By 1892 there were at least thirty-five groups recorded by the agricultural services; by 1932 some 900 dairy groups were recorded. A 1929 report noted that of the 70 million litres of milk produced in the department, three-quarters was channelled through cooperatives, the majority being processed into butter. At least ten major cooperatives, with numerous local subsidiaries, were active. This network of associations had, noted one report, 'contributed to a great improvement in agricultural production in the region and has helped to create undoubted prosperity'.[23]

Social catholicism and the peasant: the Plateau central

To move from the national to the local level of syndical history is to shift from the sometimes lofty ideological and moral pronouncements of national leaders to the more practical and prosaic preoccupations of those anxious to

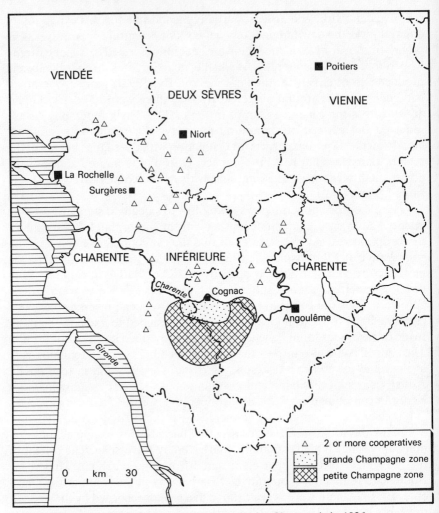

Figure 4.2 Geography of dairy cooperatives in the Charentais in 1926

establish the roots of syndicalist and cooperative activity at village level. Just what the statistics of expansion and consolidation, the arguments about peasant solidarity, the ever-increasing cooperative turnovers, statistics proudly collected by the national movement, meant at the local level is hard to establish. Only a more detailed examination of regional traditions can go some way towards answering this question

To the traveller moving northwards from Montpellier and the plains of Languedoc, the *département* of Aveyron is marked by the steep climb of the Pas d'Escallette onto the limestone plateau of the Larzac, deeply incised by the spectacular gorges of the Tarn and Jonte. Northwards the greener hills of

Figure 4.3a. The department of Aveyron

the Lévezou and the Aubrac represent the southern outliers of the Auvergne and central France (Figure 4.3a). The department is a transitional one – distinctively southern around Millau and the Larzac, more northern and Gothic around the *préfecture* of Rodez. In the early years of this century it was a difficult, isolated and, to some observers, backward region. In the north, a subsistence pastoral economy dominated, whilst only in the Ségala, a region transformed by the construction of a railway line from Rodez to Carmaux in 1904, was a modern, intensive agriculture emerging. As Béteille noted, 'the majority of the population, sunk in poverty, practised a strictly subsistent agriculture', whilst Durand pointed out that on the

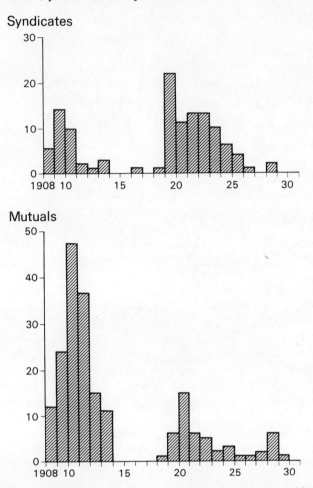

Figure 4.3b. Development of syndicates and mutuals in Aveyron 1908–30

Aubrac 'the nineteenth-century farmer cultivated the land exactly as his medieval predecessor had done'. The population was overwhelmingly rural and agricultural; only in the north-east, in the mining and metallurgical area around Decazeville, did industry intrude.[24]

The 1892 agricultural census revealed a social structure numerically dominated by the small and medium-sized peasant holding which accounted for some 80 per cent of all farmers. The large landowner, however, exercised considerable social and economic power and, together with solicitors, doctors, teachers and the priest, constituted a powerful *notabilité* in Aveyron. The region was a bastion of the church. With some 90 per cent of the population making their Easter devotions, a rate of ordination of priests which was twice the national average, and a powerful tradition of church schools, the influence of the priest, combined with the patronage of the squire was fundamental in this society.

It had been the intense catholicism of the region that had stimulated the growth of syndicates and cooperatives in the pre-war period. An alliance of priest and squire, mediated through a range of lay associations, had been instrumental in creating the Union des associations agricoles du plateau central which, in the years preceding the First World War, had developed a network of syndicates and insurance groups. These would, activists hoped, tie the peasant population to both its native hearths and its natural religion. To the republican administration, anxious to avoid conflict after the separation of church and state, the heavy involvement of the church in the development of the Plateau central was a matter of some alarm. Alongside the Plateau central a republican rival group, the Régional-Aveyron, competed for membership and influence with the support of the prefect and the administration. It was never to achieve the power of its Catholic counterpart.[25]

The rural exodus had been a key motive underlying the interests of priest and squire in creating this network. The population had fallen from 415,000 in 1886 to 369,000 in 1911. By 1921 it was down to 322,000 – the consequence, not of low birth-rates, but of massive migration to the employment markets of Paris and the cities of the Mediterranean.[26] The exodus distanced what was previously a compliant peasant population from both the spiritual succours of a powerful clergy and the social control of a conservative political élite. The town increasingly became a leitmotif for the twin evils of atheism and socialism, the countryside, the representative of order, stability and the rule of prayer and patronage.

By 1914 the syndical and mutualist movement in the department was well-established on the foundations which had been laid both by Catholic activists and by their republican rivals.[27] With the stimulus of competition an ever-increasing number of syndicates and mutuals were created by the Plateau-central and Régional-Aveyron with the support and encouragement of the national bodies to which they affiliated, the rue d'Athènes and boulevard St Germain (Table 4.2).

War put an end to the creation of new groups and, for the Plateau central, it was the diocesan organisations which took over the running of the groups.[28] But the four years of the conflict were important in consolidating agricultural insurance groups in the department, with a near doubling in membership of these groups between 1914 and 1918. The reasons for such growth are unclear though the absence of male members from the household may have prompted a reassessment of the value of house and goods by those that remained. This growth of the insurance market continued in the early post-war period with the expansion of the mutualist movement into areas

Table 4.2. *The Plateau central and Régional-Aveyron in 1914*

	Plateau central		Régional-Aveyron	
	Groups	Members	Groups	Members
Syndicates	32	2,900	0	0
Fire mutuals	76	3,630	69	1,185
Animal mutuals	32	740	0	0
Credit mutuals	32	no data available	31	688

Source: A.D. (Aveyron) 35 M 3

previously little influenced by the new ideas. The southern Causses in particular, areas of larger, isolated farms producing wheat and, increasingly, sheep's milk, proved fertile ground for the new propagandists of the Plateau central, with Maurice Anglade, a former insurance inspector, as the president and an increasingly influential activist in national syndical circles.[29]

It was towards the establishment of a viable syndical network, however, that most efforts were devoted. This was hardly surprising: early on, the leaders realised that the less 'practical' groups, such as syndicates, were unlikely to take root until other organisations – mutuals, banks and the like, were established. As Figure 4.3b shows, much of the development of the organisation in the 1920s was in syndicates rather than mutual organisations. From 1920 the Plateau central embarked on a series of conferences to convert the sceptical peasantry to the benefits of syndical action. It was the cooperative that was to prepare the ground. Steady expansion of the cooperative Rouergue-Auvergne-Gévaudan-Tarnais (RAGT), founded in the pre-war period, ensured that syndical unity, coupled with astute purchasing policy, swelled the ranks of the syndical faithful in the department.[30]

At St-Georges-de-Luzençon, a report in 1919 noted that 'the constant difficulties peasants were having in obtaining goods has led a number of them to found an agricultural syndicate'.[31] At Arvieu, 'faced with the increased cost of living coupled with the illicit profits of local merchants, the syndicate was created'.[32] A similar explanation was advanced by the president of the Vaureilles syndicate. 'Tired of being subject to the money-grabbing of certain merchants, a large number of local farmers met at the village hall to create that kernel of agricultural resistance, a syndicate.'[33] Thus it was economic advantage which, in Aveyron at least, was central to swelling the ranks of members whose much vaunted peasantist values would be extolled by regional and national leaders. However, the influence of the church continued to be felt. Locally, the Association catholique de la jeunesse française continued to urge its activists to develop the social work of the Plateau central – the syndicate, militants at la Salvetat-Peyralès were told, 'constitutes an excellent means of preventing the influx of socialist views'; nationally a series of speeches by Anglade to the ACJF emphasised the extent to which the expansion of the Plateau central placed it in the vanguard of the agricultural movement in these years.[34]

The economic activity of the organisation continued apace. The RAGT doubled fertiliser sales between 1921 and 1928 and almost trebled turnover in the same period. Estimates from turnover and the results of the 1929 agricultural census suggest that it was supplying in excess of 60 per cent of all the fertiliser consumed in the department. Its own transport service, a departmental milk cooperative, a regional abattoir and facilities for agricultural education were among the offerings held out to tempt prospective members.[35]

Solid practical facilities and the prospect of cutting costs at a time of inflation were thus integral to the movement in this period. It was on this base, not on the moral and ideological exhortations of the leadership, that the power of the regional union was built. Between 1919 and 1924, 97 new syndicates were created in Aveyron and all but half a dozen were affiliated to the Plateau central.[36] That wartime experiences may have been formative in this flourishing of group activity is evident from archival evidence. The president of the Inières syndicate near Rodez commented in 1919 that 'most of the farmers of the commune had talked in the trenches of the advantages of syndicates and cooperatives and returned to their homes keen to found one as soon as possible'.[37] The liberating effect of mobilisation was also noted by Meynier who argued that 'it was the demobilised soldier who enthusiastically joined the syndicate, who experimented with fertilisers, who developed new transport routes'.[38]

At the local level then, a practical, economically advantageous movement developed in this period. The village syndicate and cooperative were important in all regions of the department. The village of Gabriac, some 30 miles north of Rodez, and the birthplace of Anglade, established its own cooperative depot in 1921; over the next nine years some 2,600 tons of goods were delivered – a seven-fold increase in annual consumption of agricultural goods compared to pre-war days. Active mutuals for fire, animal sickness and accident were also well-established as well as a credit *caisse*. On 30 September 1930 the syndicate celebrated its twenty-fifth anniversary with the habitual banquet and speeches. 'In place of egotism and anarchy', proclaimed Anglade, 'we have substituted the values of family, profession and the good of the region.'[39] At Vezins in the Lévezou, a similar pattern of activity is evident. Founded in 1913 under the patronage of de Barrau, a local landowner, the syndicate was active in purchasing agricultural goods and establishing communal premises for manufacturing cheeses and cider. In the early post-war years, the transport facilities supplied by the Plateau central helped to keep prices low in this isolated region and membership expanded. The syndicate purchased both equipment for testing and its own land for experimentation in 1922, and by 1927 the village had its own rudimentary retirement and unemployment benefit schemes under the auspices of the syndicate. Modest though such achievements may sound, their role in creating a more secure and soundly based community was important.[40]

The importance of the Plateau central was reflected in its regional cooperative, with the widening range of goods available at special prices and in the cheap tariffs for insurance of house, goods and animals. Through the journal, *L'Echo du Plateau central*, syndical reunions and annual fairs, the practical reality of agricultural organisation and cooperation was maintained. By the end of the decade the mutuals, cooperatives and syndicates of the Plateau central were spread throughout the department and, from its base in Aveyron, had developed numerous groups in neighbouring Lozère, Cantal, Puy-de-Dôme and Tarn. The scope of its involvement in the agricultural life of the region was enormous.

Alongside these clear practical preoccupations, syndical leaders in Aveyron sought to instil a strongly peasantist philosophy. The conflict between republican lay movements and social catholicism which had preoccupied syndicalists in the pre-war years had, by now, passed and, in the 1920s, the dominance of social catholicism was reinforced. It was a triumphant era for the Plateau central. The strength of the movement and, in particular, its desire to speak on behalf of the peasantry was based in a solid network of local groups – in some 150 of the 300 communes of the department and with over 75 per cent of the agricultural population in many cantons. Such organisational strength coupled with financial and administrative power lent legitimacy to its ideological and moral pronouncements.

Three distinctive themes underlay the movement in these years – a strongly Catholic conservatism, a peasantist philosophy, and a regionalist ethos. As Barral has noted, the early decades of the twentieth century were marked by a rediscovery of the word *paysan* which increasingly lost its pejorative overtones.[41] Amongst the landed gentry and intelligentsia of the conservative right the peasant was increasingly invested with moral, religious and political qualities of the most fervent kind. Implicit in this quasi-mystical idealisation of the peasantry was a vision of order, stability, religious adherence and political conservatism. Literary and aristic rediscoveries of the peasant life meshed with visions of a return to the consensus and order of a pre-political, though resolutely conservative nation. 'You know nothing of the horrible dangers lurking behind the seductive smile of the town' the peasant was told. 'Stay in the countryside with family and faith.'[42] For the many thousands of Aveyronnais already populating Paris the counsel went unheard but those *notables* active in the Plateau central saw a stemming of the exodus as a Christian duty.

The shift from this peasantist position to the corporatism of the 1930s was not a difficult one. A resolute opposition to state intervention in the agricultural sector characterised the Plateau central though, in its early years, the possibility of picking up grants from a hostile republican administration had not been lost. But, editorials in the syndical journal noted, it was for the profession itself to decide its future and solve its problems. Such ideologies were one reason for the opposition of the Plateau central to compulsory accident and sickness insurance in agriculture; undoubtedly financial expediency on the part of the large landowner reinforced such arguments.

That the leaders of the Plateau central were resolutely conservative in spirit and action is hardly surprising. The dangers of bolshevism and communism were coupled with homilies on the untramelled virtues of private property and the family farm. The threats to these institutions came, along with the dangers to morality and the Catholic faith, from the town and the state. In June 1922, the Union centrale des syndicats agricoles held its annual congress at Rodez in recognition of the emergence of the Plateau central as one of its most powerful regional members. M. Delalande, president of the rue d'Athènes, was lavish in his praise of the Plateau central. This movement, he eulogised, 'is anything but revolutionary, it is reformist and creative . . . the very antithesis of socialism which stimulates the basest of passions and appetites . . . it represents the paragon of good sense, careful reflection and positive action'.[43]

Regionalism was a further thread in this ideological cloth. For Anglade, the fostering of regional power through the union was a vital counterbalance to what he, like many of his social peers, regarded as the excessive centralism in national life. In Aveyron this regionalist note accorded well with the predelictions of an intellectual élite anxious to preserve the cultures, traditions and dialects of Rouergue. The organisation sponsored regional folklore and, through its publications, sought to encourage local dialect and the use of *occitan*.

What then did the activity of the Plateau central in Aveyron amount to in this period? It is perhaps easier to consider the practical consequences first. The syndical movement undoubtedly did much to stimulate agricultural modernisation. It improved the amount and quality of goods essential to agriculture – fertiliser, improved seeds, agricultural machinery were all made available through the syndicate. Technical and advisory services were available from the Plateau central through headquarters staff or the syndical journal whose circulation was never below 18,000 in this period. Insurance of animals, person and house undoubtedly helped improve the quality of village life. Secondly, access to credit was a significant by-product of the movement, for the development of credit banks, especially in the developing wheatlands of the Ségala, facilitated the expensive shift from cultivation in the valleys to the plateau surfaces which, with the addition of chalk and fertilisers, greatly increased farming benefits. Total credit provision by the

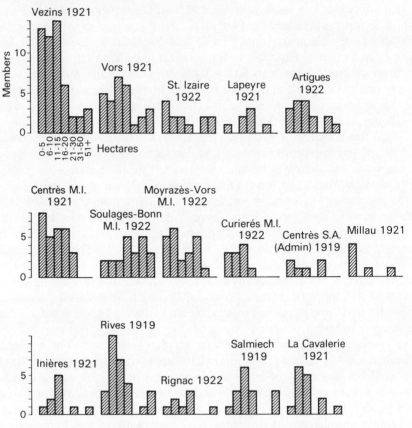

Figure 4.4 Property holdings of Plateau central members 1919–22

Plateau central rose from half a million francs in 1921 to eight and a half million francs in 1930, representing a real increase in the capacity for agricultural investment, especially in the modernising Ségala region.[44]

Assessment of the ideological aims is more difficult. Statistical examination of data on population change and levels of syndical activity in 1931 has indicated that the syndicate may well have slowed down rates of population decline but the evidence is far from conclusive.[45] The extent to which the syndicates fulfilled their much-vaunted aim of embracing all members of the rural community is also hard to judge. But it is possible, through examination of membership lists of insurance groups, to evaluate their spread of membership.[46] For the period 1919–22 these records indicate the dominance of large landowners (over 30 hectares) in the groups and the almost total absence of any agricultural proletariat (Figure 4.4).

But that the 1920s marked a golden age for the Plateau central in Aveyron is beyond doubt. Its regional power was unchallenged, its national prestige undoubted and, like many aspects of the Union centrale – of which it was a powerful part – its policies embraced both modern and forward-looking economic activity together with a romantic vision of the countryside based on a cult of the peasant.

The degree of social harmony achieved by the Plateau central is also hard to assess. That efforts were made to create a sense of contentment in the countryside is clear. The 'enemy' was portrayed as the town and the state, not the fellow peasant steadily increasing his holding or the landowner increasing the price of rented land. Syndical hegemony was total – there were, for example, no labourers' unions in the department – and, though this hegemony did not mean that there was no social tension in Aveyron, it does point up the success of the Plateau central in being able to represent the country-dweller as a largely unified and homogeneous group.

Class or community? Syndicalism in the Landes

The rural community was, of course, far from homogeneous and not all its protest movements followed the agrarian pattern typified by the Plateau central. The structure and socio-economic condition of the peasantry varied regionally and there were not inconsiderable parts of France where a peasantry, in its traditionally understood sense, did not exist. Thus in central France the forestry-workers of the Yonne or the share-croppers of Guillaumin's Allier did not fit with the characteristic image of peasant France lovingly fostered by the propagandists of the rue d'Athènes. Nor did the farm labourers of the Paris Basin, or the labour force of the large cereal and sugar-beet farms of the Nord automatically gravitate towards the patronal, paternalistic groupings of the Catholic right. To the diversity of conditions in rural France, a diversity of organisations was added.

The department of Landes in south-western France was, until the middle of the nineteenth century, composed largely of waste land and unstable coastal sand-dunes unable to be used productively. Under the Second Empire, with the personal interest of Napoleon III, coastal dunes were stabilised and large areas of land drained, afforested or farmed. The opening of the Bordeaux–Dax–Bayonne railway in 1854 further speeded up the process of agricultural improvement. Forestry work, the collection of pine resin (the *gemmage*), some cereal cultivation (with an expanding maize production in the early twentieth century) and pastoral farming became the mainstays of the region.[47]

Apart from the recent development of the inland region of the department (the so-called *Grandes Landes*) the area was also distinctive in that much of the land was held in large estates and leased under various forms of share-cropping or *métayage*. Widespread in the longer-settled southern part of the department, the region of the Adour, this form of land tenure suited

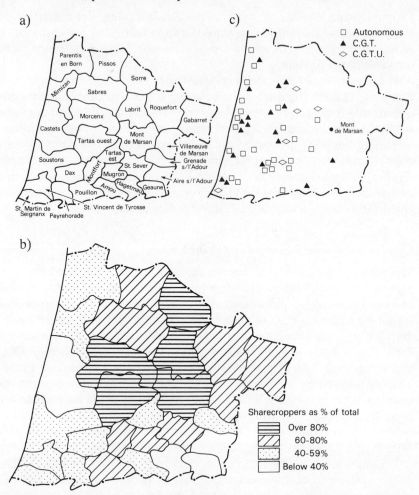

Figure 4.5 a. Cantons of the department of Landes. b. Sharecropping regions of Landes in 1929. c. Sharecropping syndicates in Landes in 1919

the largely bourgeois landowners who had bought up the newly created estates.[48] In 1912 the department had the largest number of sharecroppers in France, almost 20,000, concentrated in the central forest region and the valley of the Adour. As Figure 4.5b shows, the central cantons of Tartas, Morcenx, Mont-de-Marsan, Labrit and Sorre were dominated by this form of tenure.[49] In 1929, sharecroppers outnumbered owners by almost two to one.

The conditions of sharecropping contracts varied but, in the Landes, were usually severe. A constant subject of dispute and discontent, a prefectoral report drawn up in 1919 highlighted the worst aspect of such contracts.

Division of the harvest was usually on a half/half basis here in contrast to central France where a two-thirds cropper/one-third owner system prevailed. One of the worst aspects of the contracts was the *corvée* whereby sharecroppers had to work, unpaid, for up to 98 days per year on owners' land. Transport of material, the costs of animals, and sustenance on such *corvée* days had to be borne by the sharecropper. The severest contracts demanded a tithe of harvest produce as traditional extra payment. In some instances sharecroppers were obliged to buy wood from their owner, after, naturally enough, having cut it themselves.[50] The way in which the product of the farm was divided meant that sharecroppers were frequently in debt especially when taxes, one of the few things not shared out, were taken into account. The system bred discontent but a form of debt bondage meant that, paradoxically, the *métayer* had little option but to stay put in the hope of eventually climbing out of debt.[51]

This sharecropping system gave the region a distinctive social and economic structure which was reflected in the syndical organisations created in the 1920s. With an income estimated to be well below that of the salaried labourer in the poorer parts of France, the sharecropper was also constrained by the semi-feudal personal dependence between himself (or rather the family couple since both partners were required for labour) and the landowner. In the early years of the century, sharecroppers, together with the resin workers of the Landes (who were often sharecroppers as well) had sought to improve their position with a series of strikes. Especially severe in 1906 and 1907 these troubles led to the creation of a syndical federation which adhered to the socialist Confédération générale des travailleurs (CGT). Modelled on industrial unionism its aims were improvements in both the conditions of *métayage* and in the price the *résiniers* received for their product. But the movement petered out after 1909 in a series of internecine struggles between the communist and socialist movements for influence in the syndicates.[52]

The war acted as a catalyst for a reinvigorated syndical movement in the region. Many sharecroppers returned with strong revolutionary ideals.[53] Furthermore, rising food prices consequent upon war inflation intensified discontent with the high demands of landowners. Added to this general environment of dissatisfaction was a second element which reinforces the contrast with the Plateau central in Aveyron – a strong industrial influence. The metallurgical industry of the Boucau-Tarnos region in the west of the department provided fertile ground for powerful communist (Confédération générale des travailleurs unifiés – CGTU) and socialist (CGT) syndical activity which spilled over into the countryside. As Bonnault-Cornu notes, 'strong links between the sharecroppers and the metal workers were forged through the intermediary of sharecroppers' children who frequently worked in the factories', when the agricultural calendar allowed.[54]

In June and July 1919 the prefect reported a series of short strikes in Bas-Adour by sharecroppers refusing to pay in full the monies specified by their contracts. Seeking to examine the causes of the discontent, he was informed by his sub-prefect at Dax that outside agitation was the prime cause of the problems. Left to themselves, he suggested, the sharecroppers would remain loyal and quiescent; exposed to the corrupting propaganda of socialism and communism, social peace was threatened.[55] By September 1919 some 29 sharecropping syndicates had been created in the Landes and socialist advances in municipal elections during the same period spread alarm in the administration. By December, 35 syndicates of sharecroppers had been created (Figure 4.5c). The pattern of development reinforces the argument that the role of industrial workers was central, for the highest concentrations were not in the central forest cantons where the number of sharecroppers was high, but in the west around the forges of the Bocau in Castets canton.[56]

In the face of possible coordinated strike action by the sharecroppers and under intense pressure from anxious landowners the prefect followed a dual course of action. First he instituted a detailed inquiry into the role of external 'agitators' in the syndical movement and, secondly, sought to negotiate a solution to the problem of sharecropping contracts. In his first task he was aided by a network of investigators from the *Sûreté Nationale* and by sub-prefects avid to search out the slightest hint of communist or socialist involvement in the troubles.

An Italian forge worker, Viro, was one of the more colourful of these agitators. It was Viro who had been sent by the CGT to try to incorporate the movement into the national syndical group. A powerful speaker, he travelled the region in the summer of 1919 founding syndicates and encouraging united strike action by the sharecroppers. Reports to the prefect reveal him as a 'small, grey-looking man with a serious face and behaving like a fairground bully', whilst his co-conspirator, Lucq, appears as a 'tanned, skinny and tough-looking man, the very epitome of a sour and angry revolutionary'. Another militant, Raboutet, excited attention as 'a violent extremist of the CGT and a man to be feared . . . he has only one arm'.[57] This picture of a peaceful countryside undermined by external agitators was, no doubt, the preferred explanation of events to the conservative administration. But the prefect was equally critical of the landowners. Their intransigence and outright refusal to deal with any syndicates (they would deal only with *their* sharecroppers on an individual basis) alarmed the prefect almost as much as the spectre of a socialist or communist countryside.[58]

Through October and November 1919 the sharecropping syndicates developed, and decided in particular to demand not simply a suppression of some of the more extreme sections of their contracts (the *corvées* for example) but the establishment of a new model contract for sharecropping to be adopted throughout the region. The new contract would include a two-thirds allocation of the product of the farm to the sharecropper, for repairs and improvements to be carried out at the expense of the owner and for the expense of animals and fertiliser to be borne largely by the owner. The syndicates sought to introduce the new contracts on 11 November 1919, but the owners refused to negotiate.[59] As the prefect noted, 'they have shown themselves to be absolutely intransigent and would not even discuss the matter with the syndicates'.[60]

Early in the New Year the syndicates decided to suspend all contractual payments to the owners pending a reply to the new contract proposal. Syndical action was firm and coordinated and demonstrations ensured that syndical discipline was maintained. Landowners seeking to harvest their crops without the consent of their sharecroppers were forcibly prevented from doing so. The owners were often appalled at events: at St Martin de Hinx they accused the prefect of being too accommodating towards the sharecroppers and once again pointed to the spectre of external agitation: 'many politicians from outside', they said, 'had created the syndicates with the sole intention of awakening greed amongst the sharecropper, and inciting hatred towards the owners by dangling bolshevik ideas in front of their ignorant eyes'.[61]

The reaction of the prefect to the tension was to call the various mayors of the communes affected to a meeting at Dax on 24 February 1920. After a series of difficulties an accord was eventually signed on 11 March. As Gratton notes, between February and March 1920 some 3,000 sharecroppers had taken part in the movement and 63,000 days of work had been lost through strike action.[62] The accord marked a significant advance for the sharecroppers and an undoubted victory for the new syndical organisations. The abolition of *corvées*, longer contracts and a fairer distribution of produce were the chief features of the accord.

It did not, however, mark the termination of the conflict. A number of owners quickly evicted some 200 of their sharecroppers and the strikes spread into other regions of the Landes. This, argued the prefect, posed once more the danger of left-wing propaganda spreading in the region as new syndicates were created in areas previously untouched by the conflict (most notably in the south of the department). Demanding the application of the Dax accord to their regions, some 45 new syndicates were created in the summer of 1920. With a refusal to harvest, a series of mass demonstrations and the singing of the 'Internationale' by the peasantry, social unrest spread. Ultimately military force had to be used to expel the more militant sharecroppers from their holdings and the movement faded under legal and administrative pressures.[63]

If, in the short term, the action of these syndicates was limited, the longer-term effects were far from negligible, for these conflicts, coupled with those of 1906–9, laid the foundations for the development of a strong socialist and communist tradition in the region. The particular conditions of land holding, the semi-proletarianised position of the sharecropper and the traditions of concerted action through the syndicate, action which had improved the lot of the sharecropper through the accord of Dax (even though the accord was limited in its application and undermined by concerns for internal security and rural law and order), were to be continued in the region until the abolition of sharecropping in 1946.

The 1920s were therefore marked by the continued dominance of the rue d'Athènes in syndical affairs, by the collapse of efforts at creating a single agricultural body, the CNAA and by the establishment, after many hesitations, of a body which in later years was to become ever more important, the chambers of agriculture. But of most significance was the reinforcement of the power and prestige of the regional syndicates. Their political and moral strength depended massively on the size of membership and the extent of financial and insurance strength they could provide. The emergence and character of the Plateau central group typified, it can be argued, just such a group. However, as the study of sharecropping syndicates of the Landes has shown, not all regions of France followed such a pattern. To argue for a single typical syndical group would be to ignore the complexity of economic and social structures in rural France.

5

The economic crisis and the rise of corporatism, 1930–1940

'Before the Depression, the peasantry was for the most part passive, inarticulate, atomized. Since the Depression, the peasantry has become increasingly active, vocal, organised.'[1] This judgement by Wright highlights how important this period was in creating an 'authentic' peasant voice in the countryside. The steady promotion of the peasantry into the organisations of the rural world, the increasing recourse to peasantist doctrines and ideology and the return of a sense of pride in being part of the 'peasant community' have all been regarded as outcomes of the economic and political events of this decade. Such a view should not, however, be allowed to obscure the fact that these developments were rooted in the agrarian movements of earlier decades. What was new was the sheer number of groups now vying for peasant support.

The range of such groups was remarkable. The quasi-fascist 'Greenshirts' of Henri Dorgères, the conservative Parti agraire, the traditional syndicalism of the rue d'Athènes, the communist Confédération des paysans travailleurs or the socialist Confédération nationale paysanne all sought to seduce the electorally powerful agricultural population of some 4½ million (or 32 per cent of the economically active population of France).[2] Political gain, economic cooperation, price support for the farming community and moral conformity were advanced as arguments for peasant enrolment in the varied agricultural groups of this period.

The world economic depression underpinned this organisational ferment. Agricultural prices fell by some 50 per cent between 1930 and 1935, and agricultural purchasing power fell by over a quarter in that same period.[3] The price of wine collapsed: 154 francs per hectolitre in 1929, by 1932 it was down to 128 francs and to only 64 francs in 1935. This collapse in prices was further aggravated by two factors: production continued at a high level, particularly in the wheat and wine sectors, and the country remained committed to the import of produce from metropolitan France, especially Algeria; and the gap between agricultural and industrial products worsened from

71

1934 as a continued fall in agricultural prices coincided with a degree of stabilisation in the costs of industrial inputs into agriculture. In addition, the fall in urban revenues that accompanied mass unemployment further depressed demand for agricultural goods.[4]

These dramatic collapses in the agricultural sector were to brutally expose some of the contradictions implicit in traditional syndicalism. For some, events required the French peasant to revert to a traditional subsistence economy, to turn in on themselves, to reduce production of agricultural goods and consumption of industrial products. Yet, paradoxically, for many peasants, encouraged by the cooperatives and banks that were now such an integral part of farming life, such a reversion was impossible. Even the most modest of farmers depended on credit, was tied to new inputs of fertiliser and seed and was inextricably bound up in the national and global economy. Short-term loans to farmers, at 696 million francs in 1929, had risen to 1,248 million francs in 1935, reflecting the increasing indebtedness of the agricultural economy.[5]

At the same time, those syndical leaders who, in the preceding decade, had been so eloquent in their defence of the independence of the agricultural sector from state intervention, found themselves trapped by their own rhetoric. The very severity of the crisis, and its illustration of the interdependence of the agricultural, industrial and financial sectors, increasingly suggested that the state alone could provide the powers necessary for agricultural stability. Whilst deploring state intervention and disdaining the sullying influence of politics in the 'free' economy, agrarian deputies in the Chamber nonetheless acknowledged the necessity of a state role – exceptional means for exceptional times was the grudging justification, an attitude which, notes Barral, was common to syndicalists of both the right and left.[6]

Traditional syndicalism

Membership of syndicates stood at about two million in 1930, some 50 per cent of the agricultural population, and without doubt an impressive achievement for the movement. With the growing number of cooperatives, mutual and credit groups and the chambers of agriculture, very few peasants in France can have remained untouched by this expanding network of associations. The collapse of the CNAA in the middle of the 1920s meant that the contrast between the rue d'Athènes and the boulevard St Germain remained, though very much reduced from pre-war days.[7] But the economic conjuncture was to ensure that the organisations of rural France could not remain wedded to their traditional preoccupations of moral support and limited economic intervention. The gravity of the crisis was to provoke severe discontent in the countryside and to elicit a dual response – first, towards the creation of a more technocratic and economically rational syndicalism and, secondly, an increased support for direct political action through the development of a number of peasant parties.

One of the earliest casualties of the economic crisis was the Crédit agricole. A dual system – one supported by the rue d'Athènes, known as the Crédit agricole libre, the other largely state-supported – had developed and expanded greatly in the 1920s.[8] A collapse in farm revenues coupled with excessive commercial commitments threatened both regional and national banks. It was to be the 'free' credit groups that were to experience the severest difficulties, precipitated largely by the collapse of some of their regional banks, most notably the Plateau central.

The directors of the Plateau central had invested heavily in the creation, in 1917, of a regional abattoir at Cantaranne, near Rodez, to coordinate and market the region's meat. The early success the abattoir experienced in the immediate post-war years was replaced by chronic insolvency in the late 1920s.[9] Its collapse in 1930 forced the Plateau central to apply to the rue d'Athènes for financial support. Itself under financial strain, it was unable to meet its commitments and collapsed in December 1931. An application for state funding to allow the operations of the rue d'Athènes to continue was refused with public statements about the need for financial prudence and, in private, political glee at the embarrassment of the rival to the state-run system.[10] Ultimately, the bank was taken over by the Banque Fédérative d'Alsace-Lorraine, but this solution was not wholly satisfactory and permitted only a partial repayment of funds. The 'official' Crédit agricole, based in the boulevard St Germain, was given special advances in order to stimulate agricultural production in the late 1920s and, whilst both lending and deposits slowed up in the Depression, a degree of financial stability was maintained.

The collapse of these independent banks was a cause of great embarrassment, especially at the regional level. In Aveyron, the home of the Plateau central, republican rivals were fierce in their criticism of the group. For almost nine months the republican *Courrier de l'Aveyron* castigated the Plateau central with accusations of mismanagement and financial incompetence. It was, one critic argued, 'a so-called social organisation which amounts to nothing more than a commercial company . . . and a badly run one at that'.[11] Such polemics echoed the debates of the early years of the century when tirades against the supposedly incompetent priests and *notables* who were active in agricultural affairs dominated the local press. The strength of feeling against the Plateau central was such that, for the first time, a rival syndical organisation was created in the region to oppose it.[12]

In some regions the network of syndicates and other groups fared rather better. Gueslin's study of the organisation of credit in Alsace has shown how the strength and broad membership of the credit movement, established in the relative prosperity of the 1920s, helped it to weather the difficulties of the

Depression years. If the 'official' Crédit agricole in the region faced difficulties from 1936, because of government pressures to finance the affairs of the
Wheat Office, the independent groups which were part of the Fédération
agricole d'Alsace et de Lorraine prospered. Whilst activity did slow down in
the second part of the decade, there was no severe financial crisis as occurred
elsewhere. The Fédération was thus well able to withstand pressures from
the more extreme corporatist demagogues of the region. A relative prosperity, in contrast to the financial insolvency of the rue d'Athènes, gave the
organisation both internal pride and external prestige.[13]

It was the financial problems of the rue d'Athènes, coupled with a recognition of the severe economic crisis in French agriculture, that prompted the
emergence of a new corporatist ethos amongst certain younger syndical
activists in the early 1930s. Corporatist ideals had long been part and parcel
of conservative syndicalism. The stress on hierarchy, discipline, and Christian self-help had been a formative influence in the early movement. The
profession, through the agricultural syndicate, was envisaged as the most
appropriate body to judge matters of production and social welfare. Corporatist theorists, such as Salleron and Le Roy Ladurie, wedded the traditional
focus on the mixed agricultural syndicate as the central organisational pivot
of the rural world, with a modernising, even technocratic emphasis which
contrasted with the nostalgic peasantism of the old leadership.

Gathering around them a new generation of leaders, a number of them
progressive farmers educated at the Catholic agricultural colleges of Pur-
pan, Angers and Beauvais, this group detached the Union centrale from its
old spiritual and ideological stronghold on the rue d'Athènes and, in 1934,
rechristened it as the Union nationale des syndicats agricoles (UNSA). A
regeneration of syndicalism in the countryside followed, with a stress on a
corporatist vision of the rural world. For the new leadership, state intervention in a period of economic crisis marked a serious threat to rural
society – one of the central tenets of corporatism was to control that
intervention and to delegate questions of production, marketing and working conditions to the local and regional syndicate. For men like Le Roy
Ladurie and Salleron, whose syndical experience had been gained in the
powerful Office central in Brittany, the central role of syndicalism seemed
both natural and obvious. The example of Germany, where agricultural
affairs were controlled through corporatist organisations, provided a useful
example. Similarly, corporatist organisation of agriculture in Mussolini's
Italy had resulted in spectacular advances in production, at least in the early
stages, and provided evidence of the apparent successes of a corporatist
organisation of economic life.[14]

The Congrès syndical paysan held at Caen in 1937 marked the renewal of
both the membership and policy of the new syndicalism. Some 1.2 million
'peasant families' were listed as enrolled in syndicates, a membership figure

which, the organisers claimed, was a true and representative one.[15] As in previous periods, the bulk of the influence of the movement resided in the powerful regional unions. The Office central at Landernau was one of the most influential. Under the control of Hervé de Guébriant, it had greatly expanded its marketing and cooperative services during the crisis of the 1930s which, when wedded to the social and insurance services it had developed over the past two decades, gave the office a virtual organisational monopoly in Brittany.[16]

In south-western France the corporatist effort was spearheaded by a landowner from the Tarn, Alain de Chanterac. As was shown in chapter 4, one of the most powerful syndicates of the region, the Plateau central, had been founded by conservative social Catholics to stem the rural exodus and rebuild peasant values in the region. An emigrant society, the Solidarité aveyronnaise, founded to help those who had migrated from Aveyron, had been instrumental in setting up the Plateau central and now, some thirty years later, it played a formative role, with de Chanterac, in seeking to regenerate syndical affairs in the region.[17] Growing disquiet had been ex-pressed at the increased commercial activity of the syndicate, and the collapse of its bank in 1931 had alienated many members. Furthermore, it was argued, the very success of the regional cooperative was threatening the livelihoods of many small merchants and shopkeepers who were unable to match the prices the syndicate was able to offer. Excessive commercialism, a charge which had often been levied at powerful regional syndicates through-out France, was, it was argued, distorting the proper moral and social role of the syndical movement.[18]

This general discontent was seized upon by the activists close to the regenerated UNSA. Dr Ayrignac, an influential member of the Solidarité aveyronnaise, and de Chanterac were both active in the Plateau central in 1935 and 1936 and embarked on a propaganda campaign to recreate an active and local syndical organisation.[19] Through his journal, *L'Effort pay-san*, de Chanterac had a powerful means of spreading the new corporatist philosophy in the south-west and this programme was carried out, noted Ayrignac, 'in direct liaison with the directors of the UNSA and as part of a coordinated plan in many other departments'. The arrival of the Popular Front government led to a concerted campaign throughout the south-west of syndical reunions, the election of new board members, the breathing of new, corporatist life into the quiescent syndical movement.[20]

The preoccupations of *L'Effort paysan* reflected the concerns of UNSA in a number of respects and serve to typify what was taking place in a number of regions. First, the obsession of previous syndicates with economic activity was attacked. The real task of the syndicate, noted Ayrignac, was 'to defend the profession and sustain the peasant family' and not to transform the syndicalist into a merchant or industrialist.[21] Secondly, it aimed to create a

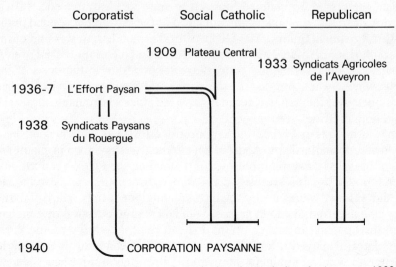

Figure 5.1 Organisational changes in agricultural associations in Aveyron, 1933–40

single, politically powerful peasant grouping in the region with which to face up to the perceived threat of the Popular Front.[22] Through 1937 and 1938 internecine conflict developed in the region between the Plateau central and a confederation grouped around *L'Effort Paysan* until, in April 1938, a single federation, the Syndicats paysans, was created and affiliated to the UNSA.[23] These changes reflected the conflicts between three traditions – a republican and social Catholic tradition, with roots going back to the turn of the century and a newer, corporatist tradition, which was ultimately to triumph under Vichy and the Corporation paysanne (Figure 5.1).

In some regions the early 1930s saw the emergence of a peasant syndicalism, led, not by the old rural élite of doctors, large landowners and solicitors, but by small peasant farmers. One of the most important of these groups was the Syndicat des cultivateurs-cultivants in Brittany. The movement was rooted in the powerful social catholicism in the region. Whilst the Office central at Landernau dominated agricultural life in the area, the action of a radical priest, the Abbé Mancel, had been instrumental in creating a Fédération des syndicats paysans de l'Ouest, independently of the Office central, in 1924. By 1928 it had a membership in excess of 15,000, grouped in some 200 syndicates, concentrated in Ille-et-Vilaine, but with some support in Côtes-du-Nord.

In contrast to most agrarian syndicates of this period, it specifically excluded from membership all those without a direct interest in farming. Only the owner–occupiers, the *cultivateurs-cultivants*, were eligible. Led by

Mancel (who frequently found himself at odds with the church hierarchy in the region), and supported by a powerful regional newspaper, *L'Ouest éclair*, the federation, like its rivals, created a series of practical institutions – insurance mutuals, an agricultural cooperative and bank, a sickness insurance scheme – designed to give practical expression to peasant solidarity and to improve the quality of country life. Whilst salaried workers were excluded from membership, good relations between owner and worker were advocated in the spirit of social catholicism.

In 1927 a Ligue des paysans de l'Ouest was founded under the auspices of the federation in order to coordinate political pressure for reform in the regional and national administration. Its manifesto was explicit as to the role of syndicates and the league: 'some farmers may think that, despite our current disunity, a common front for policy reform requires little effort . . . Don't be deceived: in the syndicates you will certainly find all those credit and mutual services to which you are accustomed. In the League, however, you can unite to make your concerns known to elected representatives . . . the syndicate will take care of your material needs – the league is there to cater for your intellectual, moral and social demands.'[24]

Whilst obtaining a considerable audience in the early 1930s in much of Brittany, the federation and league had foundered by the middle of the decade. Opposition from both the powerful traditionalists of the Office central and the church hierarchy, coupled with internal squabbles, were largely responsible. Church opposition was especially significant, prefiguring the debate which would ensue when the recently founded Jeunesse agricole catholique began to emphasise its message of peasant promotion in the late 1930s. The rise of Dorgères in Brittany further diminished the influence of the federation. In the short-term, the experiment to create an authentically peasant organisation failed, in the longer term, the experiment was to be repeated with much greater success in other organisations.

In some regions the renewal of syndical activity did not occur until late in the decade. In the wheat- and sugar-beet producing department of Aisne, in northern France, a powerful Union des syndicats agricoles de l'Aisne had, since 1919, established a weighty network of local syndicates and mutuals. Of particular importance in this region of large producers was the syndical wheat cooperative which, in 1931, had collected some 45 per cent of all the wheat produced in the department.[25] But the economic crisis of the thirties damaged both the functioning and financial stability of the union and its activity was not renewed until 1938. The chief architect of the renewal, a dynamic, 31-year-old wheat farmer, René Blondelle, was later to become one of the chief strategists of the post-war national syndical movement.[26]

It is worth dwelling on events in the regions for they reveal the roots of conflict evident in the syndical movement in this period. The old problem of organisational diversity is clear. Chronically unable to unite nationally, regional and local syndical history frequently dissolves into conflict between groups for membership and influence. In the Massif Central and the south-west, even the sustained intervention of the UNSA had been unable to ensure a unitary organisation in a region which, in social and political terms, might be expected to be favourable. Secondly, such conflicts illustrate a theme general to the syndical history of the period, the clash of generations. One of the features of UNSA was its young, technically-skilled leadership. The steady promotion of what Toussaint called the 'new peasant bour-geoisie' had been a feature of the new corporatist organisations.[27] This challenge to the old *notable* class, so dominant in the regional syndicates at the time the national groups were being transformed, was reflected in the organisational conflict which sometimes accompanied these changes. The process was, however, slow and laborious. Thirdly, syndical conflicts were a reflection of the broader politicisation of the peasantry in this period. On both the right and left peasant parties sought to elicit a direct response from the agricultural population – in the articulation of this response the in-volvement of syndicates was inevitable.

Peasant politics

The task of organising the farming community was not taken up solely by the syndical and cooperative movement. Political parties and interests were not slow in seeking to channel rural discontent into new political formations or extra-parliamentary pressure groups. The growth of political groupings was more marked on the right than the left. Ironically, at a time when the peasantry was quitting the countryside in droves, ideologues were busy extolling the virtues of the pure, unsullied country life. There was no unified peasant response to the blandishments of the politicians – much depended on local tradition and the strength of local *notables*. But it can be argued that large sections of the peasantry were attracted by the traditions of direct action established by some of the new groups and also that, as most peasants were involved in the marketing of produce and hence were affected by price collapse, there was at least some sense of a shared economic position despite the differences between peasants in terms of landholding, tenure, farm size and dominant production. There was no unified peasant response to the events of the 1930s, but there was more common ground between peasant groups than might at first be imagined.

One of the earliest peasant parties to be founded was the Parti agraire created in 1927 by a flamboyant one-time teacher who titled himself Fleu-rant Agricola. A narrowly political organisation, its first deputy (for the Puy-de-Dôme) was elected in 1932. In 1936, a dozen deputies were elected for the party but its lack of ideological homogeneity hampered its growth.[28] A more serious challenge came from the rising star of rural demogogy, Henri Dorgères.

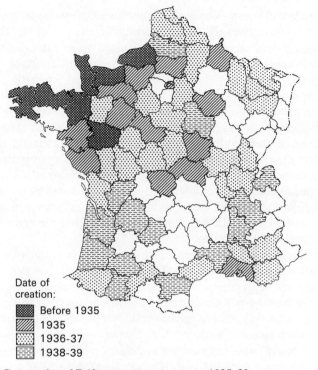

Date of
creation:

▓ Before 1935
▨ 1935
▒ 1936-37
▤ 1938-39

Figure 5.2 Geography of Défense paysanne groups 1935–39

A journalist born in the Nord in 1897, Dorgères was to become the central figure in a powerful peasant movement throughout France. As a journalist and editor of the *Progrès agricole de l'Ouest*, he had begun to campaign for an authentic peasant militancy in the late 1920s. The application of social-security legislation to the agricultural sector was the catalyst for the creation of his first Comité de défense paysanne, in Ille-et-Vilaine in January 1929. A fierce opponent of government intervention in agricultural matters, he argued that the profession, not the state, should organise agriculture. With a programme of opposition to social security and increased taxation, the movement spread rapidly. Rooted solidly in Brittany and Normandy by the middle of the 1930s (Figure 5.2), the Dorgerist blend of peasantism, corporatism and a quasi-fascist organisational structure led to the establishment of committees in some 52 departments by the end of 1937. If the origins of the movement were in Brittany, its chief financial support came from the north and Paris Basin where both large farmers and the agricultural proletariat lent support to the movement. By 1938, membership of these groups was estimated at half a million, concentrated in the *bocage* of the west, the large farms of the north and the small-farming communities of the south-west.[29]

As Orry has judiciously noted, this most powerful of right-wing currents in the thirties had complex origins, numerous allies (on both right and left) and uncertain objectives. Its support came from the peasantry, the agricultural proletariat of the *ceinture verte* around Paris and conservative intellectuals, many of whom were to become influential under Vichy. Its cultural roots, he argues, reveal these complex origins with a powerful peasant racism coupled with an exaltation of direct action and virility. These roots cannot but reinforce the complex and elusive character of so many agricultural groups in this period. In some ways the vividness of his language and the colour of his manifestations masks the more serious contribution he made. His organisations, avowedly peasantist, were organised and run by peasant members, and Houée has argued that the creation of these groups marked an important stage in the opening out of rural mentalities. 'This defensive reflex', he notes, 'opposed to both State and the town and lacking doctrinal clarity or political astuteness was nonetheless the first major peasant explosion of the industrial era.'[30]

The attitude of the traditional agricultural organisations to these developments was usually equivocal. They had, of course, always refused any kind of political engagement, seeking thereby to maintain the independence and neutrality of the movement. Such was the vigour and strength of these movements, however, that to have ignored them would have been impossible. The development of a corporatist ethos through the creation of UNSA, in 1934, coincided with the peaking of peasant politicisation through Dorgères and Fleurant Agricola and, if syndical leaders sought to maintain a *cordon sanitaire* between themselves and these noisy groups, they were not averse to channelling that discontent into increased syndical activity and membership. In 1934 a Front paysan was created between the UNSA, the Parti agraire, the Defence Committees of Dorgères and some of the specialist producer groups. A campaign of propaganda by the group, through 1935, sought to enrol peasant support for changing economic policy.

In Aveyron, for example, all the major agricultural associations of the department, with the exception of the strongly republican group, and including the official chamber of agriculture, were signatories to a document demanding a new *politique agricole*. A demonstration, in June 1935, attracted 11,000 peasants to hear Dorgères, Le Roy Ladurie and de Chanterac. A 'conspiracy of bureaucrats and international capitalists' was at the root of the problem, Dorgères argued, whilst the more measured tones of Le Roy Ladurie, secretary-general of UNSA, argued for the installation of a corporatist regime like that of Mussolini's Italy to save the nation's peasantry.[31]

The meeting, no doubt like many others elsewhere, attracted varying publicity. The Catholic press welcomed what was said but republicans distributed leaflets attacking Dorgères as nothing but a peasant fascist hobnobbing with the squirearchy of the department. A small contingent of Greenshirts was established in Aveyron and the imprisonment of Dorgères in late 1935, for encouraging a tax-evasion scheme, created some discontent but, in general, the June meeting proved to be the climax rather than the starting-point of agrarian discontent in the department.[32]

By late 1935, UNSA and its more politicised allies had parted company, partly because of the growing extremism of Dorgères, partly because of the growing self-confidence of the regenerated national syndicate. But the regional power of Dorgères remained, with some 40,000 members of defence committees in 1939 based in Brittany, Normandy, the Paris Basin and Lorraine.[33] In Brittany, for example, the tacit support of de Guébriant's Office central at Landernau helped to maintain the influence of Dorgères in the region.[34]

Socialist and communist groups

Although the decade was most clearly marked with the imprint of right-wing peasant politics, parties of the left continued their attempts to maintain or extend their influence in the countryside. In general they met with only limited, localised success: 'the efforts of socialist and communists to penetrate the peasant movement through the creation of syndicates were generally unsuccessful'.[35]

The earliest efforts had been made by the communists. In regions such as the Landes, Allier and Corrèze, efforts at enrolling an agricultural proletariat and small peasantry in syndicates which were closer to the urban–industrial conception of such groups had begun in the 1920s. One of the most charismatic figures in the organisation of communist syndicates was a small farmer from Lot-et-Garonne, Renaud Jean, who had established the Conseil paysan français in 1925 to coordinate the communist effort. Its role and influence was modest. According to Gratton, its first congress in 1926 grouped some 13,000 members in 110 syndicates – modest indeed in comparison with the massed troops of the Union centrale. But the modest nature of communist efforts reflected the view of its leaders that they should create their own groups only in areas which were not susceptible to a policy of entryism into 'bourgeois' unions.[36]

In 1929 the conseil was transformed into the Confédération générale des paysans travailleurs (CGPT). But, geographically, its influence was restricted to the north-west Massif Central, central and south-western France, and parts of Languedoc, and its traditional membership continued to be the sharecropper or proletariat. During the peasant discontent of the early 1930s, however, the CGPT was involved in protest action against land and property seizures (the same cause which was the catalyst for Dorgères) which took it outside its traditional sphere of influence into parts of Brittany, the Alps and lower Normandy. In January 1937, Renaud Jean's journal, *La Voix paysanne*, which had struggled to make ends meet, was finally taken

Parti Agraire
Communist/Socialist groups
Défense Paysanne

Figure 5.3 Geography of peasant politics in the 1930s

over by the communist party to become *La Terre* with a circulation of about 35,000 in May of that year.[37]

Socialist efforts at grouping the peasantry were, like those of the communists, limited socially and geographically. Henri Calvayrac, a small farmer from the Haute-Garonne was the animator of a Confédération nationale paysanne established in February 1933. Its strength, estimated through newspaper circulations at about the level of the communists, was based in the centre and south-west, with some isolated support in Brittany. Attempts at forming a single socialist–communist grouping were regularly made between 1934 and 1939, but met with little success.[38] The geographical implantation of both communist and socialist groups was restricted: outside of a swathe of territory on the western flanks of the Massif where Jean and Calvayrac were active, membership was small and episodic. The power base of Dorgères and the right-wing groups was much more solid (Figure 5.3).

Despite the small size of these groups of the left they readily engaged in bitter polemic with each other in their search for power and membership in particular regions. The struggles between socialist and communist in the Landes exemplifies this. As was shown in chapter 4, the particular agrarian conditions in the region had led to vigorous activity in the early twenties by both communist and socialist activists. Strike action, followed by the accord of Dax in 1920, put a temporary halt to the agitation but by 1926 trouble flared up again. A dispute over sharecropping conditions led to a series of strikes in the Adour. With two socialists as key organisers, Rey from Paris and Désarménien from Bayonne, a concerted campaign was organised to enrol the sharecropper syndicates in the CGT.[39]

It was the socialist CGT, rather than the communist CGTU, which was most successful in this period in recruiting members.[40] The first indications of a more concerted strategy by the communists to enrol the syndicalists of the region came in 1930, when a police report noted that Renaud Jean, the animator of the Conseil paysan, had been touring the region seeking members to swell the already growing communist groups in the nearby department of Lot-et-Garonne. His journal, *La Voix paysanne*, was distributed at meetings and Jean, with his 'oratorical skills and natural *bonhomie*', urged those present to join the newly founded Paysans-travailleurs and denounced the reactionary policies of the socialists in the department. But, noted one police commissioner with a certain glee, 'these meetings were greeted with little enthusiasm and the successes that the Paysans-Travailleurs had hoped for were not forthcoming'.[41]

In the early 1930s the competition between the two groups intensified, largely as a consequence of the economic crisis. One of the major casualties were the *résiniers* who were responsible for the collection of pine resin from the extensive private and state forests of the department. That many *résiniers* were also sharecroppers exacerbated their already precarious position. In 1934 there were an estimated 18,000 *résiniers* in Landes; prices for a barrel of resin prior to processing had fallen from a peak of 1,386 francs in 1926 (at that time, it was said, the pine trees were 'weeping golden tears') to 414 francs in 1931 and 313 francs in 1933.[42]

In April and May 1934 a series of strikes took place in the forest zones of the Landes over the question of price and the conditions of exploitation, for many *résiniers* worked under sharecropping contracts which, it was argued, were especially unfavourable. In 1934 the Fédération des métayers et gemmeurs du Sud-Ouest was relaunched (it had been largely moribund since the mid 1920s) by a local socialist, Charles Prat, to pressurise both local and national administrations to take action to stabilise prices.[43] Renaud Jean meanwhile continued to tour the region pressing the case for his communist Paysans-travailleurs group. The seizures of property in lieu of taxes, a feature common to many parts of rural France at this time, prompted a renewed outburst of communist activity but, once again, Jean was outflanked by socialist groups. As one police report noted, 'the sharecropper and resin syndicates have been equally active organising reunions to counter the communist propaganda'.[44] Communist implantation was confined largely to the cantons of Roquefort and Gabarret bordering on Jean's home region of Lot-et-Garonne. Elsewhere, particularly in the central Grande Lande, the CGT remained all-powerful; in 1935, it was noted, 'the influence of the *Paysans-travailleurs* is practically nil in this region; the CGT has been able to maintain its stronghold'.[45]

As with the sharecroppers, the relation between agricultural labourers and the traditional agricultural syndicates remained equivocal. For all the rhetoric surrounding the ideals of a 'mixed' syndicate embracing labour and capital, farmer and worker, the involvement of the proletariat in syndicate activity was limited. It can be argued that neither rhetoric (the virtues of the family farm, of property, of independence) nor policies (goods, services, insurance for the peasant) were calculated to appeal to the farm labourer. Gratton's analysis of the place and activity of the agricultural labourer serves to emphasise the importance of strike activity, sometimes coordinated by syndicates, sometimes not, in creating a sense of solidarity amongst these groups.[46] Indeed, as has been seen, common cause for a reform of share-cropping in the Landes was central to the creation of a regional syndical group.

Strike activity, at a peak in 1926 and 1928, tailed off in the early part of the thirties, largely as a result of fears of rural unemployment at a time when urban jobs were no longer plentiful.[47] The election of a Popular Front government in 1936 did, however, have an effect on the actions of agricultural labourers. A series of strikes in the summer of that year were, argued politicians of the right, imitating the industrial unrest of the period. A practical outcome of these conflicts was the legalisation of collective labour contracts on a regional scale which laid down conditions of work and remuneration for agricultural labourers. In 1937 a further bout of agricultural unrest occurred in the Paris Basin and the north-east.

In the Aisne the root cause of the problem lay in the collective contracts established the previous summer after a series of strikes. In the Aisne, 31 communes and over 100 large farms were affected by strike action in July and August 1937.[48] Many of the farms were owned by the Compagnie nouvelle des sucreries réunies which refused to honour collective contracts, sacked existing workers and brought in outside labour to bring in the sugar-beet harvest. Volunteers to help harvest were brought from Paris (Dorgères was especially active in organising groups) with over 40 buses roaming the countryside in search of work. Clashes occurred between strikers and volunteers at Ollezy, Lehancourt and Seracourt in the heart of the sugar-beet country. At Seracourt an attempt by strikers to push a bus containing 40 volunteers into a nearby canal was only just thwarted by mounted police. Efforts to bring in the harvest were coordinated by the Union des syndicats agricoles de l'Aisne, demonstrating clearly where the interests of the dominant syndicalism lay. By early August, however, temperatures had fallen as the volunteers, clearly more of a hindrance than a help, left the region and the strike action was ended through the mediating role of the Bourse du travail.[49]

State intervention and the crisis

If the election of a Popular Front government in May 1936 was greeted with dismay by the agrarian right, this response should not be allowed to obscure the fact that the rural electorate, and, in particular, the small peasantry, played a not inconsiderable part in that electoral triumph, with strong support from the peasantry of the centre and south-west and from the agricultural proletariat of some of the northern departments.[50] A central tenet of the Popular Front manifesto was a reform of cereal marketing in order to ameliorate the low prices and chronic instability of that sector, and the creation of the Office du blé (later transformed into the Office National interprofessionnel des céréales) in August 1936 stands as the central legacy of Popular Front farming policy. Its longer-term importance in preparing the way for increased state intervention was of great significance.

The aim of the legislation was simple, its passage and execution fraught with difficulty. George Monnet, the new Minister of Agriculture in Blum's cabinet, sought to first organise and control a seemingly anarchical wheat market, secondly, ensure an adequately remunerative price and, thirdly, institute some sort of mechanism for arriving at a final wheat price which took account of producer, processor and, for the first time, consumer needs. The mechanism was a state-run body, empowered to control all wheat imports and exports and charged with establishing a commission to oversee overall price structures. The storage of grain was to be facilitated through the creation of a network of cooperative silos funded largely through increased state subventions to the Crédit agricole.[51]

As Wright has shown, the passage of the legislation establishing the Office du blé was problematic, not only in the Chamber of deputies, where the centre-right sought to water down the bill but, more especially, in the Senate, still dominated by rural conservative interests. They branded the bill 'the handsomest Marxist monument known to legislation anywhere' which would mean 'serfdom for the French peasantry'.[52] But Monnet was thwarted only in his attempt to establish the principle of collective contracts by which producer and consumer cooperatives could negotiate contracts of purchase which would be guaranteed by government; his other aims were largely achieved.

There can be no doubt that the creation of the Office du blé marked a major advance towards the principle of sustained state intervention in the agricultural sector, an intervention which was potentially far more threatening to traditional rural élites than previous legislation on working conditions, insurance and welfare provision, legislation which had been fought by the corporatist right. What is most striking about the debate, however, was the attention devoted to the detailed mechanisms of the system rather than the fundamental principle of government intervention. Farmers, whether small or large, had experienced five years of market anarchy and falling prices, and this experience must have been important in preparing them for the experiment of greater government intervention. Behind the rhetoric of the landowning senator, more enamoured of the peasantist myth than the realities of peasant life, it is difficult to escape the conclusion that for many opponents of intervention, few real alternatives were at hand.

Some of the fiercest debate was over the structure of the committee which would control the working of the office. A political realist, Monnet was aware that, unless its structure was carefully regulated, the powerful UNSA representatives and the regional unions could simply turn the office into a fief of its own. On the council of 51 members he therefore allowed no more than 29 places for producer groups (amongst those groups were representatives of the Conseil national paysan and Paysans-travailleurs as well as UNSA) and, by requiring a three-quarters majority for price-fixing decisions, he effectively prevented the traditional groups of the rural world from disrupting the activity of the organisation.[53]

Its success is hard to evaluate. Wheat prices certainly rose from 74 francs/quintal in 1935 to 140 francs in 1936 and 180 francs in 1937.[54] But this rise was aided, at least in part, by the poor harvests of those years. A bumper harvest in 1938 put severe pressure on the office and brought fierce criticism of the creeping *étatisme* implicit in the administrative control of cooperatives, stocking policy and the make-up of the governing committee. The wheat producers' group, the AGPB, was especially critical but the ability of the office to buy and store wheat meant that such criticism could be borne. As one director of the AGPB noted, 'we can't continue to practise the politics of the ostrich – the Office has, by and large, been welcomed by the peasantry'.[55]

This guarded welcome is perhaps the most notable aspect of the creation of the office. Even in regions dominated by agrarian syndicates, realism rather than rhetoric greeted the fledgling organisation. At Landernau the powerful Office central was fearful of the effects of the office. As an organisation it was in favour of regulation, it said, but not state intervention. 'The choice', it noted, 'was between free organisation of the Profession and the kick of the collectivist boot.' But, setting aside such rhetoric, it was not slow to use the newly created system to its advantage by channelling all wheat supplies through the local syndicates to the main cooperative at Landernau, thereby enhancing the already considerable economic power of the syndicate.[56]

In Aveyron both the conservative Plateau central and the republican Fédération des syndicats agricoles de l'Aveyron gave a guarded welcome to

the office. Indeed the former group had played an important role in establishing a major wheat cooperative in the department in August 1934. Two
years later its republican rival established a second cooperative at Villefranche-de-Rouergue. But the attractions of state financial assistance
brought both syndical groups together in establishing the major cereal
cooperative silos at Baraqueville in the heart of the Ségala, the major
cereal-producing district of the department.[57] The inauguration of the silos
in November 1938 marked, according to *La Terre rouergate*, 'an event of
fundamental importance in the history of the agricultural profession in
Aveyron', bringing together rival groups in the defence of their members'
interests. The same syndical journal was vigorous in its defence of the office.
Despite its problems, it noted, 'it plays an essential part in protecting the
small producer from the speculators and financial vampires that beset the
industry'.[58]

The office was the one major institution bequeathed by the Popular Front
to French agricultural life; its long-term impact was far from negligible.
Whilst the plethora of social legislation (the paid holidays, 40-hour week,
salary increases) applied only marginally to the agricultural sector, the
economic crisis of the decade was responsible for establishing a new relationship between agriculture and the state.

A new peasant élite?

According to both Barral and Wright, the most important long-term legacy
bequeathed by the Depression era was the training and promotion of a new
peasant élite. But the evidence of a radical change in the leadership of
regional and national syndicates is difficult to find. The creation of UNSA to
some extent marked a shift from the traditional dominance of the *notable* to
a more openly farming leadership. But, despite the lip-service paid to the
peasantist basis of the new rural philosophy, corporatism, the seats of power
were still largely occupied by the bourgeoisie and large landowner. Where,
then, is the evidence for this sea-change in leadership?

Perhaps the most detailed analysis of representation in any agricultural
group has been carried out by Mora.[59] In her study of the creation and
development of the chambers of agriculture she examined the 1936 elections
to the chamber in which around 3½ million of the agricultural population
voted. Her conclusions point to a high degree of stability amongst those
individuals and groups elected. The power of the syndical and cooperative
groups in the electoral process was considerable. On average there were at
least 100 agricultural groups entitled to vote in each department for the
group slates in the chamber. The traditional syndicates were assiduous in
ensuring that their allied groups were on the chamber list. In some departments, as Table 5.1 shows, there were several hundred such groups – a

Table 5.1. *Groups registered for Chamber of Agriculture elections 1936*

Haute-Marne	535	Puy-de-Dôme	304
Pas-de-Calais	480	Nord	288
Bas-Rhin	359	Ain	283
Rhône	331	Drôme	267

National average = 100 groups
Source: Mora (1967)

testament both to the fertility of the movement and the political skill of traditional syndicalists in marshalling their forces.

That most lists were dominated by a few older-established groups is illustrated by the fact that there was very little competition between rival group lists. Only in parts of the Massif Central and the south-west (the Allier, Landes, Dordogne, Haute-Garonne) and one or two northern departments was competition evident. Analysis of those elected showed that 85 per cent were owner–occupiers and 9 per cent farmers or sharecroppers. The bias in eligibility against agricultural workers (at least two years' employment with the same employer was required) meant that only 1 per cent of those elected came into that category.[60] The chambers did not create a new class of agricultural activists or constitute a new pressure group able to override the often sectional interests of the traditional syndicates and cooperatives so dominant at this time. As Pitaud scathingly pointed out, 'Most of the members of the Chambers would be hard pushed to plough a straight furrow or to tell a two-year-old bull from a milk-cow; on the other hand at least they know how to dress well, what constitutes good taste in jewels and, of course, how to deliver a pretty speech.'[61]

It is primarily to the Catholic church that one must turn for evidence of a change in attitudes and activity on the part of the silent peasant majority. As has been emphasised earlier, the church, through the influence of social catholicism and under the aegis of the ACJF, had played an important role in the expansion of syndicates and cooperatives. The ACJF continued in existence through the 1920s, playing a part in the social and cultural life of the countryside. But its influence was declining and the example of the Jeunesse ouvrière chrétienne (JOC) founded in 1927 and the first of the Action catholique movements in France, was followed in 1929 by the creation of the Jeunesse agricole catholique (JAC).[62]

A guiding principle of this youth movement, destined to become one of the most influential in France, was that before even speaking of religion it was necessary to be fully aware of the realities of social, economic and cultural life in the countryside. Observation of everyday life, of the economic conditions of farming, of the relationships between different rural

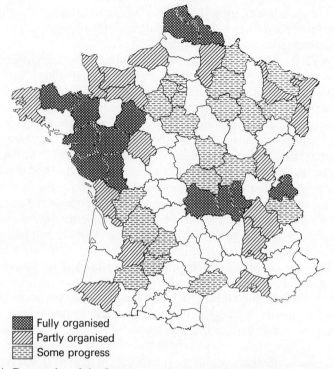

Fully organised
Partly organised
Some progress

Figure 5.4 Geography of the Jeunesse agricole catholique in 1935

groups was an intrinsic part of the JAC programme.[63] It both built on earlier roots and established radically new priorities for young country-dwellers. Its roots lay in earlier youth training programmes established by some of the larger regional syndicates who had been eager to create youth sections to their unions which would ensure continued membership. Regional unions such as the Plateau central, the Office central and the Union du Sud-Est had also established agricultural education programmes in the 1920s to fill the gaps left by an inadequate government education programme. But the emphasis on observation, on active and militant involvement in agricultural associations, on the search for Christian solutions to daily problems gave the JAC an emphasis altogether different from its somewhat paternalistic and conservative predecessor.

From a diverse series of small groups which were especially strong in Nord, Rhône, Yonne and Meurthe-et-Moselle, some 500 sections in 65 dioceses had been established by 1934. In 1935 there were at least 10,000 youngsters enrolled in the agricultural correspondence courses coordinated by the JAC.[64] Figure 5.4 shows the geography of JAC implantation in 1935. Interestingly, the strongest regions were not necessarily those which were traditionally the most Catholic for, in such regions, the novelty of the JAC met with some hostility from the Church hierarchy. Rather it points to the important role played by the local chaplain or *aumônier* whose influence was often unpredictable.

The creation of the Jeunesse agricole catholique féminine (JACF) in June 1933 was intended to provide solutions to potentially the most severe problem facing rural areas, the exodus of young women. Working conditions for women were more severe than for the men since their areas of work included both domestic and farming tasks. Any capital available to the family was spent on agricultural investments – homes lacked running water, decent washing facilities, and the most elementary privacy for both individual and couple. Isolation and the problems of cohabitation added to the difficulties of women and further encouraged migration. Whilst for the man marriage usually meant additional labour resources for the peasant farm, for the woman it meant leaving home to become a supplementary worker in an extended family whose affairs were governed not by her and her husband, but by the grandparents who owned and ran the farm. The early surveys of the JACF focused on just such problems but tended to concentrate on largely material solutions rather than engaging in an examination of the problems of sexual inequality. The JACF proved as successful as the JAC in attracting members – by 1938 there were some 12,000 militants in the movement and a journal, *La Jeunesse agricole féminine*, with a circulation of 86,000.[65]

In this period the foundations for the success of the JAC and JACF in the following twenty years were laid. The task of reChristianising the countryside was embarked upon with enthusiasm and, from the middle of the 1930s, with the full support of most of the hierarchy. The motto of the JAC, 'Observe, Assess, Act' emphasised the practical preoccupations of the organisation. The annual surveys and discussion of problems carried out by the JAC were accompanied by serious efforts to improve the quality of cultural and social life in the countryside. Thus the activity of these groups in these early years was twofold. The most obvious was a willingness to develop social life in the community through organising singing, theatrical and agricultural competitions and by holding conferences and meetings, often carefully organised to foster a sense of unity and pride (this applies especially to the annual congress and regional pilgrimages). But these external manifestations concealed a much more serious activity – the renewal of self-confidence, the development of a new élite from amongst the peasantry itself and the steady apprenticeship for positions of responsibility in the groups and associations of the rural world. This steady, incremental action was to bear rich harvest in the years to come.

The experience of the Depression – economic collapse, syndical disarray, vigorous, sometimes violent, peasant discontent, increased state intervention – were thus central to the history of agricultural groups in France.

Before 1930, the key organisations in France were traditionalist in ethos, dominated by a rural élite which was wedded to the notion of a large, fecund and Catholic peasantry, independent of town and state, unsullied by class conflict. The events of the Depression were to transform these groups. A rejuvenated syndicalism saw corporatism as a means of organising agricultural affairs and, though the old guard were not initially uncomfortable with this philosophy, its increasingly technocratic emphasis showed that a return to the halcyon days of a pre-ordained 'eternal order of the fields' was not a possibility. The creation of the Office du blé was vital – it was a symbol of the pressures for greater state regulation of agricultural affairs. Finally, in the new youth movements of the Catholic church, the foundations were laid for the flowering of the syndical, cooperative and self-help movement in the years following the Second World War.

6

Agricultural associations under Vichy, 1940–1944

The fall of France in June 1940, and the arrival in power of Pétain, marked the end of the Third Republic and the establishment of a regime whose central theme of 'Travail, famille, patrie' emphasised a return to the supposed moral order, conservatism and peasant values of the nation. That nation, wrote Pétain, 'will recover all its ancient strength through contact with the soil'.[1] The myth of peasant unity, of a timeless rural France betrayed by the cynical manipulations of corrupt politicians, was a central part of both the ideology and policy of the new regime. But these quasi-mystical pronouncements in favour of a peasant France wedded to a traditional, Catholic morality sat, at times uneasily, with a policy towards agriculture and its institutions which was sometimes radical and far-reaching. Any judgement of the four years of Vichy cannot ignore this fundamental paradox.

As in the preceding decade the economic conjuncture was highly unfavourable to French agriculture. The Occupation engendered a series of chronic crises in the agricultural sector. Manpower shortages were acute – a large number of agricultural workers were held prisoner (some 700,000 according to one estimate).[2] German requisitions of agricultural produce were considerable – annual totals of some 3 million hectolitres of wine, 7 million quintaux of wheat and 15 per cent of all milk production were withdrawn from France.[3] Even though, as Milward notes, 'the Germans met with passive, undeclared and often unperceived resistance on the peasant farm', such losses could not be avoided.[4] Overall estimates suggest that at least 15 per cent of all French agricultural production was requisitioned. Not only was current production hit by the Occupation but future production was compromised.

The increases in productivity and production since 1918 had required major mechanical and technical inputs into farming; such inputs were lacking in the war years. It became practically impossible to find spare parts for foreign farm machinery, to obtain sufficient supplies of fuel and fertiliser, or

92

to procure the pesticides and herbicides necessary for good cultivation. In such conditions production fell catastrophically – for wheat by 18 per cent to 20 per cent, for potatoes by 40 per cent, for milk by 30 per cent – during the Vichy years. Furthermore, French consumers were unable to obtain vital colonial supplies of sugar, fruit and oils.[5] In the face of these difficulties much government effort was devoted, not to solving production problems, but rather to ensuring that what was produced was equitably distributed. The Vichy period was first and foremost one of chronic food shortage.

Administrative difficulties compounded the crisis of *ravitaillement général*. The division of the country into an occupied and unoccupied zone (which lasted until 1942), the attachment of the Nord and Pas-de-Calais to Belgian rather than French administration, and the loss of Alsace and Lorraine to the Reich made overall organisation of the economy difficult. The loss of the chemical industries of the latter greatly exacerbated fertiliser shortages.[6] Added to the problem of fuel supplies, the new geographical divisions made transport of produce difficult and central control ever more problematic. The partition of the country into specific regions which were to be responsible for their own provisioning also posed severe difficulties. Thus a region such as Languedoc, dedicated to monoculture of the vine for some 60 years, was in a much more parlous position than Brittany and Normandy where polycultural farming was already established. Individual departments fought hard to be placed within one regional boundary rather than another, with departments in the Massif involved in unseemly scrambles to avoid being placed in the same food zone as Languedoc.

The immediate effects of these problems were twofold. For the consumer, rationing became increasingly severe, with the establishment of at least eight categories ranging from youngsters through manual and office workers to the elderly. Rations were estimated at an average of 1,700 calories in 1942, 1,000 calories two years later, well below the quantity needed. A widespread blackmarket developed, city-dwellers suddenly rediscovered their rural relations, the peasantry itself became envied for its privileged access to food. For the producers themselves, food shortages led to the elaboration of an increasingly complex set of regulations governing the delivery of quotas of produce to the market.[7] One beneficial effect of the shortages was a rise in relative living standards for the peasant; according to Cépède 'most observers agree that during the Occupation the standard of living of most peasants, especially in the poorer regions, rose appreciably'.[8]

The Service du ravitaillement, established in April 1939, became an increasingly powerful government tool. The scope of the Office du blé was widened to include all cereals, and similar organisations were established to deal with sugar-beet and wine. A national commission was also set up to establish regional quotas for agricultural produce. One of the most powerful local mechanisms for directing agricultural production were the *contrats de culture*. Through these contracts, drawn up voluntarily or, after February 1941, on a compulsory basis, each farmer had to undertake to produce a given quantity of products which were in short supply. Thus oil products, chronically short at this time, were especially favoured; farmers agreeing to produce the necessary crops would often receive priority deliveries of items such as fuel oil and mechanical equipment which were all but unobtainable on the official market.[9] The net effect of such contracts was limited. The problem of fraud was never effectively tackled, and pricing policy, often more attentive to consumer than producer, hardly encouraged prompt delivery of quotas.

The Corporation paysanne

It is important to emphasise these economic aspects of the Vichy period, for their practical implications were to undermine and ultimately destroy the purer doctrinal aspects of the new regime. The peasant family was to be the cornerstone and epitome of the state. The fall of France had been seen by many conservative *notables* as testimony to the corruptness, instability and anti-rural bias of the parliamentary regime of the Third Republic. Around the charismatic and venerated figure of Pétain, the hero of Verdun, the Vichy government sought a renaissance of the spiritual and moral values of the nation, values which were to be found deep in the benign soil of peasant France. In its policy towards the peasant community, the Vichy government sought a blueprint for a corporatist organisation of social and economic life.

This vision was not new and, at an early stage in the development of a corporatist regime for the farming community, many of those active in UNSA and the right-wing peasant parties in the preceding decade came into prominence. It was these leaders – Dorgères, Le Roy Ladurie, Salleron, de Chanterac – who were to play an important part in framing the early legislation on the organisation of agriculture enacted under Vichy.[10] The core of this legislation – an act establishing the Organisation corporative de l'agriculture – was brought into force on 2 December 1940.[11] In theory the act marked the triumph of the corporatists who had been so active in the last decade. Not all militants welcomed the new legislation. Augé-Laribé, for example, feared that local and regional power and experience would be subordinated to central control, whilst the specialist producer organisations, notably the AGPB, fought for a particular place to be accorded to their interests. A corporatist organisation based on specific products was, however, ruled out on the somewhat dubious grounds that, since the majority of peasants were polycultural producers, a general purpose corporation was most appropriate.[12]

The corporation placed the syndicate firmly at the heart of agricultural affairs. It was, noted Salleron, the geometric centre of the profession, and it was the organisation which was given primacy over all others. 'If this had not been done', argued Salleron, 'chaos would have resulted'.[13] Membership was to all intents and purposes compulsory, for membership of any of its allied groups (mutuals, cooperatives, etc.) was taken to imply and require membership of the syndicate. The act, furthermore, gave greatly increased powers to the syndicate as the main body charged with establishing conditions of work, legal affairs and rates of pay in the farm sector. The multiplicity of other groups active in the countryside were reorganised in a more hierarchical manner and in general subordinated to the syndicate. In his peasant charter, Salleron outlined the precepts of the corporation: the overthrow of individualism, the dominance of the general over specific interests, professional unity and the power of the syndicate to sponsor and enact legislation.[14]

The position and role of the chambers of agriculture in late 1940 were unclear. Caziot, the new Minister of Agriculture, at first accepted and then turned down an invitation to address the APPCA in November 1940 at Vichy. It seems his reticence was due to the imminent demise of both the departmental chambers and their national representative body. The law of 2 December suppressed both groups without specifying reasons. The president of the APPCA remarked drily that, 'as loyal Frenchmen we will accept the law without comment'. It was not until December 1941 that some explanation for the dismantling of the organisation was given, when Caziot argued that the role of the chambers had been interpreted too widely and that they had sought to take over affairs which were the legitimate domain of the syndicate. Echoing the debates which had surrounded the establishment of the Chambers some twenty years earlier, Caziot maintained that the elections to seats on the Chambers had introduced politics into the professional domain. In February and August 1943 further ministerial decrees anticipated the creation of a set of regional (rather than departmental) chambers. In January 1944 members of these new chambers were nominated at seventeen regional centres and, in May, the final decrees dissolving the pre-war chambers were enacted.[15] The new regional chambers, with their unspecified powers, were never properly constituted.

The new power and influence given to syndicalism reflected the demands made by advocates of corporatism in the 1930s that it should be the profession itself that exercised control and responsibility for its affairs. But this increased influence was not without costs. A much more rigid and hierarchical organisation of syndicates was established in the series of meetings of the national committee for corporatist reorganisation during 1941. At the base of the pyramid were the local syndicates – only one per commune – embracing all those associated with agriculture and initially with a nominated president or *syndic*. If its role and influence were widened, external control from the second, regional scale of syndicates was strong. After initial attempts to shift power from the departmental to the supra-departmental

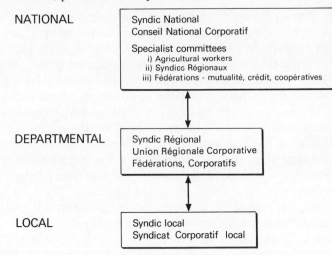

Figure 6.1 Structure of the Corporation paysanne

scale, the regional syndicates were eventually based primarily on departmental boundaries. At national level the all-powerful Conseil national, with a membership drawn from regional syndicates, cooperatives and mutualist groups and the Ministry of Agriculture, was designed to exercise control over agricultural affairs (Figure 6.1). It was from this body, not fully established until March 1943, that the direction and powers of the corporation were established.[16]

If it took only five months from the establishment of the Vichy regime to the passage of the law on the corporative reorganisation of agriculture, it was not until 1943 that the corporation could be considered as properly constituted. The reasons for this time-lag reveal much about the difficulties the fledgling organisation faced. First, it indicates that the corporatism of pre-war years was anything but monolithic. If the rhetoric was often similar the practical policies varied greatly. What role should be given to the syndicate? Should regular syndical elections be held? Where should most power reside – the local, departmental or national groups? Such questions were a chronic source of dispute between the creators of the new organisation. Secondly, there were serious difficulties over the precise relationship between corporation and state.[17] The new organisation was theoretically to end the spectre of state intervention in the agricultural world, that harbinger of bolshevism according to the right. As Salleron, architect of the new legislation, argued, 'it is through the directed and centrally planned economy and not through syndicalism that the danger of state control is increased'.[18] But the fledgling organisation quickly faced problems in its relationship with the state.

The most acute initial difficulties were with the Ministry of Agriculture. If, in theory, the two were supposed to be separate, in practice they remained closely linked. And, during a period of administrative turmoil, it is hardly surprising that the established powers and procedures of the Ministry frequently overrode the weaker structures of the corporation. Rarely was the corporation able to exercise the full range of legislative power attributed to it in December 1940. Salleron denounced this position fiercely, arguing that 'the Ministry of Agriculture has deliberately ignored the status of the Corporation through imposing an increasing number of frankly illegal decrees without reference to the Corporation'.[19] These difficulties meant that the corporation came increasingly to be viewed as an instrument of state bureaucracy able to do little other than assist in carrying out government policy on production, rationing and delivery of agricultural goods. Pressure of circumstance rather than fundamental flaws in the legislation were thus at the root of the corporation's problems in this area.

The establishment of the corporation on the ground was a difficult process which reflected pre-war divisions and quarrels between rival agricultural associations. As Cépède has noted, 'except in those regions where traditional syndicalism was strong before 1939, the establishment of corporatist organisations was long and drawn-out'.[20] A report in the middle of 1941 indicated that a swift transition from pre-war to corporative organisations was anticipated in only twelve departments. In a further 39 special committees had to be set up, whilst in 37 other departments rival syndical groups would have to be fused before the corporation could be established. By the end of 1941 regional corporations had been established in only fourteen departments – the remaining 75 had proceeded no further than the creation of organising committees.[21] Not until late 1942, almost two years after the legislation, was a regional network fully established.

The corporation on the ground – Aveyron 1940–44

The difficulties which surrounded the establishment of the corporation and the extent to which its development reflected regional nuances are well illustrated in the case of Aveyron. It was the first department in the unoccupied zone to establish its own corporation, an organisation which placed agricultural affairs in the region firmly in the hands of traditionalists. Within two months of the first AGM of the Corporation paysanne du Rouergue, a network of 290 communal syndicates had been created, 35,000 peasants held syndicate cards and the syndical journal, *Rouergue-paysan*, had a print run of over 25,000. How then was this transition achieved and, more importantly, what did the creation of the corporation mean to the farming population of the department?

The strong Catholic traditions and conservatism of the region had led to the development of a group of powerful agricultural associations which, as was noted earlier, reflected the corporatism of the 1930s. But this corporatist *élan* had led to internal conflict in the dominant syndicate of the region, the Plateau central, and it was this conflict which was sharpened when the Vichy regime was established. Since 1937 a campaign to fuse the Plateau central into a peasant front had been led by Joseph Ayrignac, an influential doctor and landowner. He argued that the peasantry with its 'strength, good sense and calm behaviour were in a strong position to counterbalance those politicians bent on destroying the nation'.[22] Whilst his efforts at creating a peasant front in the department failed, he was able to establish a Union des syndicats paysans in December 1938, with over 150 founding syndicates. Its power base lay in the uplands of the Aubrac in the north of the department; its policy, to create a unified, corporative syndical group in the region.[23]

An unequivocal welcome was given to the new regime by both groups in the department. As early as July 1940 Ayrignac published an open letter arguing that Pétain 'can count on the total support of our peasants in his work of national salvation and regeneration'.[24] The passage of the legislation establishing the unitary, hierarchical syndicalism of the Corporation exacerbated the struggle between rival groups in Aveyron as it did, no doubt, in many other departments. By the end of 1941, however, the Plateau central had lost the struggle for supremacy and, after some 30 years of dominance in the department, it was replaced by the new corporation.[25] The Vichy Minister of Agriculture, Pierre Caziot, and Rémy Goussault, president of the national Corporation paysanne, visited Rodez for the first AGM of the new organisation, congratulated Ayrignac on being the first regional *syndic*, and emphasised the new chapter about to open up for the peasantry of France.[26]

The speed of the transition in Aveyron is not especially surprising. In the late 1930s Ayrignac had established close relations with UNSA, who were now the leading theoreticians behind the new organisation. Furthermore, the ideology of Vichy represented a restatement of ideals which had been powerful in this department for almost four decades. The preservation of the peasantry, family values, Christian morality and mutual aid were hardly novel ideas here. The enthusiasts for the corporation were not newcomers. As Ayrignac noted, 'the destiny of the new organisation has been placed firmly in the hands of the defenders of traditionalism who have been active in the region for many years'.[27] The first executive committee of the corporation in Aveyron had included Anglade, founder of the Plateau central, Bouscayrol and de Pomairols from the republican syndicate groups, Perier, a Plateau central official, and two activists from the sheep-farmer syndicates of the south of the department.[28] From the administrative point of view continuity rather than change is the most striking feature of the establishment of the corporation in Aveyron. It is a reminder that change in the peasant community is rarely as dramatic and far-reaching as the national histories might suggest.

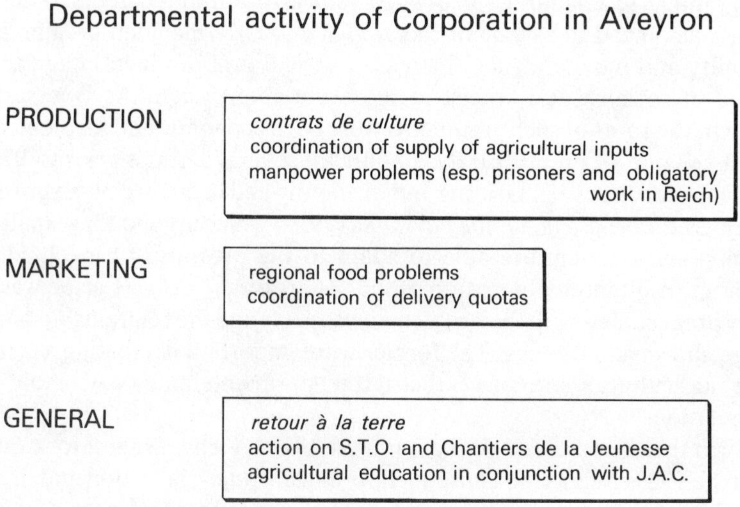

Departmental activity of Corporation in Aveyron

PRODUCTION

> *contrats de culture*
> coordination of supply of agricultural inputs
> manpower problems (esp. prisoners and obligatory
> work in Reich)

MARKETING

> regional food problems
> coordination of delivery quotas

GENERAL

> *retour à la terre*
> action on S.T.O. and Chantiers de la Jeunesse
> agricultural education in conjunction with J.A.C.

Figure 6.2 Activity of the Corporation paysanne in Aveyron

The paradox which surrounds the functioning of the corporation is well illustrated by examining regional rather than national activity. An organisation which was resolutely opposed to state intervention in agriculture was ultimately to become an instrument for increasing state control at a time of acute production difficulties. This paradox was quickly recognised by Ayrignac who wrote early in 1942 that 'unhappily the Corporation has been obliged to succumb to the pressures of the administration . . . at all costs the State and the Corporation must not be considered as the same thing'.[29]

Much of the work of the corporation in Aveyron focused on questions of production (Figure 6.2). By early 1942 six specialist advisory groups had been established for milk, wheat, potatoes, tobacco, fruit and ewes' milk. Their chief task was two-fold – to increase production and ensure delivery of quotas to the market. Food supply problems were accentuated because for the purposes of *ravitaillement* Aveyron was placed in the Languedoc region and was thus required to export considerable quantities of foodstuffs to feed the urban populations of the coast. Corporatist activists fought to change this ruling and, in 1943, Aveyron was placed in the Massif Central region. Special *contrats de culture* were also established by the corporation. These annual contracts pledged farmers to deliver specified quantities of agricultural produce to the official market in return for priority deliveries of fertilisers, seeds and other agricultural material.[30] Efforts were also made to modify the effects of the service du travail obligatoire (STO), which drained the region of manpower as did the compulsory work schemes for young people (the chantiers de la jeunesse).

One of the central aims of corporatist theorists was the establishment of a programme to encourage people to return to farming careers. The arguments advanced in favour of this *retour à la terre* included greater family stability and independence, increased agricultural production and the absence of socialist and atheist ideas in the countryside. As Boussard has shown, the roots of such arguments were both economic and ideological and had been part of French rural economy for several decades prior to Vichy.[31] Thus the link between farming and the family had been forcibly expressed in Caziot's *La Terre à la famille paysanne* (1919) which argued for a small-scale family-based agriculture able to adapt to the pressures of mechanisation without resultant depopulation of the countryside.[32] Augé-Laribé was similarly preoccupied with the problem of property and the relationship between large and small holdings. The former were important in creating a competitive agricultural structure, the latter in maintaining a sizeable rural population.[33]

Such themes emerged with great force under Vichy. Mallet, for example, saw the 1929 crisis as the consequence of over-industrialisation and drew the conclusion that only a sustained return to the land could provide a stable long-term solution. 'The economic necessity of a return to the land', he wrote, 'is fundamental to both France and to the other nations of the world.'[34] Such economic arguments, which frequently recognised the near impossibility of such a programme, were bed-fellows of ideological arguments often much less lucid. It was Pétain who best expressed such ideals. 'The earth will not deceive you', he argued, 'she demands your succour; a field which lies uncultivated is a part of France that dies, one that is cultivated anew is a part of France that is reborn.'[35] This programme, established in the Vichy years, was a touchstone for the regime – in moral, religious and political terms, a reflection of the new France about to emerge from the ashes of defeat; in economic terms, little more than a hopeless anachronism.

From early 1941 the corporation in Aveyron began to survey abandoned or poorly farmed land for the programme; marginal comments reveal diverse reasons for their abandonment: 'the owner, mentally unstable, cannot do more than cultivate her garden' (Prades-de-Salars), 'a farm which was denounced as uncultivated has, in fact, been neglected only since the outbreak of war' (Villefranche-de-Panat), 'the owner's son was mobilised and subsequently made a prisoner of war and manpower shortages have hampered efforts to improve cultivation' (Montfranc).

The programme provided an opportunity for some peasants to settle old scores. Numerous letters denounced farmers for having land which they were unable to cultivate. One farmer at Moyrazès was denounced as being unable to farm properly. After asking for the land to be ceded to him, the plaintiff requested that the letter be destroyed forthwith. Another farm in the Lot valley was, the letter-writer complained, far too large for the farmer and his one son. The letter asked whether, as the father of five children, the land might be ceded to him as his need was greater. Demands for the cultivation of common land were also made and generally supported by the corporation in the department. Demands from North Africa for the provision of farms in the department were also forthcoming though they met with little success. Applicants were usually politely informed that the severe climate and difficult farming methods made such requests impossible to meet. Popular opinion may have posed problems as well.

The success of this *retour à la terre* was not great. Of the forty-two dossiers examined in the department, only eight resulted in grants of land and none of these involved the establishment of new peasant families.[36] Such a record seems to reflect national trends well. Between 1941 and 1944 there were 1,561 applications for land. Of these only 591 were successful. As Gervais notes, 'this tiny number is perhaps a fair reflection of the anachronistic message of the programme'.[37] As the practical work of the corporation developed there was increasing confusion between it and the state. *Rouergue-paysan* consistently sought to distinguish the two – 'the corporation was not, we insist, instituted merely as the ante-chamber of government' noted one editorial,[38] whilst Ayrignac later argued that 'the Corporation in Rouergue was established without regard to any political parties and embraced members from all political persuasions'.[39] Such confusion was ultimately to prove fatal for the corporation.

An assessment of the corporation

If the Corporation was established with at least relative ease in some regions, such as Aveyron, it is evident that its anticipated role was severely curtailed by the pressure of the economic conjuncture. From being the centrepiece of a reorganised and unified agricultural profession it became, in the space of a few months, a secondary arm of an increasingly discredited state used only for enacting government legislation. That its protagonists were heartily deceived is clear from the continual resignations and reformulations Boussard traces in her detailed history of the organisation. Even in areas where pre-war corporatism was highly influential, the activity of the new organisation was restricted.

In Aisne, for example, the powerful Union des syndicats agricoles was officially transformed into a corporative organisation in March 1941, with its pre-war president, Blondelle, playing an active part in the group. In practice, however, de Sars has argued that the financial and administrative resources of the old union were safeguarded to prevent too close an association between the union and the corporation.[40] Membership was almost total amongst the farming population – 8,500 members out of 10,500 in the middle of 1942, though many of the largest farmers of the region played little part in the corporation.[41] The success of this strategy is perhaps best shown by the fact that, unlike many departments, the union was allowed to revert to its old buildings, administration and finances in 1945.

In Brittany the powerful Office central at Landernau adopted the new regime with some enthusiasm. The departmental syndicates of Finistère and Côtes-du-Nord were united in a single regional corporation with Budes de Guébriant as the regional *syndic*. It sought to carry out a range of economic and social services including discussions of the method of establishing quotas for supplying agricultural produce to the market, and for increasing animal and dairy production in the region. In 1942, the establishment of special sections within the corporation to deal with agricultural labourers had challenged the cherished myth of peasant unity, but in Brittany they were established quickly. Thus, in November 1942, a section was set up to negotiate rates of pay and conditions for agricultural workers. Despite the presence of three times as many employers as employees the commission turned down a request for a 19 per cent increase in wage rates on the grounds that it was too modest! Perhaps prompted by a fear of acute manpower shortages, a 25 per cent increase was voted.[42]

For agricultural organisations in Alsace and Lorraine the position was much more critical. The annexation of the region into the Reich was followed by a policy of incorporating agricultural production and organisation into the German model. In late 1939 the records and administration followed the evacuated populations from Alsace-Lorraine to south-western France. Altogether some 196 associations from Alsace and 61 from Lorraine migrated to the south. In August 1940 they returned, together with the evacuated population, to a region now destined to become an integral part of Germany. The Fédération agricole was split up; its syndicates were grouped with the Ludwigshafen palatinate. The personnel of both the syndical federation and the powerful mutualist groups of the region were replaced by pro-German appointees. The scope of the powerful credit and cooperative groups of the region was radically transformed – the Germans saw its chief role as being the economic support of the Reich.[43]

By late 1942 a policy of germanisation was explicit in the pronouncements of the new groups. The task of the agricultural cooperative, the leader of the corporation in Alsace, Engler-Fusslin, argued, 'was not just to aid the profession but equally to help the German people to win their battle for liberty'.[44] In the reform of the cooperative and credit sectors a policy of centralisation and concentration was followed with the intention of achieving as rapid an integration of local circuits into German patterns as was possible. By the end of hostilities, Gueslin argues, the mutualist movement in the region had embarked on a transformation from a specifically agricultural movement to one based on urban and industrial as well as agricultural capital.

The Vichy period was important for the development of agricultural organisations. Its most widely known, and most criticised innovation was the establishment of the Corporation paysanne. As has been stressed, however, it is difficult to judge the wisdom of such an innovation in the light of less than four years' activity in particularly difficult conditions. But if, as Boussard notes, the corporation represented 'the most positive creation of the *Etat Français*', the attempt to impose syndical unity by decree and to reinforce a particular peasantist image of the countryside by government appointment was frustrated from the start.[45] The economic and social conditions of France in this period only served to make the task increasingly impossible.

In practical terms little was achieved by the corporation. The holding of elections for local *syndics* in 1941 and 1942 was of value in developing a democratic base for syndicates which was built on in later years, though the leaders continued to be the representatives of the old rue d'Athènes tradition.[46] But perhaps more important than the corporation itself were the body of reforms which began to be introduced through the Ministry of Agriculture in this period. Thus Caziot, Minister from 1940 to April 1942, improved credit provision for an ambitious policy of rural house improvement and electrification, as well as instituting changes in conditions of land tenure and improving agricultural education.[47] The *remembrement* policy, which was to transform the structure and appearance of the countryside in post-war years, also dated from this period. In these positive reforms one can detect the technocratic aspect of the corporatism of the 1930s. Less obvious, less rhetorical and less flamboyant than the pronouncements extolling the bucolic bliss of the countryside, the beginnings of a rational and coordinated *politique agricole* based on the necessity for some state role in farming can be detected in these years.

Although difficult to quantify, it can be argued that the Vichy period at least helped create a new climate in rural France. Economic conditions increased both the wealth and position of the peasant, and political pronouncements of the virtues of the peasant way of life reflected both the peasantist myth and the urgent needs of *ravitaillement*. A large number of local peasants gained positions of responsibility in the new syndicates of this period and state intervention in agriculture increased to such an extent that it was to become accepted as inevitable though rarely seen as welcome. If the corporatist vision of the 1930s embraced both the economic realism of the new technocrats and the pastoral myth-making of the agrarian traditionalists, by the end of the war the policies of the former had eclipsed the rhetoric of the latter. The days of a backward-looking and archaic traditionalism within agricultural organisations in France were numbered.

7

A rural revolution? Syndicates and cooperatives, 1944–1965

In the two decades following the war dramatic changes were effected in the number, structure and role of agricultural organisations in France. The cooperative sector was greatly enlarged to embrace both the production and marketing of agricultural produce. The agricultural syndicate remained central to French agriculture; it was through the syndicate that economic and social strategies for farming were elaborated and debated and the movement continued to be a productive source of organisational innovation. The degree of state intervention, often through the chambers of agriculture, also increased from the 1950s.

A new framework for agricultural organisations

In June 1944 the government in exile in Algiers dissolved the Corporation paysanne and its constituent bodies, a decision confirmed in October 1944, and followed by the arrest of some of its more prominent members – Caziot, de Guébriant, Le Roy Ladurie (despite his resignation from the corporation some two years previously). In its place a Confédération générale de l'agriculture (CGA) was established, formed largely around an embryonic organisation created in the Resistance years, and led by Tanguy-Prigent, a young Breton socialist, who had been active in the inter-war years in creating a syndical movement to rival the powerful Office central in Brittany.[1]

The task of the new organisation was difficult. The elimination of all remnants of the corporation was in many respects a political rather than an agricultural decision, for much of its work had been useful and few of its leaders, whether regional or national, could be considered collaborators. A CGA which was strongly influenced by communist and socialist ideologies was faced with widespread peasant scepticism and reticence. In its early months the leadership of the new group was sensibly widened and, in the first congress in March 1945 a number of representatives of the old rue d'Athènes tradition were given national posts. At this congress the structure

Confédération Générale de l'Agriculture (C.G.A.)

Syndicalism

> *Fédération nationale des syndicats d'exploitants agricoles (F.N.S.E.A.)*
> Agricultural workers - represented through industrial unions
> *Cercle national des jeunes agriculteurs (C.N.J.A.)*

Cooperation

> *Fédération nationale des coopératives agricoles (F.N.C.A.)*
> *Confédération générale des coopératives agricoles (C.G.C.A.)*

Mutuality

> *Fédération nationale de la mutualité agricole (F.N.M.A.)*

Credit

> *Fédération nationale du crédit agricole (F.N.C.A.)*
> *Fédération centrale du crédit agricole mutuel (F.C.C.A.M.)*

Figure 7.1 Structure of the Confédération générale de l'agriculture

of the CGA was defined: each of the branches of association – mutuality, syndicalism, cooperation and credit – were represented on the main committee[2] (Figure 7.1).

If, in principle, the structure of the new umbrella organisation for French agriculture seemed relatively straightforward, its practical implementation was more difficult. Syndical interests were to be represented by a single, newly created organisation – the Fédération nationale des syndicats d'exploitants agricoles – with constituent groups in all departments. It is interesting that a government anxious to rid the country of all Vichy traits, nevertheless maintained a unitary syndicalism in the countryside. One of the unstated aims of the militants in the CGA was to displace the syndicate from the all-powerful position it had occupied in pre-war and Vichy days. The central place of syndicalism and its dominance by a conservative *notabilité* had, it was argued, fundamentally weakened the place of the left in the countryside. The new structure would overcome this in a number of ways.

In the first place syndicalism was given no more than an equal footing with other groups (cooperatives, mutuality) in the CGA, despite the demands of the newly created FNSEA for at least two-thirds of the seats. Secondly, in October 1945 agricultural syndicates were specifically forbidden to engage in any kind of commercial activity, such as the purchase and sale of agricultural goods – activity which had been a central part of syndical activity in the pre-war years.[3] This regulation was designed to weaken the place of the syndicate in the countryside.

Table 7.1. *Continuity of personnel in syndicates in Aveyron, 1942–46*

	Officers (%)	Executive (%)
Département	31	25
Rodez region	26	24
Millau region	24	21
Villefranche region	47	33

Source: A.D. (Aveyron) 35 M 3(6)

This internal conflict between left and right in agricultural circles was further heightened when, in the elections for posts of responsibility within the new FNSEA, held between December 1945 and February 1946, the old élite was returned in strength. As Wright noted, this perhaps represented, less the pull of older doctrinal loyalties, than the 'natural tendency of village communities to choose tried and trusted local spokesmen: the same men who had been active in the prewar peasant movement and, often, in the Vichy Corporation'.[4] Thus, in a traditionally conservative department such as Aveyron, continuity rather than change characterised the local scene. Analysis of the results of this first election revealed that almost one-third of those active in the corporation years were re-elected to power in 1946[5] (Table 7.1).

This degree of continuity was also evident at national level. At the first congress of the FNSEA on 12 March 1946, a moderate from Maine-et-Loire, Eugène Forget, was elected as president. Forget had been active in the corporation in his region and, as he himself wryly noted, his election was a compromise politically and geographically; his region was on the interfluve between the strongly conservative Paris Basin and the left-wing south-west![6] Perhaps more significant, however, was the election of René Blondelle to the post of secretary-general. With the backing of a powerful local syndicalism in the Aisne, Blondelle, who had cut his political teeth in the corporation, was to be an astute and politically influential leader of the FNSEA in these early post-war years.[7]

By 1946, then, a single, unitary syndical body, democratically elected, had been created in France for the first time. The old struggles between squire and radical deputy, catholic and anti-clerical were suspended. In the case of the cooperative and credit movement unity was not achieved until much later. Thus the dual origins of cooperation (rue d'Athènes and boulevard St Germain) were reflected in a rival Confédération générale and a Fédération nationale respectively. The unity of the mutuality movement established under Vichy was maintained – the so-called Mutuelles 1900 continuing to insure risks to animals, machinery and housing whilst the Mutualité sociale agricole was established to coordinate social security provision for the agricultural community.[8]

The complex relationships between the different organisations seeking to represent agricultural interests is well illustrated by the case of the chambers of agriculture. As was noted in chapter 6, these had been allowed to disappear in the Vichy period as a consequence of the desire to emphasise the primacy of syndicalism. Neither the government nor the syndical movement took any action to reinstate the chambers in the immediate post-war period; it was only on the initiative of the vice-president of the Dordogne chamber, Abel Maumont, that action was taken to reinstate the organisation. Sending a circular letter to all chambers in France, 72 positive replies were received and, in November 1948, a meeting of all departmental presidents was held in Paris. Not all representatives were in favour of a renewal of activity. Budes de Guébriant, for example, president of the Finistère chamber and a former activist in the Corporation paysanne, argued that a re-emergence of the chambers would compromise syndical power and representativeness.

Government interest in the chambers was non-existent; it was only when departmental chambers informed local prefects that they were renewing their activity that the central administration began to act. Pflimlin, the Minister of Agriculture, remitted the question to the Cabinet and, in November 1949, indicated that they could proceed with the renewal of their activities. The refusal of the National Assembly, in December 1950, to vote the necessary finances to allow for elections to the chambers further compromised efforts to relaunch the organisation.[9]

The structure of the various agricultural organisations and the nature of the relationship between them is of more than administrative interest, for the debates reveal that, beneath the façade of a united CGA, old tensions and rivalries continued to exist. At the heart of the difficulties was the place of syndicalism. Whilst no longer divided into separate, rival unions it was nonetheless engaged in a struggle for power and influence. In the early Liberation years their chief opponents were the cooperative groups formerly part of the boulevard St Germain, and a struggle between Blondelle, at the head of the FNSEA, and Lamour at the CGA marked national agricultural life until 1950. By a strategy of using the voting strength of the powerful specialist associations (the wheat, sugar-beet and wine producers – Blondelle was an influential member of the first of these) the FNSEA gradually replaced the theoretical power of the CGA with its own, practical strength. By November 1953 the ambitious projects of the CGA had failed and its role had been reduced to simple administrative coordination. As Houée pointed out, 'the professional organisations had once more rediscovered their traditional animosity and cleavages'.[10]

Similar difficulties were evident in the relationship between the FNSEA and the chambers. The reemergence of the latter posed problems over the question of representation. If chamber elections were to be held, who was to be considered as representing agricultural interests – the syndicate, the CGA, or the chambers? In the end, the granting of finances to the chambers for elections in March 1952 was made conditional on acceptance of an accord with the CGA and FNSEA. This accord, signed in February 1951, gave the prime representative role in agriculture to the syndicate. The chambers were not permitted to pronounce on agricultural matters without prior consultation with the syndical and cooperative movement. Their role, the accord noted, was limited to the 'study and realisation of projects of general agricultural interest such as professional education, technical progress in farming and infrastructure'.[11] As Mora notes, 'the Chambers became little more than study groups for the technical improvement of agriculture and for the servicing of other agricultural bodies'.[12] Blondelle further reinforced the central position of syndicalism when he was elected president of the national chamber in 1952, defeating Pierre Martin, president of the CGA, by 58 votes to 24 with 15 abstentions.[13] The fact that so many delegates either voted against Blondelle or abstained was a measure of the divisions between those holding office in agricultural groups.

The problems of unity

The history of the national syndical movement in this period was one of rivalry between those active in the CGA, generally on the left, and the old rural élite who had been active in the corporation. But at the local and regional level, syndical activity varied enormously. The reason for such variation lay in the implicit contradictions of a unitary syndical movement. By the early 1950s, the dominance of the FNSEA in national agricultural life had been fully consolidated. But real power within the syndicate lay in only a few hands. The powerful departmental syndicates of the Paris Basin and the north, together with the specialist organisations, dominated the national executive of the FNSEA. Technically skilled, well-educated and well-placed in their local syndicates, men such as Blondelle and Forget represented the interests of the more advanced regions rather than the small polycultural peasant of the south and west. National syndical power was thus compromised both geographically and socially: geographically because power and controlling interest at national level was vested in a group drawn from a restricted region; socially, because the interests of the small producer were less well represented.[14]

These conflicts were reflected in syndical policies in the ten years or so following the Liberation. Much of the lobbying effort of the FNSEA was devoted to the issue of pricing policy. Thus the question of parity between industrial and agricultural prices was a continuing theme in union demands,

Table 7.2. *Membership of the FDSEA 1946–57*

Département	1946	1950	1957
Aveyron	22,000	4,500	8,400
Corrèze	22,000	11,000	7,000
Dordogne	16,000	2,000	3,800
Lot	11,000	4,000	3,000

Source: A.D. (Aveyron) 35 M 3; Tavernier (1969)

particularly with the increasing volume of debts incurred as agricultural modernisation proceeded apace. This concentration on pricing policy inevitably favoured the large producer over the small – the greater the volume of product, the greater the overall benefit. In June 1951, Blondelle sought to exercise a more direct link between syndical demands and government by a programme of *action civique*, in which deputies who agreed a programme of agricultural reform would be fully supported in their electoral campaign by the FNSEA. This attempt at direct political intervention met with only limited success and the experiment was not repeated.[15]

More dramatic was the extent of agricultural unrest in this period. Many departmental syndicates had become increasingly adept at organising demonstrations, market boycotts and produce strikes in support of higher farm prices. In July 1953 the wine-producers of the Midi, faced with overproduction and price collapse, organised a series of road blocks and coordinated the resignation of hundreds of village mayors in protest at the economic situation. In October and December of the same year a whole series of protests in the small farming regions of the Massif Central and Charente was organised by the so-called Comité de guéret, who drew up their own programme of action and reform at odds with the more restrained action of the FNSEA.[16] Two consequences flowed from these events: first, an attempt was made to reform the archaic agricultural market. A threefold structure was put in place in October 1953 embracing a consultative committee of producers and marketing organisations, two intervention organisations for milk and meat empowered to purchase and stock excess produce should a price collapse threaten and, finally, an agricultural guarantee fund to provide financial and technical backing for the intervention groups.[17] Secondly, the activity of the Comité de guéret showed the extent of unease felt by many departmental federations with the direction of national policy.[18]

The concerted rivalry and struggles evident at the national level in fact concealed a disenchantment with the movement in many departments. Whilst membership stood at 1·183 million in 1946, by 1950 it had fallen to only 742,000 and, in 1957, was still lower at 647,000.[19] Perhaps more serious than the overall fall in membership were the geographical patterns of the change. The fall was most marked in the south and west – at the 1950 FNSEA congress 23 out of 90 departmental federations were unable to pay their affiliation fees because of membership falls. In some instances membership had more than halved in a ten-year period (Table 7.2).

Regional examples of syndical history in this period are instructive in showing the contrasting fortunes of the movement. In Aisne, Blondelle's home department, the powerful pre-war Union des syndicats agricoles de l'Aisne took over the tasks of the FDSEA and created an influential and thriving union in the late 1940s.[20] In the immediate post-war period syndical membership was very high – Keeler gives a figure of 95 per cent of all farmers in the department in 1947. One of the most powerful arguments in favour of membership was access to scarce and sometimes rationed goods through the syndicate and, as the supply of goods improved, membership fell to about 72 per cent in the early 1950s.[21] But that figure was still an impressively high one and reflected the popularity of the syndical policy of concentrating on parity of prices between the industrial and agricultural sector. As Keeler notes, 'appeals for peasant unity in Aisne focused primarily on the common interests of large and small farmers in the price of the one product which nearly all of them produced: wheat'.[22]

The union was also able to expand its influence through a series of practical initiatives which were made possible largely because of the sound financial base of the organisation. With high membership, a subscription scheme based on farm size, and an administrative structure overhauled in the late 1930s, the union took a series of initiatives in the technical improvement of agriculture in the department. The number and scope of departmental cooperatives were expanded to include cooperatives set up to repair war damage and to improve the marketing of potatoes, maize, tobacco and milk. Much effort was given over to a series of commissions to improve the quality and market value of milk – a shrewd move to maintain syndical membership in the Thiérache region to the north-west of Laon, where milk rather than monocultural wheat was important, and where membership had traditionally been rather low. Local, small-scale initiatives seem to have characterised syndical activity in this period in a search for a more constructive and practical syndicalism which might move beyond the mass demonstration.[23]

Led by Blondelle, the union, reflecting no doubt its membership of larger monocultural producers, reiterated the importance of national policy on prices. The term peasant, hardly appropriate to the 350 hectare wheat farms of parts of the department, was employed without hesitation by the syndical journal, *La Défence paysanne*, and the *action civique* and demonstration were seen as the main public manifestations of syndical power.[24] But beneath this visible strength lay a vital network of local services, technical help and cooperative activity which led to the union becoming an increasingly important cog in the agricultural development of the Aisne.

The experience of the department of Aveyron was a very different one. The transition from the corporation to the FDSEA had not proceeded with anything like the smoothness that was evident in Aisne. If, in the syndical elections in early 1946, turnout was a respectable 65 per cent of eligible farmers, the network of local groups across the department existed largely on paper alone. By 1950 membership had fallen to one-fifth of the 1946 figure, the union lacked any administrative resources and local activity was almost nil.[25] The reason, Laurens, the president, argued, was financial: 'now that rationing is no longer with us', he commented, 'many cannot see the point of paying a subscription to a syndicate which seems to offer nothing tangible in return'.[26] A second reason was advanced by the Catholic press. The links between syndicalism and mutuality, which were so vital in the pre-war movement, had now been broken, leading to an organisation which lacked creativity and limited its role to one of demonstration and complaint.[27] Without the financial resources of a department like Aisne, and with a clientele much more diverse than the large wheat farmer, the fortunes of syndicates in Aveyron were, like many other departments in the south and west, at a low ebb in the early 1950s.

In the Charente, syndical difficulties were reflected in the development of two groupings in the immediate post-war years. Of particular significance were the contrasts between the Cognac and Confolentais regions of the department. In the former region a long tradition of viticulture, the dominance of the major houses such as Hennessy, Martel and Hine, and the generally weak hold of the Catholic church made the area a bastion of radicalism with a powerful regional tinge. In the poorer Confolentais, bordering on the north-west of the Massif Central, a strong communist tradition had developed pre-war and been expanded by the Resistance movement. The only way in which more conservative interests could undermine this political influence was through syndical activity.

The establishment of the FDSEA in the department, in 1946, elicited a series of conflicts between a radical wing in the Cognacais and the more conservative and Catholic syndicalists of the Confolentais. The official, leftist, FDSEA faced increasing difficulties in collecting subscriptions from the Confolentais and, in 1949, with strong support from viticultural interests, a committee was formed to create a dissident syndicate. Efforts at reconciliation failed and, in February 1953, the FNSEA excluded the 'official' Charente FDSEA from membership and recognised only a newly founded departmental union as the official syndicate. This syndical split was, as Maresca notes, reinforced by the social and economic contrasts between their geographical heartlands. The old FDSEA drew its support and leadership from viticultural interests and an essentially modernist peasantry, whilst the newly established and officially recognised UDSEA drew membership from migrant Catholic farmers, attracted to the region through the migration syndicates active in Brittany in the post-war period.[28]

Catholicism and the peasant: the Action catholique

Much of the literature describing the changes in leadership and policy of the syndicates in the 1950s, and their influence on the broader cooperative movement, contains strong hagiographical elements. The broad sweep of events is undoubtedly an attractive one as a new generation of authentic peasant leaders, many of them from the more geographically isolated regions, swept to local and national power and embarked on a massive modernisation of structures and mentalities in rural France. What this work further emphasises is the formative role played by the Catholic church in both the education and training of the peasant mass and, more importantly, the creation of a new élite from the small and middle peasantry to take control of the organisations of the rural world. The chronology, organisation and consequences of these changes are central to an understanding of agricultural organisations today.

As was noted in chapter 5, the creation of the Jeunesse agricole catholique (JAC) in 1929 was a reflection of the need both for improved leisure and education facilities in the countryside, and the perception on the part of the church hierarchy of the need to reChristianise the agricultural milieu. The growth of the JAC, and its sister movement the JACF, had been spectacular in the 1930s and, during the Occupation years, the educative and organisational work of the church continued. Relations between the corporation and the JAC were not always cordial for the former, at least in some regions, sought to integrate the youth movements of the church into its organisations.[29] But an agreement in June 1942 between the youth movement of the corporation and the JAC meant a degree of freedom for the latter, at least in the unoccupied zone.[30] In some areas relations were not troubled. In Maine-et-Loire, a positive relationship developed between the two organisations with the departmental corporation, in which Forget, later to be president of the FNSEA, was active, happy to leave the organisation of the youth movements to the church.[31] In Aveyron a similar spirit prevailed and the JAC and JACF consolidated their power considerably in this period because of the general absence of any other kind of leisure facilities in the countryside. It was, noted Laur, a period of steady preparation and consolidation for future years.[32]

The range of activity of these youth groups and their adult equivalent, the Mouvement familial rural, was four-fold. Its primary role, and one which was fundamental to its philosophy, was education. In general the level of education in rural areas was especially poor and agricultural training was very sparse. The task of the JAC was to improve the self-awareness and confidence of the peasantry through education. Stress was laid on work done by the local group to educate themselves. Local surveys of village life, of agricultural methods, of the role of credit or mechanisation were central to

Table 7.3. *Subscriptions to 'Action catholique' journals in Aveyron, 1952*

Region	Subscriptions	As % of males aged 14–24
Ségala	1512	17.2
Aubrac	292	18.3
Lévezou	48	12.3
Causses	520	19.6

Source: Archives Abbé Bion (Rodez)

its philosophy for its leaders argued that if the peasants themselves discovered the problems of their environment the search for solutions would be greatly facilitated.[33] As one observer noted, 'it is impossible to create an authentic JAC movement without using the local survey and enquiry as a means of awakening the milieu'.[34] Each year a particular theme was adopted for study – in the late 1940s these included mechanisation, agricultural work patterns and housing conditions. The problems of cohabitation and sanitation – chronic problems in many rural areas – were a constant preoccupation.[35]

Alongside the survey more general education courses were run in many departments. As a priority, agricultural correspondence courses had been developed in many regions to fill the gaps left by a largely inadequate state provision. Equally important were a series of graduated courses for young people designed to provide both technical and social skills. Special *stages d'éveil* for fifteen year olds taught often reticent, shy and poorly educated youngsters how to read and write critically, the skills of public speaking and money management. For eighteen year olds, the *stages de réflexion* concentrated on agricultural problems and introduced questions of social life, cohabitation and farm management to the young men and women of the community. Special study visits to neighbouring regions or, occasionally, abroad, emphasised agricultural improvement, the adoption of new techniques and the importance of solidarity between farmers in different regions. Such courses were designed to fill the gaps left by a school education which was frequently episodic and short and to give peasants the self-confidence to face the difficulties of the post-war period with their own solutions.

Perhaps the most striking aspect of the JAC and JACF in the early post-war years was their emergence as a mass movement. At a time of rationing, economic austerity and lack of leisure provision, their role in organising theatrical competitions (the *Coup de la joie*), local fairs, religious pilgrimages and holidays was widespread and popular. In Aveyron, for

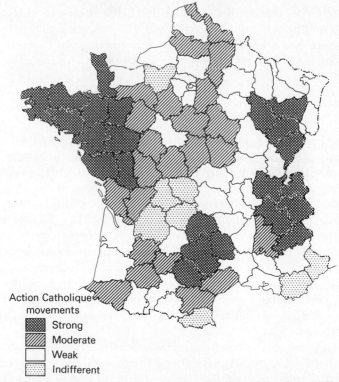

Action Catholique movements
- ▓ Strong
- ▨ Moderate
- ☐ Weak
- ░ Indifferent

Figure 7.2 Geography of the Action catholique in the middle of the 1950s

example, the 1949 *coup* attracted some 2,000 participants – a reflection, noted *Le Rouergat*, of the 'immense need the rural world has for leisure and entertainment'.[36] The 1947 pilgrimage from Aveyron to Lourdes was attended by 2,000 young men whilst 3,500 young women made the same trip a year later. Subscriptions to the JAC press in the department were high. Analysis of the 1952 subscriptions in the department to the two main journals reveals that as many as one in five of all males in the age group 14–24 held subscriptions (Table 7.3).

Examination of the attendance figures at the JAC congress at Lourdes in 1952 reveals a similar picture of a highly successful and popular mass movement in Aveyron with some cantons sending as many as 25 per cent of their young men on the pilgrimage.

These Catholic organisations were undoubtedly powerful national movements in this period. If the geography of the groups reflected the patterns of strong catholicism in France their influence in the bastions of Brittany, parts of the Loire valley and the Vendée, Alsace-Lorraine and the Moselle and parts of the Massif Central (Aveyron, Lozère, Puy-de-Dôme) was considerable (Figure 7.2). Few areas were untouched by the groups. National circulation of the movements' journals fluctuated at around 75,000 in the late 1940s for the JAC and 110,000 for the JACF.[38] Some 70,000 young men and women came to the 1950 congress of the movement at the Parc des Princes in Paris for a festival of sport and leisure and to demonstrate the strength of this new peasant self-confidence. A year later, at a series of provincial rallies, close to a quarter of a million members of the movement gathered for similar meetings. No syndical organisation could have excited such interest and gathered such numbers.[39]

But these movements were as much concerned with training a new élite to take control of the organisations of the rural world, as with creating a mass movement. This emphasis upon peasant promotion to representative positions marked a departure from the traditional attitude of church organisations, which had been largely to leave the control of syndicates and cooperatives to the traditional representatives of the peasant – the priest, squire, or large landowner. For the leaders of the post-war movement, perhaps sensing that the traditional élite was both compromised by the Vichy experience and disappearing rapidly, service and activity in syndicates and cooperatives was 'a task of great importance which we have ignored up till now'. This particular task was to depend on a new, militant élite: 'we have to engender a new set of leaders from our milieu in order to render our institutions more humane and our world more Christian'.[40]

Thus one of the paradoxes of the movement was that, whilst aiming its message at a very wide constituency, it sought, in practice, to create a new élite in the countryside. If earlier studies of the JAC have tended to be rather uncritical in their descriptions of the work and influence of the movement on certain key figures, recent work, in particular by Maresca, has been more sanguine in its judgement. First, however, some consideration of numbers is important. National membership of the movement in the early 1950s was estimated at several hundred thousand, but active militants were far fewer. It is impossible to give a national estimate but regional examples serve to emphasise the point. Maresca's study of the JAC in Meurthe-et-Moselle, one of the most powerful departmental federations, emphasises the small numbers of real militants in the department and in particular stresses the bourgeois origins of many of the militants. She disputes the view that the JAC naturally threw up a rural élite; the process was much less spontaneous than earlier histories have suggested.[41]

An examination of the movement in Aveyron further emphasises the small number of militants involved. A survey in 1942 put the number of activists at about 240, whilst in 1948 there were no more than 150 at a time when some 3,500 attended the annual JAC congress in the department. Throughout the 1950s the number of militants rarely exceeded 250.[42] Evidence from activists during the period reinforces this conclusion: 'an élite movement above all with a strong cultural and social emphasis',[43] 'a mass

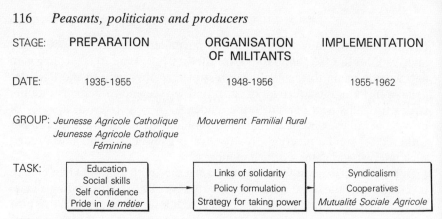

Figure 7.3 Action catholique and the seizure of power

movement only in its early stages . . . it rapidly became characterised by small groups reflecting on specific problems'.[44] Studies from both Brittany and Anjou, centres of JAC activity, reinforce this vision of a movement having its most profound effects not on the milieu as a whole but rather on small, influential groups within that milieu.[45]

What sets of values were imparted by the movement to this small group of activists? The importance of taking up posts in agricultural organisations was seen as a prime duty. The national movement explicitly argued for the creation of a new group of leaders: 'for centuries the solicitor, squire, and teacher have been at the head of our institutions . . . today peasants themselves, artisans, shopkeepers are leading our syndicates and presiding as mayors'.[46] In his *Motorisation et avenir rural* René Colson, secretary-general of the JAC between 1943 and 1948, emphasised that the changes taking place in agriculture threatened the family structure of farming and that the only solution lay in association and cooperation.[47] This theme of cooperation was constantly reiterated by the movement. As one departmental chaplain noted, 'the family enterprise can only survive through forming voluntary associations with others . . . the cooperative is our best means of saving the family farm'.[48] Thus these militants rejected the view that economic salvation lay through traditional peasant conservatism and sought instead to develop the economic power and productivity of family farmers in a rational and coherent manner. It was a progressive and modernist view of the future of agriculture in their regions.

This message was reinforced through national journals and, more particularly, through the meetings of militants at local level. The stress on observation gave militants the necessary experience to formulate problems and pose possible solutions. The message was economic as well as spiritual – what was distinctive about these movements was the attempt to apply Christian principles to the creation of a humane economic system which would avoid the twin excesses of capitalist individualism and socialist collectivism. And, equally distinctive, was the emphasis on action – on the application of such principles through involvement of members in the syndicates, cooperatives and mutual groups of the rural world. As Colson argued, 'the rural militant lives in an environment where discussion and debate have only a minor place; it is action that has most effect'.[49]

The seizure of power

By the early 1950s the influence of the JAC and MFR on the organisations of rural France was becoming increasingly visible. It was in this period that their role began to shift from the stage of preparation and training to implementation (Figure 7.3).

The clearest expression of this influence can be seen in the way militants of the movement began to take control of departmental syndicates, cooperatives and the Mutualité sociale agricole. One of the most important mechanisms for this seizure of power was the Cercle national des jeunes agriculteurs (CNJA). This group was founded in 1947 by the CGA, with a largely technical and educative role for young farmers – the organisation of study visits, for example, was one of its chief tasks. As Lauga notes, the JAC was far more successful in attracting a dynamic and active membership – a fact which, in some areas, led to friction between the two organisations.[50] The disappearance of the CGA in 1954 caused the group to opt initially to constitute its own, independent organisation but it soon decided to become a formal part of the FNSEA with its own representation on the national committee. Its membership was restricted to farmers, their wives, and sons and daughters between the ages of 18 and 35, and it created both a national committee and departmental groups.[51]

By the early 1950s the first generation of JAC militants, trained in the late 1930s and Occupation years, and increasingly active in the CNJA, were beginning to assume posts of responsibility. In 1954, one survey estimated that at least one-third of mayors of rural communes were *anciens* of the JAC.[52] The role of these militants in departmental syndicates was also increasingly important as the old rural élite was steadily replaced by peasant militants. This process was perhaps the most striking consequence of the Catholic action movement in rural France, for it was to lead to a radical change in national syndical policy and leadership. Individual biographies serve to illustrate how the change took place.

André Laur was one of nine children born to a family with a small farm in Aveyron. Whilst six of his brothers and sisters had pursued their education up to the age of 17, he left school with no more than his *certificat d'études*. He joined the JAC at an early age; 'the general education it provided was especially useful – specific technical education', he noted, 'came rather later'. By 1942 he had become the departmental president of the JAC in Aveyron, concentrating in particular on setting up the educational courses of the group. In the immediate post-war period there was a new spirit amongst the farming community: 'undoubtedly there was a conflict of generations for many organisations were very closed to the young . . . with my getting married and setting up home my preoccupations changed and I joined the MFR'. It was through the MFR that the process of change was articulated: 'the JAC at that time did not take direct initiatives in these matters – it saw its task as helping to form future generations'.

In 1949 elections were held to the Mutualité sociale agricole and this provided the opportunity for action. 'At that time syndicalism and the Mutuelles 1900 were somewhat inaccessible and these elections provided an opportunity to put what we had learnt into practice . . . Yes, I suppose you could say there was a kind of MFR mafia at the time . . . but it was ideas and a philosophy we were trying to advance and not particular individuals.' Laur was completely inexperienced – 'I'd had only a one-day course at Lyon organised by the MFR . . . the great advantage of this first post as administrator was that it gave me access . . . access to people, to office help, to documentation.'[53]

It was through a small group of MFR activists that the Aveyron FDSEA was rejuvenated in the middle of the 1950s. Marcel Bruel, a small farmer from Capdenac in the north-west of the department, had been active in the pre-war JAC movement – 'I was not especially Catholic', he notes, 'it was a question of temperament rather than philosophy and the JAC in Aveyron had kept well clear of the Corporation.'[54] The FDSEA was in a parlous position in the middle of the 1950s, and it was through a group of MFR militants – Bruel, Laur, and Cazals – that the syndicate was revived and rebuilt. A green 2CV, purchased with a loan from the Crédit agricole, was instrumental in facilitating the constant round of meetings in this, the fourth largest department in France. Equally active in the CNJA, Bruel was proposed by that group for the post of secretary-general of the FNSEA in 1960 and won with a comfortable majority.[55]

Michael Debatisse was born in the middle of the 1930s in the Puy-de-Dôme, and owed much of his training and administrative skills to the local JAC group. 'The JAC gave us a method of analysis, embryonic but efficient, and the desire to take action which would reflect our system of values . . . it served as a buttress for the agricultural revolution of the 1950s.'[56] From positions of responsibility in the regional and national JAC, Debatisse gravitated to the CNJA and, in 1958, became its secretary-general. It was Debatisse who, more than any other individual, represented the new force in rural France – it was his book, *La Révolution silencieuse*, that first brought this sea-change in rural France to the attention of a wider public.[57] A small family farmer, the policies he espoused sought a rational, sound future for the family farm which recognised that not all peasants could remain on the land and that migration of some farmers was essential if those that remained were to survive. In 1950, he later argued, 'No one would have thought that there would be mass unemployment in the industrial world; we thought we could leave the land and find a job without difficulty.'[58]

Louis Sesmat, born in 1934 on a medium-sized farm near Nancy, provides another example of this promotion. From the age of 16 he was active in the JAC, especially strong in this part of France; the fact that many of his brothers and sisters participated undoubtedly aided his integration into the movement. 'The JAC was a veritable training school for us', he notes, 'for it showed us how to seek out those people who could help us, it taught us to understand economic mechanisms and how to express ourselves clearly . . . it provided marvellous opportunities.'[59] At the age of 24 he became the national president of the JAC, and from an early age was active in the agricultural organisations of his region – president of the CDJA and administrator of his local Crédit agricole; 'the form of responsibility has changed over time, the responsibility itself has always been there'.[60]

Bernard Lambert was born in 1931 near Nantes where his parents had a small share-cropping farm in a region which was traditionally conservative and Catholic. Lambert joined the JAC just after the war and, like Debatisse, set about educating himself with enthusiasm and appetite. In 1951 Lambert took over the family holding with his elder brother and, at the same time, assumed national responsibilities with the JAC (1954) and the CNJA (1956–8). For Lambert, the very success of the JAC was testimony to the inadequacies of rural schooling, and its emphasis on action echoes that of many other militants of the period. 'Amongst all the church movements of the period', he points out, 'the JAC had the great merit of being the least clerical . . . and, without doubt, it has formed men of action, fully in contact with the realities of the milieu.'[61]

Such individual examples could be multiplied many times, reinforcing the view that the arrival of this wave of new militants, active at local, departmental and national level and trained in the JAC and MFR, was the single most important transformation of the post-war period. But, as Maresca has cogently argued, some cautious reassessment of the role of these groups is appropriate. In her study of agricultural leaders in Charente and Meurthe-et-Moselle, she has argued that the spontaneity of these changes has been overestimated by historians and activists of the period. In particular she argues that many new militants in fact came from solidly established and comparatively well-off families. Such families frequently possessed greater social and cultural advantages than their neighbours. The JAC, she argues, provided a club, a closed society within which promotion to posts of power could be facilitated. It enabled the middle peasantry, the agricultural bourgeoisie, to reinforce their social and cultural power. That the economic policies of the JAC and MFR sought explicitly to promote the medium-sized family farm lends further support to her argument.[62]

This interpretation is certainly a valid counter to the accounts of the church-trained militants of the period which perhaps overemphasise both the spontaneity of their promotion and the poverty of their background. But the criticism should not overshadow the very real role played by these groups in the promotion of an authentic peasant class for the first time. In many regions, notably the Massif Central and the west, this was a very real characteristic of the movement – the very intensity of the struggle it often promoted between the traditional agricultural bourgeoisie and the new peasant militants is testimony to this. If Maresca's analysis forces one to look more critically at the role of these groups and presses for a more differentiated interpretation of the movement it will have served a valuable purpose.

As was emphasised earlier, majority control of the FNSEA in the middle of the 1950s was vested very much with the large farming interests of the north and Paris Basin. This controlling interest was reflected in the importance it gave to pricing policy in negotiations with the government. Certainly agricultural unrest focused on this specific issue. If the demonstrations of 1953 had led to some reorganisation of agricultural markets to try and avoid massive price fluctuations, the problem was far from solved. However, the partial success of the FNSEA lobbying policy in this period reinforced its tendency to focus most of its efforts on pricing problems. Agricultural unrest remained high, however, with strong agricultural support for both the communists and the Poujadists, amongst whose number Henri Dorgères secured election in Ile-et-Vilaine.[63] The achievement, in 1957, of a degree of price support in the Laborde decree allowing price indexation for certain agricultural products marked the high point of this strategy.[64] As Gervais commented, 'at the moment when the Fourth Republic was about to disappear the capitalist sector of the agricultural economy benefited from an income largely guaranteed by the state'.[65]

With the advent of the Fifth Republic, accepted by referendum in September 1958, the legislative framework negotiated through the FNSEA was, at least superficially, favourable, with a degree of regularity in the market and legislation on the indexing of agricultual products. The new regime was, however, to rapidly disturb that apparent harmony. In December 1958, as part of a series of economy measures, price indexing for the agricultural sector was abandoned. With it the central achievement of the FNSEA disappeared. More significant, however, were the beginnings of a rapport between gaullism and the young farmers of the JAC and CNJA. By this time the regional transformations carried out by these activists were beginning to have a national impact. Bruel was now secretary-general of the FNSEA and Debatisse, at the same post in the CNJA, launched a fierce attack at the 1959 FNSEA congress on the obsession with prices. As Lauga notes, 'without denying the importance of prices, the CNJA insisted on the need to increase farm sizes and to develop a concerted policy of agricultural investment . . . it marked the start of the battle between price and structure'.[66]

ORIENTATION LAWS

1960

1　Establishment of policy principles - priority support to medium-sized farm; financial aid for installation of young farmers

2　Reform of agricultural tenancies

3　Creation of *Sociétés d'aménagement foncier et d'établissement rural* (S.A.F.E.R.) for property reform

4　Action to reduce extent of uncultivated land and the creation of priority rural action zones

5　Modifications to *Fonds d'orientation et de régularisation des marchés agricoles* (F.O.R.M.A.) to improve agricultural processing and marketing

6　Restructuring of *Sociétés d'intérêt collectif* (S.I.C.A.) schemes to foster creation of more cooperatives

1962

1　Property reforms - notably the creation of the *Groupements agricoles d'exploitation en commun* and establishment of the rights of the S.A.F.E.R. to priority land purchasing

2　Strengthening of power of agricultural producer groups

3　Creation of *Fonds d'action sociale pour l'amélioration des structures agricoles* This provided for:-

　　i) Funds to encourage older farmers to retire through the *Indemnité viagère de départ* (I.V.D.)
　　ii) Migration of farmers to larger holdings
　　iii) Special aid to farmers in difficult regions

Figure 7.4 The Orientation Laws of 1960 and 1962

If the most immediate effect of the abandonment of indexing was the massive agricultural demonstrations in the summer of 1959, a less apparent trend was the increased involvement of the CNJA with the elaboration of a new *politique agricole*. The government drew two lessons from the experiences and policy statements of the young farmers. First, it was made aware that the real beneficiaries of a concentration on prices were the large, capitalist farmers of certain regions. Secondly, it was attracted by the economic rationalism of their arguments: the recognition that agricultural restructuring (and the implied disappearance of many thousands of 'uneconomic' farms) sharply contrasted with the blanket preservation demanded by the communist or right-wing political parties. The young farmers' movement was thus accorded a perhaps disproportionate place in the elaboration of policy: 'the collaboration between gaullism and the CNJA went well beyond simple tactical considerations; they shared the same conceptions regarding the relationship between state and economy, were at one in their wish to transform agricultural structures, and agreed that the replacement of the old guard in the syndical movement by young militants could only be in the national interest.'[67]

The consequences of this negotiation and contact were to be found in a new agricultural charter, the *Loi d'Orientation Agricole* of April 1960, supplemented by a second *Loi* in 1962. This proposed a series of new regulations and objectives which were intended to accelerate the reform of agricultural structures (Figure 7.4).

The package was remarkable for a number of reasons. In the first place its comprehensive emphasis on structural reform without provision for blanket price support showed the influence of the CNJA in its elaboration. Secondly, it defined the clear social and economic objectives of farm policy; the preservation and development of farms 'worked by two units of man-power in such conditions as will permit the rational utilisation of capital, land and techniques and the maintenance of an adequate revenue'.[68] The legislation creating the SAFERs was especially important, for it recognised that some sort of control on land accumulation was an essential prerequisite for a farm policy which required an overall increase in the average size of farm holdings. If the economic arguments of the young farmers recognised that many farms would go to the wall, the new legislation provided the mechanism for a more rational redistribution of such land as the exodus freed.[69]

Within twenty-four hours of its publication, the Senate and all the agricultural associations, with the single exception of the CNJA, voiced their opposition to the legislation. In the summer of 1961 rural France saw some of its most bitter demonstrations, with the destruction of voting urns at Pont l'Abbé in Brittany, the occupation of the *préfecture* at Morlaix, and further trouble in the Massif Central and the south-west.[70] In many regions an active campaign of opposition to the new laws was coordinated by the FDSEA. In the Aisne, Blondelle's own union argued that 'there was absolutely no need for such structural reforms – it is prices that are the problem . . . one can only deplore the tendency of this government to sacrifice the present for the future'.[71] For other regions, notably in the south and west, indexation of prices without structural reform was a nonsense. What the events of 1960 and 1961 showed was the contrast which existed between the aptitude of farmers to adopt new techniques and their general inability to exercise real economic power. The reaction to the law reinforced once more the signifi-cance of social and geographical differentiation in the farming community.

By the middle of 1961 only two parts of the legislation had actually been put into operation and in September, Pisani, the new Minister of Agricul-ture, set in train the elaboration of a complementary set of laws which would make the 1960 legislation more operational. This was finally passed in the National Assembly in August 1962. It was more practical than the first law and, largely resigned as it was to the role of government intervention in agriculture, the FNSEA reluctantly accepted it.

By the early 1960s, then, a series of radical changes had taken place in the key organisations and policies underpinning French agriculture. The rejuvenation of the agricultural syndicate, helped by the role of the Catholic church, had laid the foundations for a new set of structures in the agricultural economy. For the family farm, now the acknowledged cornerstone of agricultural policy, to survive, the place of cooperatives of all types and scales was central. In this respect the link between syndicalism and economic organisation of farming was of particular importance.

The development of group agriculture

The philosophy of the new rural élite taking its place in the CNJA and FNSEA was based firmly on the realisation that, for the family farm to survive and prosper, individualist tendencies had to be overcome. Cooperation between a few individual farmers or between farmers in a particular region or system of production was essential. Since the Liberation, then, a whole network of cooperatives developed to permit a more rational utilisation of means of production, the better marketing of agricultural produce and a more secure and stable economic environment for agriculture.[72]

Syndical involvement in such organisations was important from the outset for, to many, syndicalism and cooperation were the two chief weapons of the peasant and could be separated only with difficulty. If the roots of cooperation were very deep in rural France, and, as has been argued, cooperatives had played an important part in the pre-war syndical movement, the two decades following the Liberation were distinguished by an explosion of new forms of cooperation at all scales and with diverse purposes. Houée has identified two broad categories: those concerned with improving production conditions at the level of the farm and those aimed at stabilising market conditions. Both owed much to the influence of the new generation of syndicalists.[73] We can take Houée's analysis further and differentiate cooperatives according to scale, origins and objectives as in Figure 7.5.

Some of the earliest efforts at cooperation in this period were to be found at local level. The Centres d'études techniques agricoles (CETA) were small groups (between ten and fifteen farmers) who met regularly to exchange information and experiences and to set up a joint programme of agricultural improvement using the skills of agricultural technicians. Initially strongest in the large farming regions of the Paris Basin, by the late 1940s they had spread to traditional polycultural areas, often under the impetus of the new militants. From fifteen in 1951, their numbers expanded to 994 in 1962 and their role as catalysts of change in particular regions is especially significant.[74] Their overwhelming emphasis on increased production and productivity reveals the dominant mentality of the period.

At the same time the Coopératives d'utilisation du matériel agricole

SCALE

Local	- usually production oriented (C.E.T.A., C.U.M.A., G.A.E.C.)
Regional	- usually product oriented - meat, milk, wine (S.I.C.A.)
National/multi-national - usually product oriented - cereals	

ORIGINS

Syndicalism - especially local and regional

Government - especially national

Chambers of agriculture - especially local and regional

OBJECTIVES

Technical improvement
(C.E.T.A., C.U.M.A., Banque du Travail)
Property structures
(G.A.E.C., G.F.A.)
Market organisation - single or multi product

C.E.T.A. - *Centre d'études techniques agricoles*
C.U.M.A. - *Coopératives d'utilisation du materiel agricole*
G.A.E.C. - *Groupement agricole d'exploitation en commun*
G.F.A. - *Groupement foncier agricole*
S.I.C.A. - *Société d'intérêt collectif agricole*

Figure 7.5 Structure of agricultural cooperatives

(CUMA) developed as small-scale cooperatives. The majority were created in order that a group of farmers could purchase expensive items of machinery or to enable particular farming processes to be carried out more easily.[75] Their role was, however, more than purely technical: as Houée notes, 'they provided a kind of apprenticeship for farmers sowing the seeds of professional solidarity and developing methods of proper accounting on the farm'. Their numbers had increased to 9,100 by 1960.[76]

One of the most important consequences of the Orientation Laws was the flexibility it gave farmers to adapt their own property conditions to their needs. The Groupement agricole d'exploitation en commun (GAEC) allowed farmers to group their lands as one unit for purposes of taxation and farming, but continue to retain property rights and a guaranteed input into farming decisions. In theory their creation marked a major change in farming mentalities in sacrificing the god of individual property ownership on the altar of agricultural progress. In practice, the vast majority of

GAECs were created between members of the same family, the association representing a mechanism for avoiding the subdivision of farms and for giving younger members of the family a greater stake in the farm enterprise.[77]

Given the emphasis on problems of parity between agricultural and industrial prices in syndical activity in this period, it is not surprising that considerable efforts were made by syndicalists to create marketing cooperatives for particular products and regions which might help to stabilise conditions at a time of rapidly rising production. By the late 1950s, the major expansion of regional and national cooperatives had taken place within the cereal sector. The powerful Union nationale des coopératives agricoles de céréales provides a good example. Created in 1945, it united some 600 cereal cooperatives, the majority of which had been founded in the thirties. From the outset it sought to maximise its economic power through mergers and negotiation at both national and European scale. By 1955 the scale of its investments had made it the largest cereal-stocking agency in Europe. However, the links between local, regional and national groups were often poorly controlled and lacked financial rigour. Many cooperatives remained financially insecure and poorly run.

The arrival of a new group to positions of power in syndicates and cooperatives marked the start of a new rigour and professionalism in the cooperative movement. The programme of improving agricultural returns required that the profession exercise careful control over the market and, in 1966, a single cooperative union, the Confédération française de la coopération agricole was set up. The process of amalgamation of cooperatives, the increased scale of operation and the greater influence of the movement over production decisions were all consequences of this change in leadership. The effects on the cooperative sector will be more fully examined in the following chapter.

If the internationalisation of the cooperative sector was not to emerge until the late 1960s, the most striking development in this period was the emergence of regional cooperatives catering for particular products. The SICA (Société d'intérêt collectif agricole) formula was widely employed for these new cooperatives. Particularly widespread in areas rejuvenated by the new syndical militants (notably the Massif Central and Brittany), they were often set up as part of a broad syndical programme combining demonstrations with a more practical marketing programme. They were frequently created to deal with milk, meat and poultry, products traditionally much less susceptible to cooperative processing and transformation than cereals and sugar-beet. The relationship between the cooperative, syndical and Catholic action groups can best be illustrated through local case-studies.

Brittany in the early 1960s had experienced some of the most violent agricultural demonstrations in France and was a region in which the Catholic church had played an important part in creating a new group of militants. The agricultural structures of much of the region had been transformed by a massive intensification of forage production – geared towards milk and meat production coupled with an expansion of the poultry industry – often linked to the growing involvement of agri-business in production and marketing. Yet massive advances in total output and productivity had taken place within structures still dominated by the family farm and a marketing system which was archaic and artisanal in character. Much of the unrest of this period was not caused by misery but rather by the extreme rapidity of development.[78]

For Flatrès, farming mentalities, shaped as they were by the JAC, and moulded into action through an increasingly powerful syndicalism, were the key factor in what he termed the 'second agricultural revolution' in the region.[79] The rejuvenation of syndicalism came from diverse sources but one of the most influential figures was Alexis Gourvennec. Trained in the JAC, he became the first president of a new artichoke committee in Finistère in 1958 at the age of only 22. The problems of that sector illustrated the dilemna of Breton farmers – massive increases in production had taken place with full government support whilst the marketing structures remained undeveloped. At the time Gourvennec and Marcel Léon were also engaged in a battle with the older syndical leaders in the department – there was, he argued, a total lack of communication between leadership and base in the late 1950s.

The demonstrations of 1960 and 1961 changed that. With Gourvennec at the head of the FDSEA, demonstrations were organised focusing on the immediate pricing problems but also calling for a constructive reform of marketing networks. The second complementary law of 1962 reflected many of these pressures from the base. In the same year, following a visit to Holland to examine marketing conditions there, he founded an SICA at St Pol-de-Leon, in the heart of the vegetable producing region of Finistère. Within a few years its membership exceeded 4,000, it exercised a virtual monopoly in the supply of artichokes and cauliflowers and, through this monopoly, it was able to ensure fair prices for the local producers.[80] Later efforts at improving the marketing of Breton produce was to lead to the creation of Brittany Ferries in 1973, with Gourvennec at the head of the new organisation.

Morin, in his study of the commune of Plodémet in Brittany, has provided an example of how agricultural change was channelled through the JAC-trained élite into cooperative ventures. A rejuvenated syndicalism in the late 1950s, achieved largely through the new Catholic activists, played its part in the demonstrations which swept through Finistère in 1962. A CUMA between thirteen farms in the commune had been founded in 1962, and the syndicate had helped to bring about a degree of *remembrement* in the commune. But efforts to group pea producers in order to achieve better prices, a motive which had led to successful cooperatives in the St-Pol-de-Leon region, foundered here, as the traditional canning plants weakened producer unity by offering higher prices if peasants would continue to market through the usual channels. The new ethos was not always able to triumph over peasant individualism.[81]

A further example of the economic role of the new élite comes from the region of Anjou. One of the key motors of economic change in the region was the Coopérative agricole la noelle d'Ancenis (CANA). Created in 1932, primarily to undertake cereal stockage, it had some 3,000 members by 1939 and offered a range of services to its regional clientele – supply of seeds and fertiliser, collection and storage of apples, production and marketing of wine. Its diverse character, offering a wide range of services and products, was reinforced when, after the war, it relocated at the town of Ancenis, with good communications and room for expansion. Taking over a number of rival groups in the early 1950s, the cooperative prospered and became involved in processing and marketing both dairy and wine products, as well as an involvement in the meat market. During this period it became the main channel for the promotion of a JAC-trained élite characterised by a well-developed technical education and an emphasis on specialised milk and meat production. A dynamic committee brought about a remarkable expansion in the group. The amount of milk treated in the CANA tripled between 1958 and 1966; in the same period, overall turnover trebled with the number of employees rising from 290 to 600. As Peyon noted, 'the local milieu and its powerful catholic groups, syndicalism and a well-organised Crédit Agricole created the right sort of conditions for an economic mobilisation of the region's farmers through the cooperative.'[82]

For Lambert, this new mental climate was crucial to the emergence of the cooperative. He has identified two main social networks in the region; the first based on polycultural farmers integrated through the traditional fairs and comice agricole, the second on specialised producers, often trained in the JAC, meeting through the cooperative and the syndicate. 'Everything appeared possible to this new élite', notes Lambert, 'structural reforms, control of economic power, even the beginnings of a political breakthrough.'

It was this close-knit social group that was responsible for the creation of a regional CETA in 1952, and six years later a network of Groupements de vulgarisation agricole was created to encourage technical progress and innovation amongst the specialist producers. The map of JAC implantation in the 1950s, Lambert argues, corresponded very closely to the pattern of agricultural cooperation through the CETA and the activity of the regional CANA. The JAC was the catalyst for most of the economic transformations of the region – it played a formative role in introducing a new capitalist ethos into the countryside.[83]

A third example of these connections comes from Aveyron. In the immediate post-war years considerable emphasis was placed on the cooperative as
a means of speeding up technical change in farming methods. As early as
1947, the syndical journal, *La Volonté paysanne*, had noted the dangers of
ever greater production: 'this intensive production at ever lower cost may
rapidly become the most certain mechanism by which the small family farm
in regions like ours will be destroyed'.[84] At times of agricultural unrest in
1953 and 1956, one of the first acts of the FDSEA had been to establish
departmental cooperatives for meat and milk after first organising boycotts
of the traditional marketing circuits.[85] The dairy sector was *par excellence*
the area for syndical intervention. In a department heavily dependent on
milk yet characterised by small-scale production (an average delivery per
farmer of only ten litres per day in 1955) good marketing was essential. The
FDSEA led by Bruel, played a formative role in setting up the Coopérative
agricole laitière aveyronnaise in December 1959. A merger with the private
La Ruthenoise organisation in 1961 meant that the share of the cooperative
sector in overall milk production in Aveyron rose from 21 per cent in 1950 to
34 per cent in 1962.[86]

Syndical action was not confined to the large-scale cooperative. Bruel
argued that 'amongst all the cooperative developments in which syndicalists
can take pride, the most significant has been the CUMA'.[87] The geography
of the CUMA in Aveyron was compared with that of syndical membership
and a chi-square test showed that there was a significant relationship between the two, reinforcing the anecdotal evidence of these links.[88] Finally,
membership lists of cooperatives and syndicates in the department both in
the late 1940s and in the early 1960s show the strong links in personnel
between the two groups.

The early 1960s can be said to have marked something of a watershed in
the evolution of both the structures and organisations of rural France.
Wright's *Rural revolution, La Révolution silencieuse* of Debatisse, Mallet's
Les Paysans contre le passé were all written in this period and testify to the
sense of change, of transformation and of confidence in the future development of the countryside. With the advent of the Common Market and
the continued expansion of production and productivity, future horizons
were promising. As Wright concluded in the early 1960s, 'One can at least be
sure that the French peasantry has outgrown its passive and negative role;
that its voice will be heard henceforth in the shaping of its own future, and
that of France.'[89]

8

The deceptions of progress 1965–1985

It was that newly found voice which, through the passage of the Orientation Laws in 1960 and 1962, and the rejuvenation of the syndical and cooperative movements, embarked on a programme of agricultural 'modernisation' which was central to the economic and social philosophy of the new revolutionaries. If the revolution itself was achieved in a spirit of united militancy, moulded by the church and brought to fruition through an alliance with gaullism, carrying through the aims of the new movement was a much more testing proposition.

The process of change set in train by the events of the early 1960s, based as it was on the creation of farms *à deux unités de travail*, created winners and losers and clearly exposed the different interests of farmers. Conflict between large and small farmers, between farmers of different regions, between the cooperative and private sectors of the burgeoning agro-industrial sector, and between the profession and the state continued to influence the programmes, membership and development of agricultural organisations.

The variety of such organisations can appear at times bewildering, with a labyrinth of private, official, economic and political groups involved in the process of agricultural policy-making and implementation. The chambers of agriculture have played an important role in coordinating agricultural programmes; at national level the Permanent assembly of departmental presidents (APCA) seeks to influence government agricultural policy. Negotiation between the syndical movement and government was, until reforms were attempted in the middle of the 1980s, channelled solely through the two 'official' syndicates – the Fédération nationale des syndicats d'exploitants agricoles (FNSEA) and the Centre nationale des jeunes agriculteurs (CNJA). Behind this façade of official unionism, however, is a regionally powerful group of 'dissident' syndicates. Most notable is the Mouvement de Défense des exploitants familiaux (MODEF). The main economic organisations in the countryside are coordinated through national groups with the Crédit agricole, the Confédération française de la coopération agricole (CFCA), and the Fédération Nationale de la mutualité agricole (FNMA) organising their respective sectors of the agricultural economy. The expansion in the number of such groups has been one of the most striking aspects of recent years; never has rural France been more densely covered with such organisations than at present.[1]

Syndicalism since 1962

The complementary Orientation Law in 1962 was, as has been indicated, largely unopposed by the FNSEA, unlike the 1960 legislation which had provoked the hostility of all the agricultural pressure groups except the CNJA. This change largely reflected the extent to which the activists of the CNJA had succeeded in taking power at departmental and national level. The most articulate of these militants, Michael Debatisse, became assistant-secretary of the FNSEA in 1964 and secretary-general four years later, cementing the arrival of the new rural elite.[2] Membership of the FNSEA has remained stable at around 690,000 in 1963 and 650,000 in 1980, although these figures are considered somewhat higher than actual membership because of the inclusion of CNJA members and members of the specialist producer groups. It is significant, however, that the FNSEA has been able to enrol about 50 per cent of its potential membership in recent years, a figure which is higher than the industrial trade unions.[3]

Syndical policy has shown a marked consistency since the changes of the early 1960s. The creation of an economically rational family-farming system, enshrined in the Orientation Laws, has continued to be a central policy aim of the FNSEA. Both structural reform and pricing policy have been key elements at annual congresses. 'The economic model we are seeking to create,' noted the 1976 congress, 'is the medium-sized family farm; we wish to emphasise the importance of personal responsibility in an enterprise at a human scale.' The same point is made in more recent documents: in 1986 it argued that 'agricultural policy must have as its target the medium-sized farm at a human scale in which decision-making and responsibility is exercised by the farming family.'[4]

This degree of consistency in general policy objectives is reinforced when the practical policies of syndicalism are examined. A firm opposition to large increases in farm sizes has been maintained through fear that the larger agricultural enterprise may compromise the decision-making ability of the farmer. Hence the strong support given by the union to land-reform programmes such as the SAFER and IVD which, in theory, should free land for distribution to create viable family farms. A policy of cooperation or *cogestion* with such policies is evident at all levels with syndical activists playing an important part in the decision-making bodies that have guided structural reform programmes since the early 1960s. Continued support for *l'agriculture de groupe* has also been evident. This focused initially on the marketing and processing sector but the increasing size and complexity of such groups has meant that syndical influence has perhaps declined in comparison with the 1950s and early 1960s. Nonetheless the involvement of syndicalists in such groups remains strong.

Small-scale producer cooperatives, particularly the GAEC and GFA, have continued to be supported both nationally and regionally by the FNSEA, which has pressed for increased resourcing and flexibility for property reforms. Decentralisation of some of the reform organisations after the 1980 Orientation Laws (which modified the detail but not the broad thrust of those of 1960 and 1962) led the syndicate to express concern over the lack of financial resources for reform programmes considered essential to the survival of family farms.[5]

The commitment of the syndicate to the reform programme has meant that from local to national level the organisation provides a panoply of services to farmers. Not the least of such services has been a knowledge of the increasingly complex and bureaucratic organisations which are involved in agricultural planning. Thus, whilst the responsibility for technical and infrastructural reform in rural France remains divided between the services of the chamber of agriculture, the departmental Direction des services agricoles and the Ministry of Agriculture, the ability of the syndicate to guide its members through the often labyrinthine corridors of power of these groups constitutes an important membership benefit. As Chombart de Lauwe has argued, 'Only those organisations which can work in close collaboration with public bodies serving agriculture will achieve the support of the farming community.'[6] One of the most distinctive features of recent syndical history has been the extent to which such collaboration has been achieved and the syndicate has become almost a corporatist client of a centralised state.

It can be argued, however, that this process has not been without its difficulties. It had been the collaboration of the CNJA and the technocrats of the Fifth Republic that had produced the structural reforms of the new legislation and provided the mechanisms for increased syndical involvement in agricultural planning. What the legislation provided was the framework within which the profession, through the syndicate, could exercise control over its destiny. One of the paradoxes of the 'rural revolution' was that it created a whole series of institutions through which a new élite could consolidate its power and influence.

The setting up of regional SAFERs, the development of the policies to encourage elderly farmers to retire from the profession on condition that they ceded their land to young farmers, and the increased attention given to professional training in both technical and social aspects of farming, re-quired the involvement of the departmental and national syndical move-ment. Equally important has been the expansion of advisory and technical services emanating from the chambers of agriculture within which the syn-dicates themselves have a very strong representation. As Keeler has pointed out, this expanding network of advisory groups and restructuring organis-ations meant that, from the early 1960s onwards, the FNSEA provided 'all of the essential services of a corporatist client', enabling the government to develop a 'symbiotic corporatist relationship' with the organisation.[7]

Through the late 1960s and 1970s, Keeler argues, the involvement of the union in planning and executing agricultural policy compromised its inde-pendence. The relationship between state and syndicate became, for the first time in its history, dependent and symbiotic, as syndicalists became integral to the machinery of agricultural planning through their consultative and executive role in such institutions. In 1975, for example, FDSEA presidents were also presidents of at least three of the 31 SAFERs. Equally, union delegates held at least 9 of the 16 seats on the ADASEA committees (Associations départementales pour l'aménagement des structures des ex-ploitations agricoles) which play an important role in coordinating and executing decisions on agricultural restructuring. Similar influence was also maintained on the Services d'utilité agricole de développement com-missions, which play an important part in subsidising union programmes for professional training and the women's section of the FDSEA. Many depart-mental chambers of agriculture are dominated by the syndicates: in 1975, three-quarters of all union presidents were members of their respective chambers, whilst 45 per cent were on the executives of these bodies.[8]

Given the dominant direction of the FNSEA towards structural reform in collaboration with government agencies, it is appropriate to consider the appeal of syndical policy. To what extent can its claim to represent the interests of all farmers be justified? One of the consequences of the rural revolution of the late 1950s was a recognition on the part of syndical leaders that not all farms could be maintained through state and syndical action. The promotion of the medium-sized family farm entailed the inevitable disap-pearance of many thousands of small-holdings and the resignation of many elderly farmers to the fact that theirs would be the last generation to farm.

For Tavernier, this reformist programme has determined the orientation of all subsequent syndical policy. He has argued that CNJA policy, which became the accepted orthodoxy in the middle of the 1960s, implicitly identi-fied three agricultural groups. The first, large-scale capitalist enterprises, required no government help and necessitated few structural reforms other than a ceiling on enterprise size. A second group, modernising family farmers, were to be the chief object of the reform programme. Finally, a rump of small, often elderly, farmers, usually farming in the marginal regions, was doomed to disappear as the price for the reforms which would help the second group to survive. This transformation in syndical policy from one of blanket preservation in the early 1950s to rationalisation in favour of a particular group less than a generation later was the most remarkable consequence of the rural revolution.[9]

Support for the dominant syndicalism at national and departmental level, however, cannot help but reflect the consequences of this policy. For the large capitalist farming regions of the north and Paris Basin the real power of the union has been built less on national policy than on the provision of local services. If the changes of the early 1960s had led to some diminution in their influence they were able to reassert power through the specialist producer groups. The creation of the Common Market further reinforced these trends; the specialist cereal and sugar-beet producers were able to secure power at Brussels through the accord of December 1964, which transferred agricultural decisions to a European framework. The fixing of a common cereal price within Europe from July 1967, a process in which the AGPB, rather than the FNSEA, plays the key role illustrates how the interests of the large producer were reasserted in spite of the emphasis on structural reform. That a much greater proportion of the CAP budget continues to be spent on price support rather than structural reform may in no small part reflect the consequences of decisions taken in the early years of the community.[10]

Support for the FNSEA at departmental level has remained high in these regions of capitalist farming, and in the elections for the chambers of agriculture the dominance of their lists has been consistent.[11] Such power reflects the ability of the union to provide a range of services to its members. Keeler's study of the Aisne serves as an excellent illustration of this process.[12] A department with a traditionally strong syndical movement, almost 95 per cent of its farmers belonged to the union in the middle of the 1960s. The key to its power lay, not in the mass demonstrations that had animated syndicalism in Brittany and the Massif Central in this period, but rather in the range of services and facilities it offered its members. Between 1955 and 1974 the budget of the syndicate increased by 300 per cent in real terms, and a decentralisation of personnel through the creation of paid cantonal secretaries meant that the union became the first contact for farmers seeking advice on land purchases, taxation, subsidies and infrastructural improvements. As Keeler notes, 'the farmers of Aisne have been brought into and kept within the union fold through the provision of manifold services which are vital to the professional life of the farmer'.[13]

This process provided Keeler with the evidence for a corporatist interpretation of the union. Its role, he argued, had become increasingly indistinguishable from that of the chamber of agriculture or the ADASEA. Much of the cost of this network of services provided by an ostensibly independent syndicate was in fact borne by the state through the chamber of agriculture.

Table 8.1. *Average farm sizes in Aisne, 1970–80 (hectares)*

Region	1970	1980
Thiérache	26	31
St Quentin-Laon	62	72
Soissonais	62	71
Tardenois-Brie	38	42
Valois	90	94
Champagne	77	83

Source: Chambre d'agriculture de l'Aisne (1983)

The training of syndical cadres and the services of the young farmers' groups were, as in many other departments, effectively paid for through the state. Even in Aisne, however, the power of the union was not unchallenged, for its appeal was primarily to the larger farmer. Thus membership was higher in those regions of the department characterised by large-scale cereal production. As Table 8.1 shows, these larger units dominated in the Champagne and Valois regions; in the Thiérache and Brie, characterised by smaller farms and an orientation towards dairy farming, membership was lower. The Thiérache was the only region registering some support for the dissident MODEF in elections to the chamber of agriculture.

It is difficult to measure the appeal of FNSEA policies to those farming groups which fit into the second category outlined by Tavernier, middle-ranking farmers who have sought to modernise their holdings. One indirect way of assessing this is to examine the rate of adoption of some of the structural policies advocated both by government and the syndicate. Certainly some of the earliest SAFERs were established in those regions most influenced by the syndicalist wave of the early 1960s. Auvergne, Languedoc-Roussillon and Marche-Limousin were amongst the first creations; perhaps not surprisingly, those of Picardie, Ile-de-France and Flandre-Artois were created only in the early 1970s. Naylor's analysis of the take up of other parts of the programme, such as the IVD, and the installation grants for young farmers, indicates a strong concentration in Brittany in particular. Equally the pattern of GAEC approvals shows high levels in much of Brittany and parts of central France.[14]

It remains difficult to evaluate the vitality of the dominant syndicate from such broad indicators. It is at departmental and local level that the tensions of the movement begin to appear in the contrasting perceptions of farmers on different paths of development. Burguière, drawing on the results of a major interdisciplinary project in the commune of Plozévet in Finistère, reveals many of the latent conflicts within the syndical movement. Despite its location in a region amongst the most syndically active in the early 1960s, the 'rural revolution' in the commune was short-lived. Two types of farmers are identified: the small peasantry with no hope of economic viability, and the 'modernising' farmers bedevilled with property and marketing problems. Crucially, the very presence of the former group represented an obstacle to the economic survival of the latter.

If, in 1961 and 1962, as syndicalists in the region took to the streets, membership and support for the FDSEA was widespread, by 1964 it had tailed off dramatically. The JAC group which had animated the local syndicate 'was unable to effect any change in the conservative mentalities of the majority'. The realisation that a part of the community was to be allowed to disappear in order to save a group of modernising farmers quickly spread amongst the marginal farmers, many of them elderly and many with communist sympathies. By the middle of the 1960s the syndicate had only a quarter of its former members and recruited support almost solely from those farmers who had begun the process of modernising their farms. Apathy was widespread and, by a nice irony, many elderly communists 'refused with horror the vision of a France covered with collective farms which the young Catholic activists seemed to offer'.[15]

In Aveyron the resurgence of syndicalism in the early 1960s appears to have lasted rather better. If the seizure of power by a new élite was the most striking aspect of the period, the real roots of change lay in the continued activity and importance of the young farmers' groups.[16] Above all the emphasis on *formation professionnelle* is striking, with enormous stress placed on this type of training. The influence of the church and the continued role of the JAC and its replacement, the Mouvement pour le rassemblement des jeunes chrétiens (MRJC), mean that, according to one militant, 'Aveyron fared rather better in membership and activity than some other departments'.[17] The emphasis on cooperatives of all types continued. Thus the number of CUMAs increased steadily throughout the period, the majority being created by militant syndicalists. The same conclusions applied to both the GAEC and the Banque de Travail.[18]

It would appear that these developments, initiated with such optimism in the 1960s, began to be regarded more critically in the early 1970s. Certainly conflict between the CDJA and the FDSEA over national policy towards rural depopulation began to be apparent. The number of farms in the department had fallen from 28,490 in 1963 to 22,527 in 1970 and by 1977 had fallen below 20,000.[19] Whilst recognising the need for land to be released to help small farmers adapt, the very pace of decline began to alarm some syndicalists, especially in view of the problems it posed for the more isolated and depopulated areas of the department. A continued fall in the agricultural population began to threaten the survival of services essential to life in the countryside, particularly in view of the large agricultural contribution to the social and economic life of the community.[20] After a decade or so dedicated to the rationalisation of agricultural structures and the continuance of the rural exodus, some questioning of policy began to take place.[21]

The impression that power is exercised by the same group of militants who had taken control in the early 1960s is widespread. Certainly that influence remains very strong with Cazals, Bruel, Laur and Lacombe still active nationally and locally, the latter as secretary-general of the FNSEA. Given the strength of training and educative programmes in the department, it seems likely that a smooth transfer of power between generations can take place, albeit later rather than sooner. If the policies of the CNJA and the FNSEA, elaborated out of the melting-pot of social catholicism and gaullism in the early 1960s have, explicitly or implicitly, accepted the disappearance of large numbers of farmers, how then have these farmers reacted? Furthermore, given the conclusions that can be drawn from such policies, to what extent can the claim of the FNSEA to represent all agricultural interests be upheld?

A dissident syndicalism?

When the new *politique agricole* was elaborated in the early 1960s, four groups were involved in negotiations with the government: the CNJA, FNSEA, the specialist producers (dominated by the wheat and sugar-beet groups) and the chambers of agriculture. The dominance of the first two groups as the syndical organisations which 'best' represent agricultural interests has continued in the process of negotiation and argument with government.[22] For the FNSEA, such a position lends strength both to the organisation and to farming interests. As Debatisse has argued, the syndical movement has achieved for the agricultural world 'what most industrial unions dream of – a united and unitary syndical movement'.[23] At the 1986 FNSEA congress this position was again reinforced: 'only our syndicates', it was argued, 'can organise national demonstrations, negotiate with government at all levels, show an active local syndicalism in all regions, and fully represent the preoccupations and interests of all farmers'.[24] A fierce defence of the sole negotiating rights enjoyed by the FNSEA and CNJA in its contacts with government has been carried out since the early 1960s.[25]

As has been noted, however, the economic policies and, indeed, activity of this dominant syndicalism has left sizeable sections of the agricultural community with a sense of isolation, and three currents of dissident syndicalism have developed since the early 1960s: the Mouvement de défense des exploitants familiaux (MODEF), the Fédération française de l'agriculture (FFA) and the Paysans-travailleurs (PT). Each group has a not insignificant membership amongst sections of the community, a strong base in certain regions and a demand that it be represented in negotiations with public bodies, a demand consistently rejected by the FNSEA and by the government prior to 1981.

MODEF is the oldest of these groups. In the early 1950s a number of departmental federations faced conflict with the national federation because of both policy disagreements and their difficulties in meeting the financial demands of the national body. The agricultural demonstrations of 1953 had also led to the creation of the Comité de guéret, an informal coordinating group with a membership drawn particularly from four departmental federations which had been expelled from the FNSEA (Landes, Charente, Haute-Garonne and Corrèze) together with representatives from a number of other regions, notably in the south and south-west.[26] Some six years later these informal contacts crystallised into the creation of the MODEF at Toulouse in April 1959. Its objective was first and foremost the defence of the small family farmer and its membership remained concentrated in the south and south-west with the excluded federations and those active in the Comité de guéret forming the initial membership.[27]

The new policies of the early 1960s reinforced the determination of MODEF to provide an alternative syndical organisation for those farmers who felt threatened by the structural programmes so vigorously pursued by the FNSEA. Membership grew steadily. In 1962, at the first congress, there were some 74 representatives from 31 departments, in 1968 67 departments were represented.[28] The influence of the left, in particular the Communist Party, is undoubted, for the party played a not inconsiderable part in the creation of the Comité de guéret and communist activists were important in setting up the MODEF. For Chombart de Lauwe, such influence fundamentally weakens the syndical representativeness of the organisation: it represents, he argues, 'nothing more than a party instrument to infiltrate communism into the countryside'.[29] But such a judgement ignores both the widespread support that the group has gained, and the obvious politicisation of the FNSEA as a consequence of its policies begun in the early 1960s.

What support, then, has MODEF been able to gain? One way of measuring this is by examining the results of the elections to the chamber of agriculture. In 1964 and 1967 the syndicate gained between 15 per cent and 20 per cent of the vote in those departments (almost all in the south and west) where it presented lists. The results of the 1970 and 1976 elections showed a much wider clientele. In 1970 it gained almost 33 per cent of votes cast in those 64 departments where it presented candidates and ensured representation in 23 departmental Chambers of Agriculture. Its best results were obtained in areas of family farming (south-west, central, parts of western France), with only tiny support in the north, east and Paris Basin. In 1976 it received about 24 per cent of the vote in the 71 departments where it presented lists.[30] In the 1983 elections its national support was estimated at about 10 per cent (Table 8.2).

Table 8.2. *Support for the MODEF syndicate, 1964–83*

	1964	1967	1970	1974	1976	1983
Départements contested	21	38	64	65	71	79
Percentage of votes	4	13	22	23	24	10
Seats won	28	24	37	37	51	No data available

Source: Tello (1976); Boussard (1983)

It is evident, therefore, that the MODEF, sometimes portrayed as essentially an organisation built on the old and the marginal in French agriculture, is far from being a marginal syndical force. In membership terms its strength lies in the west and south-west, predominantly amongst the smaller farmers, although it also has support in the larger farming regions of Normandy and north of the Paris Basin (Figure 8.1). The strength of the syndicate is all the more paradoxical when it is realised that it has not been allowed any representative role in government negotiation. Until 1981, and the arrival of the left in power, negotiation and discussion continued to exclude the MODEF on the grounds that it represented, not a syndicate, but a political organisation. Attempts by the socialist government in the early 1980s to ensure that the dissident syndicates are represented in negotiations with government have met with only tentative success. The FNSEA, not surprisingly, has strongly opposed such moves. The success of MODEF continues to call into question the vision of a united agricultural community promulgated by the FNSEA. At local level, in particular, the lack of representation of MODEF and other dissident groups on commissions lends support to the argument that the dominant syndicalism has sought to use public bodies to maintain its hegemony. The setting up of the departmental *remembrement* commission in Creuse illustrates this point. As Table 8.3 indicates, there was no relationship between votes cast in the elections to the chamber of agriculture and seats granted on the commission.

What kind of policies, then, does MODEF advocate? A long opposition to aspects of the Orientation Laws has been a fundamental part of their platform. It explicitly recognises that structural change towards the ideal 'economically viable' farm, employing at least two people, will in reality involve the disappearance of many thousands of smaller units. The first laws in 1960 and 1962 were in part responsible for the creation of the syndicate; its opposition to the 1980 Orientation Laws has been equally strong. Perhaps as a consequence of this somewhat negative programme, much of its policy is centred on the problem of price parity and if its demonstrations have an immediacy and vigour often lacking in the dominant syndicalism of the FNSEA, this may well be the reason.[31]

Table 8.3. *Representation on the 'remembrement'*
committee in Creuse, 1985

Syndicate	Votes 1983 (%)	Seats on committee
FDSEA	45	10
MODEF	20	1
Union pour la Creuse	27	1
Paysans-Travailleurs	8	0

Source: MODEF

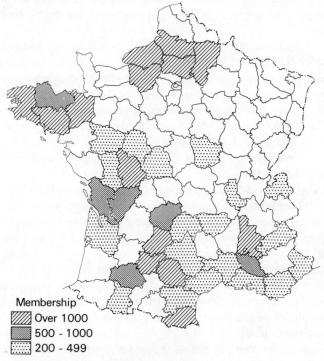

Membership
Over 1000
500 - 1000
200 - 499

Figure 8.1 Geography of the MODEF in 1985

A fierce opposition to the European Community has been a consistent policy theme. The widening of the market and, in particular, the accession of Spain and Portugal, represents, it is argued, a fatal blow for the small farmer. Not surprisingly, support for MODEF has been strong in the south (regions such as Provence and Rhône-Alps), whose fruit and wine products have been especially exposed through enlargement. Whilst supporting in principle certain aspects of community policy, its main opposition rests on the problems of price: 'MODEF is happy to see the development of measures to lower pollution, to develop rural tourism, to seek new markets for agricultural products . . . but only on condition that the future of family farmers is preserved by allowing production and sale at the right price.'[32]

The second major dissident syndicate, the Paysans-travailleurs, represents a very different section of the agricultural community though, without the right to any representation nationally, it often makes common cause with MODEF. The origins of the group are, however, less clear because its clientele is less apparent. A strong opposition to the theme of agricultural unity espoused by the FNSEA characterises their programme but, unlike MODEF, its supporters tend to be found amongst those farmers who have taken the path of modernisation and investment but failed to reap any benefits.[33]

Many militants of the movement were trained in the Catholic action groups which had produced the revolution of the 1950s but, through their experiences, were drawn to rather different conclusions regarding the development of agricultural structures. In particular, the massive investments required for agricultural modernisation, the increasing role of agribusiness in the drawing up of contracts of production (particularly in the poultry sector), and the greater vulnerability of these farmers to national and international market fluctuations led to some dissatisfaction with FNSEA policies in the late 1960s.

If, as Tavernier argues, this movement did not start from a fixed theoretical position, Lambert, one of the founders of the syndicate, has nevertheless articulated the problems such farmers faced.[34] For him, the adoption of the modernising path has increasingly placed the farmer in the position of a proletariat. Huge debts mean that the enterprise is condemned to a relentless search for greater production, and vertical contracts fundamentally compromise independence, leading, Lambert argues, to an increasing loss of both the means of production and their control. In such conditions, the reformist policies of the FNSEA disguise the truly subservient position of the farming community.

In the late 1960s, this current of thought sought to bring about internal change in the FNSEA and aimed, in particular, to change the direction of policy in the unions of the west where the disillusion of this group was most widespread. The events of May 1968, in which Debatisse, secretary-general of the FNSEA, was the sole syndical leader to come out in strong support of de Gaulle, increased tensions within both the national and regional movement. But in 1970 Lambert, active in organising demonstrations in the summer of 1968, lost his post as secretary of the powerful Fédération régionale des syndicats d'exploitants agricoles de l'ouest. The rupture between the dominant syndicalism and a dissident group widened from this point leading to the creation, in the early 1970s, of a loose alliance of local syndicates which were coordinated into the Paysans-travailleurs group.[35]

The recent efforts of this group have been focused on securing adequate representation on the chambers of agriculture and pressing for national recognition. Whilst not as successful as MODEF in securing votes, it has nevertheless managed between 10 per cent and 15 per cent in chamber elections.[36] Its support in its heartland, western France, has often been above 20 per cent, yet it remains completely dominated in agricultural decision-making bodies by the FNSEA. Thus, in the Côtes-du-Nord, the MODEF and Paysans-travailleurs secured 42 per cent of farmers' votes in the 1983 chamber elections yet had no representative place in the Direction Départementale de l'Agriculture commissions. The whiff of corporatism at local level remains strong. As one journal noted somewhat acidly, 'the FDSEA, which has a monopoly of power on property transfers through the SAFER, frequently makes use of our enforced absence to secure advantages for its members.'[37] Whether such accusations are justified is hard to judge but clearly the strength of dissident syndicalism makes the monopoly position of the dominant syndicate increasingly difficult to justify.

The third dissident group, the Fédération française de l'agriculture, is much less powerful than MODEF or the Paysans-travailleurs. A highly conservative organisation, strongly opposed to the structural policies of the FNSEA, it represents the old agrarian ideology of the inter-war years, and is localised in three departments, Indre-et-Loire, Morbihan and Puy-de-Dôme. With less than 5 per cent of the votes in the chamber of agriculture elections in 1975, its influence remains small, although it was able to contest elections in 33 departments in 1983.[38]

The character and policies of syndicalism are thus in a state of flux in the middle of the 1980s. If the dominant movement continues to press for structural reforms capable of maintaining an economically viable family-farming structure, the ever-increasing investment in property and machinery required to sustain that policy has inevitably created tensions. Chombart de Lauwe, commenting on the current position of the movement, has argued that the increasing politicisation of farmers themselves has led to a modification of the role of the syndicate; it can be argued that the FNSEA itself, in its policy of ever closer collaboration with the government (it is hardly coincidence that one former secretary-general, Debatisse, opted for a government post in 1979, another, François Guillaume, became Minister of Agriculture under Chirac in 1986) has created such tensions itself. The establishment of a Confédération paysanne in April 1987, between the dissident syndicates opposed to the hegemony of the FNSEA, seems likely to increase the debate and controversy surrounding the policies of both the dominant syndicate and its cooperation with government policy. The link between politics, the syndicate and the process of agricultural change, usually implicit rather than explicit in the history of the movement, remains as significant an issue today as it was in previous decades.

The chambers of agriculture

The departmental chambers and their national coordinating body, the APCA, constitute an increasingly important group in the elaboration and implementation of agricultural policy. The expansion in their role and activities has been one of the more striking features of the recent history of rural France. After a period in the 1950s when the syndical movement sought to constrain the role of the chambers, the technical and social changes of the *Trente Glorieuses* have now given them a greatly enlarged role. Two particular activities stand out: consultation, and the coordination of technical change. In carrying out these activities they benefit from greater financial security than the syndical movement because they receive income from a tax on property paid by all farmers.[39]

In its consultative role, the scope of activity has been widened as the range of structural measures introduced has increased. Article 2 of the 1960 Loi d'Orientation stipulated that the APCA had a right to be involved in discussions on policy with the Ministry of Agriculture.[40] Much of this power is in fact exercised through a range of government commissions and economic councils. In recent years the role of the APCA has been important in securing changes to legislation on such matters as regional policy and representation on regional councils (1972), greater representation of agricultural interests in the drawing up of *plans d'occupation des sols* on the peripheries of urban areas (1976), and modifications to SAFER legislation to ensure greater public awareness and discussion of policy and decisions (1977).[41] At the European scale, the body serves as a member of the Comité des organisations professionnelles agricoles, through which it is mandated to represent French agricultural interests.[42]

At the departmental scale these consultative powers are also important, hence the interest of the various agricultural syndicates and cooperatives in ensuring representation in the chambers, usually through supporting a particular list for election. Whilst the method of election has been regularly modified, in principle, most interest groups have at least the opportunity to influence policy through elections to the chamber. Figure 8.2 shows the structure of the most recent electoral college. Through regular plenary sessions, the chambers can comment on questions of agricultural policy and formulate responses to particular departmental and national issues. Thus, the precise syndical colouring of the chamber can have a close bearing on the types of responses formulated and the degree of open criticism and comment offered by it on particular issues.

Alongside these consultative roles, the chambers have created and co-ordinated an increasing range of technical services as well as directly

Departmental Chambers of Agriculture

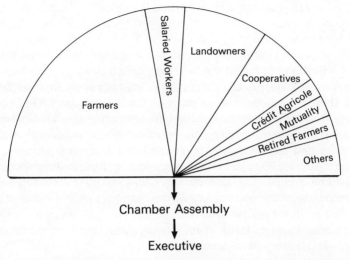

Chamber Assembly

Executive

Figure 8.2 Electoral college of the departmental chambers of agriculture in 1983

subsidising other organisations involved in the agricultural sector. Most departmental chambers have created a Service d'utilité agricole du développement through which technical advisors are funded to aid agricultural development and to coordinate those groups concerned with development issues. Similar groups have been created to deal with the specific problems of pastoral farming regions. Some chambers have also created specific organisations appropriate to the agricultural needs of their regions. Laboratory services can be subsidised through the chambers and schemes for hiring particular items of machinery (e.g., drainage and irrigation machinery) have also been created. A concern with improving housing conditions (Haute-Vienne) or with regional weather-forecasting (Meurthe-et-Moselle) typify this kind of intervention.[43]

One of the most important and expanding roles of the chambers has been in widening the provision of technical and professional training. This ranges from schemes to help the training of young farmers through the creation of Centres de formation, to the provision of schemes to train people for posts of responsibility in syndicates, credit and cooperative organisations. Such provision has reinforced the symbiosis between different organisations in rural regions. Some 43 departments offered these kinds of training courses in the middle of the 1970s, whilst individual departments had created their own Centre de formation for courses on the use of machinery (Loire-Atlantique), the economics of pig farming (Aveyron) or the development of social skills (Finistère).[44]

The chambers have played a major role in coordinating the range of structural measures applied to agriculture since the middle of the 1960s. Thus, legal and property services within the chambers help to inform farmers on procedures for *remembrement*, for grant-aided infrastructural improvements and for application to regional SAFERs for land allocations. Equally important is the role played by the chambers in determining minimum farm sizes in different regions. Such decisions are crucial, for access to preferential loans from the Crédit agricole depends on whether farms are above these minimum sizes. Land purchases from the SAFER are also possible only if the resultant holdings are above the stipulated minimum. If the new policies introduced in the sixties were the product of syndicalism, their execution has undoubtedly revitalised and, in some respects, politicised the chambers. Competition for seats and arguments about the representation to be accorded to different syndical groups are based upon a clear understanding of the important role the chambers play in the implementation of agricultural policy. That role, perhaps less visible in the early 1960s, has come increasingly to the fore, moving these bodies to the forefront of policy formulation and implementation.

Organising the economy – cooperatives and the Crédit agricole

The growth of cooperatives of all types and scales has been one of the most remarkable phenomena of the last three decades.[45] In the middle of the 1980s, four out of five farmers were members of at least one agricultural cooperative. The cooperative sector itself employed close to 150,000 people and, in some areas, notably Brittany, the Paris Basin and the southern Massif Central, such employment accounted for over 15 per cent of all industrial employment. The desire of Catholic activists in the late 1950s to graft a powerful and economically rational cooperative movement onto the deep roots of cooperation in the countryside has been reflected in the massive expansion of the movement since then. The substitution of mutual cooperation for capitalist integration seems, at least to judge by the number of cooperatives, to have been a success.[46]

At the local scale, cooperation has continued apace. The CUMA and *Banque du travail* are now an integral part of agricultural life in many areas. Nationally, the power of processing and marketing cooperatives is striking. By the late 1970s, some 70 per cent of all cereals were marketed through cooperatives, as was 50 per cent of milk, 60 per cent of *vin de table* and 30 per cent of all meat.[47] The cooperative sector has continued to grow in importance as the organisation and control of the processing and marketing of agricultural products has become crucial to the maintenance of farming revenues.

The geography of this movement reflects, not surprisingly, regional agricultural specialisations. Meat cooperatives, strongest in Brittany and the northern Massif Central, are spread throughout the country, although the closed world of the *maquignon* remains the most difficult for the cooperatives to penetrate. Milk cooperatives are concentrated in three main regions: western France (especially Normandy and the Charentais), the southern Massif Central and eastern France. Other patterns include a concentration of viticultural cooperatives in Languedoc and, to a lesser extent, the Bordelais and Champagne, and powerful cereal cooperatives in the Paris Basin and north-east. It is in this latter region, furthermore, that strong linkages between producer and processor have led to vertical integration, particularly in the sugar-beet sector. Brittany (for poultry) and parts of the south-west (for vegetables) also exhibit such linkages, tying the farmer to the cooperatives and, indirectly, to the multinational food-processing companies.[48]

This expansion of cooperatives has taken place primarily at the regional and national level through the amalgamation of smaller, local cooperatives into ever-larger groups. Some of the largest and most influential cooperatives were established through the concentration of smaller groups (often founded with strong syndical influence) in the middle of the 1960s. One of the best known, the group SODIMA (Société de diffusion des marques alimentaires), was established in 1965 through the amalgamation of twelve regional dairy cooperatives. These cooperatives have continued to collect and process milk from their regions but are able to use trade marks created by the national group (Yoplait for yoghurts, Candia for milk) to market the product. Thus the member groups have been able to maintain and nurture their regional links with suppliers whilst benefiting from economies of scale for marketing and publicity both nationally and internationally.[49]

Inevitably, such expansion has shifted the cooperative movement from its local roots and its links with the syndical movement which were previously so powerful. The changing place of cooperatives in the national economy was recognised in legislation passed in the early 1970s which realigned their statutes and, in particular, removed their exemption from company taxation. Fewer privileges were accorded to larger cooperatives – henceforth they were forced to compete on equal terms with their private competitors. A harsher economic climate and stricter, more professional administration has inevitably changed the image of the movement.

It has been this opening out of the cooperative sector to full competition that has led Klatzmann to write of how the 'grand illusion' that the cooperative could provide the panacea for all agricultural problems has been cruelly exposed. Many cooperatives established in the heady climate of the early 1960s were inefficiently run and failed to exert sufficient control over the quality of goods delivered by members; as Klatzmann notes, 'there remains a fundamental conflict between commercial efficiency and a respect for the basic principles of cooperation'.[50] The collapse or take-over of many such cooperatives disappointed many and a distancing of grass-roots syndicalism from the cooperative movement has resulted. By its commercial structures, its links with the highly capitalised food-processing industry, and its stricter financial controls the cooperative increasingly has more in common with the multi-national processing firm than the village CUMA.

The relationship between the market and producers has continued to concern the syndical movement. In recent years the development of vertical contracts in farming has alarmed many syndical leaders. For Lambert, economic systems which tie farmers both to particular suppliers of goods and to the marketers of the final product have fundamentally compromised the independence of the former. Agricultural policy is increasingly made, not in the chambers of agriculture or at the Ministry, but in the boardrooms of the booming agribusiness sector. It was a realisation of this fact that brought Debatisse, then president of the FNSEA, into the Barre government in 1979 as minister with responsibility for the food-processing sector.[51]

If cooperatives of processing and transformation have increasingly moved away from the base, the place of production cooperatives remains more local. As has been seen, syndical interest in new forms of cooperation at farm level was an important factor in the technical and social changes of the early 1960s. Such interest has continued through to the present day. The continued emphasis in FNSEA policy documents on the survival of the 'viable' family farm has resulted in a constant search for new forms of property ownership. In particular, syndicalists have searched for ways of separating fixed capital investment in land from capital required for modernising and running the farm itself. With ever-spiralling land prices and increasing farm indebtedness, two particular solutions, the GAEC and GFA, represent means of reducing overall costs of land purchases by associating two or more farm units with consequent benefits in tax and interest payments. The take-up of such innovation has been steady rather than spectacular, with about 28,500 GAECs created by 1983. Concentrated in the west, Paris Basin and the Massif Central, they now cover about 4 per cent of the total agricultural area and some 5 per cent of full-time farmers. The GFA has been most widely used as a means of easing the transfer of holdings between family members – about 6,400 had been created by 1980.[52] The development and implementation of such reforms has, unlike the processing sector, remained an important part of syndical policy both in national negotiations and through the departmental chambers of agriculture. Together with *remembrement* and the SAFER they reflect the continued interest and involvement of the syndicalist movement in questions of structural reform.

The close nexus between farming, syndicalism and the state is well illustrated by the phenomenal development of the Crédit agricole. In its

Table 8.4. *Crédit agricole loans, 1970–85 (million francs)*

	1970	1975	1985
Short-term	13,832	33,191	86,705
Medium-term	37,219	91,221	392,428
Young farmer	3,832	6,128	18,159

Source: INSEE (1982; 1986)

origins and development it was always closely linked to the organisation of the profession itself, and, from the late 1950s, it has played an increasingly major role in the modernisation of rural France. The expansion of its activity coincided, quite deliberately, with the Orientation Laws, for the loans policy of the bank, determined largely by the state, was geared towards the consolidation of the medium-sized family farm. The bank provided the means for the implementation of the new *politique agricole* of those years. The increased indebtedness of the agricultural sector reflects in no small part the funds advanced by the Crédit agricole to enable the land purchases and technical modernisation of the *Trente Glorieuses*.

As with the cooperative sector, however, its very growth and development has distanced it from its predominantly rural and agricultural roots. Massive expansion in the number of employees from 2,000 in 1950 to over 63,000 in 1981, coupled with an increased recourse to the non-agricultural sector for both funds and lending portfolio, has meant closer links with commercial banks. Thus, a reform of its statutes in 1971 allowed a wider range of loans to be offered to, for example, rural, rather than agricultural members.[53]

Notwithstanding such developments, however, the Crédit agricole continues to exercise enormous power in the countryside and to foster equally strong loyalty from farmers. At least 90 per cent of its local advisory members are farmers, its regional *caisses* have been able to maintain a not inconsiderable degree of independence, whilst the network of local and mobile banks has given the organisation an influence and power unparallelled elsewhere in Europe.[54] The expansion of its loans to farmers has been striking. Between 1950 and 1963 its long- and medium-term loans rose from 630 million francs to 13,000 million francs.[55] Subsequently this expansion has continued as the bank has financed, with considerable government subsidy, the technical and infrastructural modernisation of the countryside (Table 8.4).

If the Crédit agricole has increasingly had to move away from its agricultural roots, it has continued to play an important role in providing the necessary finance for structural reform in agriculture. Its long-term loans for land

Table 8.5. *Crédit mutuel agricole in eastern France,*
1955–79

Percentage of active population in membership			
	1955	1968	1979
Alsace	9.7	17.6	31.4
Morelle	2.8	7.9	19.5
Lorraine	0	0	8.7
Franche-Comte	0	0	3.9
All regions	7.1	13.8	16.7

Source: Gueslin (1982)

purchases and medium-term loans for the installation of young farmers are generally state-subsidised at around 2 per cent below market rates. According to Naylor, some 70 per cent of all finance for the structural programme comes from the bank.[56] For the small 'uneconomic' farmer, however, access to credit has become increasingly difficult because of the thresholds for landholdings below which loans will not be made. In the middle of the 1970s these stood at about 16 hectares, serving to reinforce the structural policies of both government and the FNSEA. The importance of such subsidised loans in the overall costs of agricultural policy has increased from some 2 per cent in 1962 to 4 per cent in 1970 and over 7 per cent in 1982.[57]

Alongside the state credit sector, the 'private' mutual credit organisations, heritors of the old rue d'Athénes tradition, continue to be of some importance. Thus the independent Crédit mutuel in Alsace and Lorraine has continued to play a key role in its region, building on the roots of the inter-war years. As Gueslin has shown, its regional role remained of major importance, increasingly so in the 1960s and 1970s.[58] With an average annual increase in loans of some 11.5 per cent in real terms in the period 1950–80 (in constant francs) the mutual has, according to Gueslin, 'an exceptional place in the region with no real equivalent anywhere else in France'[59] (Table 8.5).

The changes which have taken place in agricultural associations since the 'rural revolution' of the early 1960s have been manifold and, above all, have served to modify the way in which those changes should be interpreted by historians. The optimism of that period has been replaced by deepening concern about the structures and survival of that dominant image created in those years, the medium-sized family farm. Within the syndical movement, the myth of unity has been inevitably and brutally exposed by the structural policies which activists of the early 1960s elaborated with the young Gaullist republic. As the scale and complexity of the agricultural economy has grown so the inevitable rupture between the syndicates, cooperatives and banks active in the agricultural world has widened. As policy reviews, the problems of overproduction and public-spending constraints continue to call into question the dominant agricultural strategies of the last three decades, the optimism of that first generation of militants has been replaced by a sense of foreboding. The direction of policy will undoubtedly reflect the way in which such sentiments shape the character and responses of agricultural associations in the future.

9

Representing the community – the place of salaried labour and women

Two particular groups, women and the salaried worker, have been almost totally absent from the activities of most agricultural organisations. Yet their role in the process of agricultural change has been of enormous significance. The salaried worker has been particularly important in certain farming regions but his or her status and position in the community has rarely been fully recognised by the major farming groups. Equally the role of women has been central to French agricultural development, both for the multiplicity of economic tasks they have performed and for the part they have played in such issues as the rural exodus and economic change. It is worth reiterating the fact that the favoured farming unit of the early 1960s, the two-labour-units farm enshrined in the legislation and characterised as units of male labour, required as much input from the female as the male member of the farming family.

Salaried labour in French farming

The place of salaried workers in French farming constitutes something of an enigma. A vital and numerically important part of the agricultural community in the middle of the nineteenth century, they increasingly disappeared from view as statisticians and commentators sought to emphasise the emergence of a peasant France for political and social reasons. Yet, as Table 9.1 shows, salaried workers played, and continue to play, a not inconsiderable role in French farming despite the powerful image of a nation anchored to the family farm employing primarily family labour. If the statistics indicate the family farm becoming increasingly dominant (with salaried workers declining from about a half to a third of the numbers of owner–occupiers between 1892 and 1985) the place of salaried workers continues to be significant.

The definition of salaried workers has varied from one census to another, making overall comparison difficult. Thus in the 1892 census a distinction

150

Table 9.1. *Salaried workers in agriculture 1892–1985*

	1892	1929	1955	1975	1985
Workers	3.0m	2.0m	1.15m	0.4m	0.25m
As percentage of farmers	54	56	50	36	30

Source: Barral (1968); Klatzmann (1978); INSEE (1986)

was made between agricultural day-labourers (*journaliers*) and live-in workers (*domestiques*) whose conditions of work and remuneration varied considerably. In 1929 this distinction no longer operated; instead, the census distinguished permanent and temporary salaried workers, a distinction which recognised the reality of the small peasant farmer who may have worked as a labourer on larger farms to make ends meet at certain times of the year. Since 1955, the distinction between permanent and temporary labour has been maintained, but with the addition of a further category, the *aides familiaux*. This group, generally members of the family (chiefly elder sons), receive certain social benefits from the state whilst working on the family farm, and cannot really be considered as salaried workers with only their labour power to sell.[1]

It is not easy to characterise the extent and geography of salaried labour because of these definitional problems and also because of the sheer diversity of social and economic positions the term embraces. In its truest sense, that of an agricultural proletariat without any resources other than labour power, the extent of salaried labour was considerable in the early decades of the century, but has declined relatively and absolutely since then. But the statistics do not fully convey the reality of salaried work in the countryside which was, and has remained, essential to many family economies. The recent development of part-time farming with husbands and, more frequently, wives, working outside the agricultural economy, further complicates the picture. Even today, however, salaried labour in its strictest sense constitutes around one-third of all manpower in French agriculture, taking on an importance which is belied by the silence of many texts on the role, problems and organisation of such workers.

Whilst the employment of a salaried proletariat has been widespread in French farming, there are distinctive geographical patterns. Much of this work-force has traditionally been employed in areas outside the family-farming regions. Regions of *grande culture* such as the Paris Basin (notably the departments of Aisne and Marne) and parts of the south-west, the viticultural regions of Languedoc and the Bordelais, and the market-gardening regions of the Rhône valley, constitute the core areas where in recent years, salaried workers have made up over 10 per cent of the active population.[2] Only on the larger farming units has any sizeable salaried labour force been employed – forestry is the only other sector, often classified with agriculture, where salaried workers are important.

The place of salaried work in agriculture has long been a subject of debate amongst economists and historians. For marxists, the relative decline of this sector has contradicted the argument that, in the logic of capitalist development, agricultural production would inevitably lead to larger farming units, the disappearance of the family farm and the extension to the rest of France of the large, capitalist unit dominant in the north and the Paris Basin. This has patently failed to happen and has led to a series of mental gymnastics seeking to explain contemporary developments in French agriculture whilst remaining within the rigorous logic of marxist economic theory. Recent debates on the changing patterns of foreign and domestic capital investments or on the role of petty commodity production in the farm economy can be placed within this corpus of work. Thus the family farm has been regarded, not as inimical to, but rather as an important part of capitalist production through its use of exploited family labour producing unprofitable products in marginal regions.[3]

Within the agrarian perspective, too, with its belief in the social and economic virtues of a middle peasantry, the role of salaried workers has been problematic. For many, the place of the salaried worker was essentially temporary for, with the accession to property consequent upon the restoration of farming to a central place in the economy, the proletariat was offered the prospect of improving status through the purchase of land. A vision of upward mobility amongst the poorest group in rural society was to be a palliative to the short-term deprivations of low salary and often desperate living conditions. The moral and economic arguments for a return to the land were marshalled, in part at least, to maintain social peace and cohesion in the countryside through holding out the prospect of property ownership to those at the bottom of the ladder.

Salaried workers and the syndicate

The representation of the salaried workforce in the agricultural syndicate has always been tied to those images of the rural world held by the proponents of the movement. For the agrarian founders of peasant syndicalism in the late nineteenth century, the distinctiveness of rural and agricultural life lay in the mixing of groups and classes to form an organic, unified whole. The syndicate was to be open to all groups, the landless labourer as much as the absentee landlord, for only through this mixing could the class-based conflicts of the town and factory be avoided. This ideology was explicit in the discourse of syndical leaders at the turn of the century: 'in agriculture, the line separating capitalist and worker does not exist as it does in industry', noted one theorist. 'The interests of capital and labour are so closely intermingled that antagonism becomes impossible and the efforts of all are directed to the same end.'[4] That end was the creation of a peasant nation, the means, accession to property, was the chimera held out to the landless labourer and *domestique*. Through such an organic unity, social harmony would be achieved. For de Rocquigny, the progress of the mixed syndicate represented 'the best means of consolidating peace in the countryside through the *entente cordiale* of all agricultural classes'.[5]

The same philosophy appeared in numerous other treatises of the period. Most came, not surprisingly, from the pens of the *notables* and bourgeoisie active on the rue d'Athènes. For Gailhard-Bancel, the development of mixed syndicates allowed for 'rich and poor, large and small landowner, tenant farmer, sharecropper and worker to meet and to overcome mutual prejudice and antagonism . . . allowing peace and harmony between those who owned and those who worked the soil'.[6] Such sentiments were somewhat removed from reality, for at least two reasons.

First, as Gratton has shown, very few agricultural labourers actually joined the syndicates set up by the rue d'Athènes or boulevard St Germain.[7] Augé-Laribé was equally forceful in disentangling rhetoric and reality and noting the tiny numbers of agricultural labourers in these mixed syndicates.[8] Analysis from regional studies involving detailed examination of syndical records reveals this same feature. Secondly, the failure of the general syndical movement to attract those who owned least into their ranks is reinforced by the early emergence of class-based syndicates in the countryside catering solely for the salaried workforce and rejecting the myth of agricultural unity propagated by the majority syndicates.

Given the enormous difficulties faced in organising such a geographically and socially diverse group as salaried workers, it is nonetheless significant to note the development of class-based syndicalism in areas such as the Paris Basin, the woodcutters of the Cher or the viticultural workers of the Médoc or Roussillon. Clearly such groups were not attracted to the idea of general purpose unions set up to prevent open conflict and argument. Gratton identified over 1,100 strikes between 1890 and 1935 amongst agricultural workers (though a part of this total includes groups such as sharecroppers, whose identity as landowner or proletariat is difficult to place) with an annual average of 6,000 workers involved in strikes and 55,000 workdays lost each year in this period.[9]

The diversity of conditions amongst this workforce was increased with the intensification of the rural exodus in the years which followed the end of the First World War. One estimate suggests that between 1926 and 1931 almost two-thirds of all those leaving the countryside were agricultural workers. This exodus brought about a secondary influx of foreign workers, especially Poles and Spaniards, onto the devastated farms of the north and the Paris Basin, with an estimated 136,000 such foreign workers in 1929.[10] The Union centrale set up an office to help farmers recruit this foreign labour force. Often poorly educated and badly paid, these migrant workers further exacerbated the problems of organising this sector.[11]

It was in the inter-war period that the socialist CGT and communist CGTU began to increase their involvement amongst the salaried labour force, with the Fédération des travailleurs de l'agriculture demanding, for example, parity of salaries between workers in agriculture and industry, an eight-hour day, limits on the use of foreign workers and a code of safety in agriculture. With the reunification of the two syndical wings in 1936 and the wave of strikes and social legislation of the Popular Front, the federation grew rapidly in influence in the countryside, increasing its membership to some 180,000 members in 2,000 syndicates. With an estimated 7–8 per cent of all agricultural workers enrolled in their syndicates, it achieved a proportion higher than at any time previously, or indeed since.[12]

With the creation of the Corporation paysanne, the desire to develop a unitary, mixed syndicalism re-emerged strongly once more. At an early stage it was argued that the worker should enrol in the same syndicate as the landowner or peasant.[13] Later, however, particularly as the regulating power of the syndicate increased, their different interests were recognised through the creation of special social sections, with a membership drawn from both worker and employee (though with a numerical superiority for the latter).[14] The task of those bodies was to resolve issues of remuneration and conditions of work, though ultimately their power was limited by the growing straitjacket imposed by government decree.

The place of the agricultural worker in decision-making was theoretically increased under the new organisations which followed the Liberation. The Confédération générale de l'agriculture included specific sections for agricultural workers in its decision-making structures on an equal footing with the FNSEA. The two main syndicates involved in recruiting agricultural workers were the Fédération des travailleurs de l'agriculture (CGT) and the Fédération des syndicats libres des travailleurs de la terre, which was part of the Christian CFTC.[15] The collapse of the CGA in the early 1950s saw any real input by these groups into the overall framework of agricultural policy disappear.

By the early 1960s then, the place of the salaried worker in relation to general policy and decision-making in agriculture was increasingly marginal. This may well have been a consequence of the agricultural revolution of those years. The increasing size of farms, the drive towards a rationalisation of farming structures, the clear goal of creating medium-sized family farms were instrumental in destroying the belief, however mythical it may have been, that the salaried worker might accede to the property ladder. In the discourse of the new revolutionaries of this period, the JAC-trained militants, the new technocrats, the proponents of a rational capitalist farming with a human face, the voice of the agricultural worker was remarkably silent. Yet, as surveys both then and now continue to stress, the agricultural worker remains poorly paid, often poorly housed, isolated and with a level of education well below either his urban counterparts or his farming neighbours.[16]

That the agricultural worker had little part to play in the dominant syndicalism of the FNSEA was clear from the events of May 1968, when the union, under the leadership of Michel Debatisse, was amongst the first to rally to the support of de Gaulle against the demands and demonstrations of the major national trades unions. For Bourquelot, the events of May 1968 inspired the same sorts of fears amongst the new rural militants as had the Popular Front amongst their conservative fathers. The training of the JAC, explicitly rejecting class struggle, was, she argues, no barrier to their adopting markedly patronal stands in their relations with those unions representing the agricultural workers.[17]

Today this stagnant or declining sector of the agricultural economy continues to be represented by the large industrial unions. The Fédération générale de l'agriculture is the most important representative body, gaining around 40 per cent of the vote at elections to the Mutualité sociale agricole, with various other groups – the CGT and CGT – Force ouvrière – soliciting the remainder of the vote. Policy is geared primarily towards the extension of social and industrial legislation to the agricultural sector. In particular, the legislation establishing a minimum salary was applied in agriculture only after prolonged pressure from the salaried workers' unions. The diversity of conditions and payment (payment in kind, provision of lodgings through the tied cottage) has militated against united demands for the application of policies already fully implemented in other sectors of the economy.

If the productive sector of the agricultural workforce is declining, however, those employed in the organisational and food-processing sector have continued to grow in the last two decades. More than 130,000, for example, are employed by agricultural cooperatives, and equally large numbers are to be found in the para-agricultural sector – the Crédit agricole and mutuals for example. Klatzmann estimated that at least 600,000 people were employed in the processing sector in the late 1970s.[18] The role of syndicates in these sectors will undoubtedly continue to affect the policies and programmes elaborated by the main farming unions. It may well be that the role of the salaried agricultural worker, far from diminishing as the statistics might suggest, may in fact become increasingly important. It is a salutary reminder to note that the major farming unions, the representatives of the productive sector, now represent less than half of all those actively employed in agriculture as a whole.

The place of women in agriculture

Les paysans se marient pour avoir un ouvrier. Aux Antilles, on achète un nègre, en France on épouse une femme. (Michelet)

The family has long occupied a central place in literature on peasant society and economy. In the Chayanovian model of this economy, production and consumption needs were primarily a function of changing family size and work capabilities, with the objectives being as much genealogical as economic. Peasant farming strategies were, first and foremost, family survival strategies and, therefore, female labour was as important as male. Peasant society, with its circumscribed spatial and temporal boundaries, saw the matrimonial unit as part of a domestic economy, with carefully defined tasks according to age and sex and with a specific relationship to the requirements of the community as a whole.[19]

The importance of the complementarity of male and female labour in the peasant community of late nineteenth- and early twentieth-century France has been emphasised by Segalen. She has argued that production was organised by balancing the skills of male and female rather than through the overt, explicit dominance of male over female. Within what she terms the 'familial economic strategy' which emerged in the nineteenth century, the extent of cooperation between male and female was crucial.[20]

Numerous regional studies have emphasised the importance of both male and female labour to the farm economy. Each sex had its own, specific tasks just as each age group within the peasant community filled particular roles. Thus, in late-nineteenth-century Normandy, male labour was directed primarily towards the two main cash products – apples (for cider production) and meat. The prime concern of the female was with dairy products, seen at that time as providing a subsidiary income. Even with the emergence of dairying as the major income-earner in the early twentieth century, women continued to fulfil the main tasks in dairy production. A more common pattern was a division between work in the fields (especially the physically onerous and symbolic tasks such as ploughing) which remained the domain of men, and work in the farmyard (eggs, poultry, the kitchen garden) which reverted to the women.[21]

In nineteenth-century Languedoc a strict division of labour between the sexes operated. Whilst the heavy tasks in the fields were taken on by men, women's labour was equally important for such skilled tasks as harvesting the grapes and directing all milking on the farm. The manufacture of cheeses and butter were in the hands of female labour, except, significantly, when they constituted the major revenue of the farm. In regions where artisanal production was important, female labour was crucial – the raising of silk worms and the fabrication of cloth, for example, in regions such as the Cévennes.[22] This division of labour in Languedoc was reflected in the distinctiveness of male and female space. Around the *oustal* the presence of the woman was continuous, whereas in the fields and around the traction animals, men dominated. This same pattern frequently recurred at a larger scale when the women were especially important at the local markets (for selling the secondary farm products – vegetables, poultry, eggs) whilst the men frequented the fairs where their power as the buyers and sellers of animals could most appropriately be displayed. As Roubin has argued for Provence, 'compared with the extensiveness and diversity of the male world, the woman's domain presents narrow spatial limits and great internal cohesion'.[23]

In the case of Brittany the historical role of women in the peasant economy has traditionally been seen as highly subservient. But at least part of the evidence for this subservience has come from the spate of folkloric and travel writing which began in the early nineteenth century as the region was 'discovered'. As one traveller wrote, 'the women are first and foremost the slaves of the farm. They work the land, clean the house and will only eat after their husbands and sons who speak to them rarely and with authority'.[24] Whilst such extracts reveal the importance attached to female labour, their value as reflections of the peasant family is less certain. Many of the early folklorists of the region recorded, not what they saw, but what their moral and social code, their bourgeois culture and their political values taught them to see.

What is most striking about these local and regional studies is the narrow interdependence of male and female – the peasant economy was first and foremost a family economy and the contribution of female labour at least as important as male. Such studies have frequently emphasised the differences between male and female labour, male and female space – as Segalen notes, 'for the women, the family, the intimate, the hidden, the sexual; for the men the social, the public, the technical, the economic, the political' – but the interdependence of the two was crucial.[25] Gender relationships may have been legitimised through community pressures, through the social doctrines of the church, or through power and dependence between the sexes, but their existence meant that the strength and longevity of the farm unit required family rather than specifically male labour.

Such relationships have altered with the progress of agricultural modernisation which has subjected the farm economy to both internal and external pressures. The onset of much greater agricultural specialisation has been a key factor in reshaping the sexual division of labour. In areas of cereal monoculture, for example, increased farm size and the employment of salaried labour, coupled with the diminishing need for the cash products of the farmyard (eggs, poultry, etc.), has increasingly relegated women to specifically domestic tasks. As before, she is preoccupied with household matters but now plays little or no role in those tasks which bring in revenue. Mechanisation has further freed women from some of the more onerous tasks but, at the same time, may well permit other women to carry out those tasks more easily. The relationship between technical change and labour divisions has not, therefore, been unidirectional. The precise impact of such changes can also be a function of farm size.

In the Beauce, for example, the precise division of labour is primarily a function of farm size. On the smallest farms both husband and wife play a role in income generation, the husband through work in the fields, the wife through her control over the few farm animals left. On medium-sized farms, division of labour reflects the number of salaried workers employed and, in particular, the degree of specialisation. Where arable farming has fully replaced an arable/pastoral polyculture, the degree of female labour is drastically reduced and, note Mendras and Jollivet, 'their use of time is very similar to that of an urban housewife'.[26] On the largest farms the tasks of the husband have become essentially managerial whilst the wife, completely freed of farming activities, centres her activity on the household alone.

This pattern, identified for a *pays de grande culture* such as the Beauce, differs from polycultural farming areas although, even there, technical change and greater specialisation continue to affect relations between the sexes. Thus in the Mauges, between the Vendée and Anjou, the degree of involvement of the woman in the farm economy has been constantly reduced over time. Female participation in revenue-earning activity has been limited to looking after the chickens, rabbits and hens which also help provide for household needs.[27] In the case of Languedoc, Mendras and Jollivet have identified clear changes over time. Whereas in earlier generations male and female labour were strongly complementary, they identify an increased distancing of female labour from the prime agricultural tasks carried on outside the farm buildings themselves.[28]

Similar changes have been found in Brittany. There, the development of specialised pastoral farming has meant that involvement of women in working in the fields has been greatly reduced. But in contrast to some other regions, male did not replace female labour in the stables and animal sheds. Instead, argues Audibert, the spheres of female influence have, if anything, widened, and the intermingling of male and female space has increased rather than decreased over time. But if the working involvement of women has remained considerable, the space within which women operate has been reduced. Amongst the first victims of modernisation have been places of female sociability – the communal water well or the village wash-house have vanished along with the local baker or butcher, replaced by the travelling shop. The links of dependence and solidarity within the community, perhaps traditionally stronger amongst women than men, have equally been subject to erosion.[29]

Alongside these internal pressures for change, largely the product of agricultural modernisation, external influences have continued to reshape the relationship between husband and wife. The rural exodus in particular has brought sharply into focus the changing relationship between men and women in the countryside. For Lagrave, it was the exodus, and the realisation of the disparity between male and female expectations of country life, and male and female rates of exodus, that first prompted serious research on the place of women in traditional and modern agriculture.[30] For Segalen, the strong correlation between traditional polycultural farming areas, high rates of celibacy and high educational attainment amongst girls cannot but suggest that women have and are continuing to vote with their feet and leave the countryside.[31] The recognition that the urban environment offered potentially better living conditions has been an especially powerful force amongst rural females.

Coupled with the somewhat negative influence of the exodus, the importance of women in the process of agricultural modernisation has been increasingly recognised. Thus Moscovici has emphasised the extent to which women were major forces in farm modernisation. Their espousal of both the images and artefacts of modernity in the early 1960s was vital in creating a mental climate for change in rural France. Their role as catalysts has furthermore given them an importance in the process of change which is belied by their relative absence from the discourse of those syndicates, cooperatives and other groups seeking to represent the agricultural world.[32]

Morin's study of Plodémet in Brittany laid considerable emphasis on the role of women in the process of agricultural change, calling them the 'secret agents of modernity', a phrase accurately reflecting their absence from public gaze. Dissatisfaction amongst the women of the community with both working and living conditions was a potent force for change in Plodémet. For married women such dissatisfaction was reflected in pressure to modernise the home, for unmarried women, poor living conditions were a sufficient incentive to migrate to the town. The attractions of secure employment, steady incomes and decent sanitation were far from negligible.[33]

The place of women and women in their place?

The role of women in the syndicates and cooperatives of the rural world prior to 1945 was practically negligible. To judge by the frequency with which their membership and place is discussed in both national and local studies, the concept of association appears entirely foreign to at least half of the population of the countryside. It is very difficult to penetrate their silent obscurity, for the traditional view of women, the view most fervently propagated in the discourse of agrarian leaders, was that their place was internal to the farm and household, rather than in contact with the world of trade, marketing and agricultural techniques. The Countess de Keraflech-Kernezne, observing the place of the woman in Brittany in the middle of the 1930s, expressed this vision of a woman's role: 'keeping the man on the land by creating for him an agreeable interior, where he can find, after a hard day, the relaxation and modest comforts he has earned; charming rural life with her gaiety, courage and good humour; ennobling it through her moral influence, her example, her virtues and her prayers; finally, bringing up numerous children to a love of the land and of their father's occupation'.[34]

Within this short extract are revealed many of the underpinnings of male–female relationships which were central to the agrarian ideology of this period. Thus the activity and role of women was viewed as confined to the household, to the *foyer*, where her prime task was to create a comfortable environment for husband and family. The production of a large, healthy family, a vital source of labour on the farm, was a second requirement of the 'good' wife; in fulfilling this function the vitality of the countryside would be maintained. This vision, reinforced by pronatalist propaganda and incentives, took on particular force in the Vichy period.[35] Finally, in confining her attentions to the domestic environment, in focusing her efforts on the 'beneficial' skills of cooking, cleaning and good humour, she would be distracted from the seductive and morally repugnant glitter of the town.

Whilst such a vision was belied by the often back-breaking and dirty work that women actually performed in the countryside, its mythical power was central to understanding the place of women in agricultural organisations up until at least the Second World War. What evidence exists indicates that only a tiny number of women played an active role or even enjoyed membership of agricultural syndicates or cooperatives until at least the early 1950s. The creation of syndicates and mutuals in the years preceding the First World War had rested on the considerable economic advantages membership could bestow. Since, traditionally, economic power rested in male hands, membership was confined almost entirely to them. In the published literature on the development of local and regional syndicates in the period 1900–30 evidence of active female involvement was almost nil.

That women could play an effective role in such groups is, however, clear from the development of these movements during the First World War. In the years of conflict, many local syndicates and mutuals survived only through the active involvement of women. In Aveyron, Lozère and the Puy-de-Dôme, for example, the running of countless local groups remained in female hands during this time – interestingly enough some of the highest rates of growth in the mutuality movement took place in those four years. Significantly, however, their role was restricted to the local scale – at the departmental and regional level, activity continued to be coordinated and administered through the exclusively male church hierarchy.[36]

The absence of women from the organisation and functioning of such groups appears all the more striking in the light of the tremendous importance attached to women in the discourse of agrarian leaders. In fact, that men should speak on behalf of, and legislate for an essentially silent female body was entirely in accord with the code of values prevalent at the time. Central to the agrarian ideology was the stemming of the rural exodus; to this end the place and role of women was crucial. Numerous regional and local syndicates sought, as part of their range of policies, to create institutions which would stem the flow of women from the countryside.

The establishment of agricultural schools for young women, the Ecoles ménagères agricoles, was due to action both by individual groups (syndicates, the Catholic church) and the state. Legislation in 1918 created special courses for young women in rural areas, with a practical education aimed at inculcating those 'specifically female skills' (cooking, housework, care of babies and children) without which men would be unable to carry out 'their' tasks on the farm. As Caniou has emphasised, such schools, whether under the tutelage of the state or other organisations, continued to educate and instruct women according to the dominant, patriarchal values of the period, by emphasising solely domestic household tasks as representing the feminine contribution to the farm unit.[37]

These schools were sometimes established by regional syndicates. Thus the powerful Union du Sud-Est created a mobile school to visit the villages of its region. Usually staying for one week in each village its programme was aimed at encouraging the 'womanly' qualities of its clientele with the ultimate aim of slowing down the rural exodus. An imitation of bourgeois values (an emphasis on household management, on the potential for modernising the village home, on modern cooking methods) was viewed as one way of discouraging the drift from the countryside.[38]

In the region served by the Plateau central this same message was relentlessly forced home. The syndical newspaper, *L'Echo du Plateau central* and, later, *le SOC*, had its own 'Coin des Femmes', marginalised in both position and content, throughout the twenties and thirties. It concentrated, not surprisingly, on subjects such as cooking, family life, needlework, or domestic equipment, subjects seen by its male editors as serving both the 'real' needs of women and the ultimate interests of men. A travelling school was also established by the syndicate and in some villages, fixed schools were established to inculcate the feminine virtues.[39] Such schools served to underpin the vision, central to this agrarian organisation, of a fecund and populous countryside. In one or two villages the syndicate took more positive, practical action in setting up workshops to encourage artisanal and handicraft work by women.

What remains most striking in this period, however, is the gap between the place occupied by women in the discourse and ideology of many syndicates and mutualist groups and the real involvement of women in influencing the policies of such organisations. The myth that their role was essentially a household and domestic one was at odds with their equal contribution to the economy of the farm, but this myth served to reinforce patriarchy in the countryside and to exclude women from involvement in the circuits of economic life. The view that agriculture was an essentially masculine occupation and that, by extension, agricultural organisations, in reflecting male preoccupations, were entirely representative, was to remain a powerful barrier to the fuller involvement of women in agricultural affairs.

The rural revolution – a new role for women?

From the middle of the 1930s a steady promotion of the peasantry began to take place in the organisations of the rural world, a promotion which would finally bear fruit in the changes of the 1950s and the elaboration of the new *politique agricole* of 1960–2. What role, if any, did women play in these changes?[40]

If the part of the JAC in the promotion of the peasantry has been greatly emphasised, the part played by its feminine equivalent, the JACF, has been rather less studied. Like its masculine counterpart, its aim was to both educate and provide entertainment. Central to the first of these aims was the recognition that young women constituted the group most vulnerable to the rural exodus. The importance of local surveys, questionnaires and a knowledge of the milieu as a preliminary to action was as central to the JACF as the JAC. The kinds of questions posed were, however, somewhat different for, as one history notes, the JACF adopted the method of the JAC *en le féminisant*. Whereas in the latter group questions of agricultural techniques, the adoption of machines, engagement in syndicates and cooperatives were constantly reiterated, for the former, annual surveys tended to focus on household themes with, for example, a series of inquiries on the need to lighten female work loads in the fields in order to free time for 'their more important' domestic and household tasks.[41]

The conservative, patriarchal character of the JACF should not, however, be overemphasised. For a body which was at least semi-confessional, the influence of a morality centred on household and family is hardly surprising. At the same time, however, the organisation increasingly called into question the severe living conditions in the countryside – the lack of running water, the absence of washing machines, the cramped living conditions and, above all, the problems of cohabitation which faced so many families in post-war France. As with the JAC a system of *stages* was established to help with education at a time when the provision made for technical training in agriculture for women was limited.[42]

In general, however, the reflections of the organisation can be characterised as internal and family oriented. The very considerable physical load carried by women at this time in many parts of rural France perhaps made such reflections inevitable. For a church anxious to stem the exodus and maintain the tradition of large agricultural (and Catholic) families, such a focus is hardly surprising. Thus militants of the movement have tended to stress its impact on internal family life rather than external professional matters. For one militant, there was 'much less focus on conflict and power, on the notion of *concertation* than in the JAC – our task seemed to be one of enabling men to carry out their professional tasks'.[43] For another the JACF helped 'primarily to break down the isolation we felt . . . it provided opportunities for leisure and taught us to fulfil our domestic tasks competently – caring for our *petit élevage* . . . looking after the kitchen garden'.[44]

Coincident with the expanding role of both the JACF and the Mouvement familial rural came the period of economic expansion and agricultural modernisation, the *Trente Glorieuses*, which was to fundamentally alter the place of women in agriculture. The elaboration of the new structural policies in the early 1960s was anchored to the full development of the family farm, a farm able to provide work for at least two labour units per year. The economic role of women was implicitly recognised in this unit, the cornerstone of the Orientation Laws. But the legislative place of the woman was non-existent, for legally the farm remained in male hands, it was his labour which was recognised and costed, his was the signature required for economic transactions.[45] Yet the steady reduction in the salaried labour force and the reinforcement of the family farm meant that female labour was ever more significant in the farm economy.

Equally important has been the development of part-time farming. In 1970 some 21 per cent of farmers engaged in work outside the farm; ten years later the figure stood at 22.3 per cent. The proportion of family members engaging in such external work rose from 26.8 per cent in 1970 to 33.1 per cent in 1977, emphasising the importance of such systems.[46] If, as Rinaudo has stressed, this interdependence of occupations within peasant farming has long historical roots, its contemporary importance is undiminished. The increasing emphasis in the documents of the FNSEA on the farming *family* rather than the *individual farmer* reflects an increasing recognition of the economic role of women.[47] Many wives now take part-time or full-time work outside the farm – especially in the white-collar and service sector. The number of wives of farmers working outside farming has increased from 13 per cent in 1970 to 20 per cent in 1980.[48] The income from such work often proves crucial to the survival of the farm, further reinforcing the importance of women in the agricultural sector. Coincident with such changes has been the increasing dissolution of the one–farm–one–family unit as the basis of social and economic organisation. The increased importance of property structures such as the GAEC or GFA and the ever-widening cooperative and mutualist networks which tie individual farmers together have also restructured the place of women. These processes have had at least three effects.

In the first place it can be argued that the very pace of technical and structural change in farming has irrevocably altered the role of women. For Segalen, for example, the net effect of such changes has been to increasingly distance the woman from the farm enterprise. She speaks of women becoming 'housewifed' as technical sophistication, and multi-farm structures emerged in the early 1970s. Alternatively, her role became ancillary, albeit an important ancillary, through acting as secretary or accountant for the enterprise.[49] This view, however, appears somewhat contradictory, for it can be argued that such changes may well reinforce rather than reduce the role of women on the farm. By fulfilling increasingly specialist roles, or by taking on work outside agriculture, the importance of women may actually have increased, although their direct involvement in the production process is reduced.

Secondly, these technical changes, in conjunction with broader social and political movements towards a more equal treatment of women, have led to an important debate within agricultural organisations over the precise status of women. In the model of the family farm elaborated after 1960, the place of women was essentially ancillary in the eyes of the legislator for, like older children on the farm, they were classified as *aides familiaux* without legal rights, salary or a clear place in decision-making on the farm. This position, especially when contrasted with the important role they played in running the enterprise, led to considerable pressure from women for a legal recognition of their place. As Mendras notes, the legal rights and responsibilities of both partners could have been incorporated within new property structures such as the GAEC: this was not conceded by the legislators, whereas agreements between father and son, the most widespread form of the GAEC, were facilitated.[50]

Pressure for reform in this area led to the incorporation of a special *statut de co-exploitante* in the new Orientation Laws of July 1980. For the official historians of the FNSEA, this statute constituted 'the response of the profession to the legitimate aspirations of women in agriculture'.[51] Through this legislation, the right of women to take decisions on the farm (through signing commercial contracts for example) was upheld. But, as Lagrave has noted, both the legislation, and statistics, have continued to regard the *chef d'exploitation* as male. Thus he could sign agreements using all the goods and land of the farm as collateral without consulting his wife. She, on the other hand, could sign such agreements using only her own land and goods as collateral. 'The small advances made in this statute', notes Lagrave, 'mask the continued inequality of male and female rights'.[52] To argue that farming represents the unity of a couple's work is, she contends, a nonsense since it implies a division of work, legal rights and benefits which, in practice, does not exist. Debate over the character and application of this legislation continues today.

The extent of female involvement in agricultural organisations since the onset of the rural revolution has thus remained restricted. During the 1950s, when the promotion of peasant militants was considerable, female involvement in agricultural organisations was limited. Much of that involvement was in areas viewed as traditionally in the female domain – thus there was some involvement in the Mutualité sociale agricole or in the more localised parish and departmental social or educational groups. Involvement in syndicates, cooperatives or the Crédit agricole was minimal. One of the reasons for this was the weight of tradition. Even if the extent of domination experienced by women varied between different regions and social groups, such organisations were seen as occupational rather than social and, as such, the domain of the men who exercised the occupation of farming rather than the women who were an adjunct or aid to that occupation.

It was not until the 1980 statute which established, at least in part, the professional place of women in agriculture, that women were allowed to take a full part in the running of agricultural cooperatives and the Crédit agricole. Prior to that women could not serve equally on the executive and administrative bodies of these groups, for female votes (unless they were widows of farmers, who now were farmers in their own right) were not even counted. Only those professionals with shares in the group had status.[53] That meant that only the male, classified legally and statistically as the *chef d'exploitation*, had voting rights. The debate over the precise statute accorded to women thus goes far beyond legal pedantry – it is central to the place and voice of women in agriculture.

The degree of female involvement in agricultural syndicates remains small although it has undoubtedly increased recently. That syndical affairs had a marked influence on the lives of women cannot be doubted. Its role in the elaboration of agricultural policy, discussions of such questions as cohabitation in rural areas, the extension of social legislation to farming or the extent and level of female involvement in farming affairs has meant that the syndicate has exercised an influence far in excess of the influence women have on the running of such institutions. The number of departments where women have exercised real power within either the FDSEA or the CDJA is very small. The examples of Anne-Marie Crolais in the Côtes-du-Nord or Michèle Chezalvielle in the Corrèze are perhaps the exceptions that prove the rule.

Anne-Marie Crolais, for example, from a poor peasant family near St Brieuc, experienced enormous difficulties in becoming a militant in the syndical affairs of the region. Her first involvement in agricultural organisations came through a course organised by technicians from the chamber of agriculture on the economic and organisational problems of the region. In 1975 she went, with her husband, to a meeting designed to relaunch the CDJA in the department and found herself elected vice-president and subsequently president of the organisation. The chief opposition to her involvement came, she notes, not from her husband but from her father. A militant syndicalist in the early 1960s, he was unhappy – 'Women have no place in such affairs,' he would argue, 'you would do better to look after your children and house than charge around the country from one meeting to the next'.[54]

It is possible, however, to detect an increased involvement by women in agricultural demonstrations and protests. Since the 1960s demonstrations involving women have, according to Berlan, played an increasingly important part in the suite of protest measures employed by syndicates to make their voice heard. But Berlan, in examining in depth two particular sets of protests – amongst the *viticulteurs* of the Aude (in 1967–72) and milk producers of Finistère (in 1980–1) – has stressed that such involvement does not necessarily reflect a greater place and consideration for women in the profession. In both areas female membership of syndicates was low and their use in demonstrations was primarily to create an image of a united, forward-looking *métier du couple* which was, in fact, at odds with the realities of female subservience.[55] The demonstrations failed, she argues, to bring forward the key issue of the legal statute and rights of women in agriculture. As she notes in her conclusion, much progress still has to be made 'before the subjugation of women both within the unions and within the world of farming is ended'.[56]

Associated with such difficulties is the problem of recognition for practical skills. In a profession in which farming skills, the *métier*, are highly regarded, the uncertain place of women can be a barrier to electoral success in agricultural organisations. As Maresca has noted, successful syndicalists have traditionally had to demonstrate skills and expertise in managing the farm. Professional excellence in farming skills and continued activism in syndicates have tended to go hand in hand.[57] Such a position poses considerable problems for male representatives (the financial compensation for farmers absent as representatives is small); for women the traditional conservativism of the milieu coupled with their uncertain legal status compounds the difficulties.

The place of women both in agriculture and in the organisations of the agricultural world currently constitutes a major area of debate and discussion. A return to the old positions of dominance and inequality is untenable but, as recent debate has shown, the profession and its organisations remain undecided on the direction and pace of change. Such changes may well be of crucial importance to the survival of the family farm, a unit which has been the favoured objective of the *politique agricole* since the early 1960s.

10
Conclusion

Since the beginning of this century, the social and economic fabric of farming life has dramatically altered. One hundred years ago, the conservative, ignorant, individualistic peasant, sunk in the obscurity of generations of mud and toil, was a powerful part of political, artistic and literary mythology. Such images remain far more mythical and illusory now than was ever the case a century ago. But if technical changes – the mechanisation of arable and pastoral farming or the drive for ever greater production and productivity – have been the most visible aspect of the transformation of rural France, the spread of new forms of cooperation and association has been no less important. In these changing patterns of social, cultural and economic solidarity, endlessly reshaping the social fabric of farming, lie many of the explanations of the origins, character and future direction of agricultural change.

Associations and the farming community

Images of individualism and isolation in rural France are undoubtedly at odds with the range of associations that, at various times, have received widespread support from the farming community. How then were these groups created? Central to this book has been an emphasis on the importance of local and regional traditions and on the political context within which farming issues were formulated. Without an appreciation of this context, many associations appear simply utilitarian in character and limited in their social impact. Throughout their history political forces have been a major influence, shaping the development of syndicates, cooperatives and mutuals in the countryside.

At the turn of the century, the foundations of rural cooperation and organisation were greatly influenced by political responses to the separation of church and state. Undoubtedly syndicates and cooperatives emerged to meet real economic needs, but their consolidation into the powerful regional unions of the inter-war years reflected the ideological conflicts of this period. The renaissance of social catholicism, coupled with the rural exodus, were important in the emergence of local and regional association. The ideas of cooperation and mutual aid were nurtured by the clash of social conceptions stemming from Catholic and republican circles.

Politics were equally important in later periods. The emergence of class-based syndicalism in the countryside, albeit on a smaller scale than the majority agrarian movements, drew directly on socialist and communist ideology. The importance of political alignments in the development of the peasant movements of the Depression years was equally influential in shaping both the political policy and economic responses of farming leaders. The association between the young *jacistes* of the 1950s and the Gaullist movement was crucial in shaping the Orientation Laws which were to have such a profound effect in the countryside. The winners and losers of that *politique agricole* continue to debate the potential and problems of the farm sector within political circles. Cooperatives or the Crédit agricole are not immune to such influences; their role as agents of state intervention in agriculture has become increasingly important as a corporatist alliance between a dominant syndicalism and the government has emerged.

Underpinning this analysis of agricultural groups has been the belief that the process of agricultural modernisation is shaped as much by political and ideological decisions, as by the seemingly relentless march of agricultural structures and technology. The farm economy has not 'modernised' in a political vacuum. Increased farm sizes, for example, have resulted, in part at least, from conscious decisions by farming associations to withdraw support for some sections of the farm population and maintain it for others. Such decisions were, and continue to be the result of, intense internal debate and dissent within farming groups, debate which both reflects regional differences, and continues to reshape the agricultural geography of the nation. The increasing recourse to the cooperative sector for the transformation and marketing of produce reflects decisions by farmers and their representatives to influence the workings of the market. Such decisions were, and are, political ones. The strength of opposition to the Office du blé in 1936 serves as a reminder that the role of farming organisations in influencing economic policy is a deep-rooted one. From the protectionist debates of the 1890s to the quota systems of the 1980s, the development and character of agricultural associations cannot be divorced from their regional bases and political contexts.

If the political environment of these groups needs to be emphasised, their practical role is equally important. To the peasant farmer of the 1920s, the syndicate meant first and foremost, agricultural goods. The fertilisers, seeds, machinery and advice made available through the union were essential to the modernisation of agriculture. At a time when the quality of goods available was often highly variable, this practical, pragmatic function was important. If the link between goods and the syndicate was broken in 1945, other agricultural groups sprang up to fill the niche. The cooperative, legally distinct from the syndicate, was nevertheless frequently allied with the syndicate in terms of location, administration and even personnel.

The development of the farming mutual also served real practical functions. Insuring against loss of animals, home, goods or providing personal accident and sickness benefits were banal but very important benefits to countless village communities. They taught self-reliance and communal solidarity, for the well-being of the mutual demanded that proper care of goods and animals be exercised. The mutual (and especially the Mutualité sociale agricole) also helped train countless peasant militants, placing them on the first rungs of a ladder leading to positions of regional and national power.

The economic benefits of cooperation were, and remain, very important. In the early decades of the century, most cooperatives were for the supply of goods to farmers. The Depression showed that they could fulfil a more central function in overcoming the structural weakness of the countryside in marketing its produce. The realisation that control over marketing circuits was essential led to the expansion of regional and national cooperatives in the fifties and sixties. If that progress has faltered with harsher economic times, the place of the cooperative is undisputed. The development of local cooperatives for machinery, exchange of work or the cooperative farming of land has also brought clear practical benefits.

The profession and the state

The way in which the farming profession sought to organise itself is also central to an understanding of the history and contemporary character of the French *politique agricole*. Whilst professing a deep disdain for politics, the syndical movement has always sought, through direct or indirect means, to influence government policy. In the 1920s it was largely through the channels of the powerful national bodies, the rue d'Athènes and boulevard St Germain, that farmers or, more accurately, those who saw themselves as the representatives of farmers, put pressure on the state. Such pressure was more often negative than positive. The long campaign waged by agrarian traditionalists against the introduction of compulsory state accident and sickness legislation into the agricultural sector in the 1920s typifies such intervention. Similar opposition to the radical social legislation of the Popular Front also characterised the movement.

The 1930s marked something of a watershed in this respect. On the one hand, a powerful corporatist doctrine emerged amongst farming leaders. It was a doctrine which explicitly argued that the state should not intervene in the farm sector but should instead delegate power to the syndicates to enable them to carry out the tasks themselves. What was novel about such a conception was its recognition that intervention of some kind, planning of some kind, was essential. If there had to be planning, it was argued, let us, rather than the state carry it out. At the same time, the conditions for much greater economic intervention were created by the collapse of agricultural prices. Only the state had the resources (administrative as well as financial) to tackle the problems of production and marketing and, after initial hesitations, syndicalists accepted the necessity for such national organisations as the Office du blé. Crucially, then, the basis for a corporatist relationship between profession and state was laid in this period.

The Vichy period saw the consolidation of this state–profession nexus although, as has been shown, the economic conjuncture of those years made the experiment an abject failure. But, despite attempts to wrest power from the syndicates in the late 1940s, their place in the elaboration and execution of policy was reinforced by the rural revolution of the 1950s. The Orientation Laws gave the syndicate an active role in refashioning the landscape through its direct input into the mechanisms created to bring about those changes. Current syndical policy cannot help but reflect the contradictory pressures of such a position: seeking to criticise, from an independent stance, the elaboration of policy yet intimately involved in the very execution of that policy at local and departmental level.

It would be wrong, however, to see the syndicate as the sole political body in the panoply of organisations active in rural France. As was stressed in chapter 8, the place of both cooperatives and the Crédit agricole is especially important. As the former are forced to become larger in order to maintain their competitiveness, how can they maintain their links at the local scale? Does the increasing recourse to contracts with the all-powerful food-processing multi-nationals compromise the principles of 'capitalism with a human face' which were such a powerful catalyst for cooperative expansion in the late 1950s? As farm indebtedness increases the policies of the Crédit agricole have become central to agricultural strategy. The application of minimum levels for farm sizes, the continuance of loans for products currently in surplus, support for the *remembrement* and SAFER policies are all subjects of fierce debate within both the bank and other, agricultural organisations.

The rich and diverse history of agricultural associations in France serves to emphasise the central importance of human agency in the process of economic change. The cooperatives, mutuals and syndicates of the rural world both reflected and shaped the world in which they developed. Their creation cannot be understood without an appreciation of the particular context of period and place; their activity was important in influencing the direction and pace of change. In creating new bonds of solidarity, in cooperating to overcome conditions of scarcity or overproduction, the farming community sought to shape its own destiny in some, however imperfect, manner. Equally, the role of the Catholic church in educating a new militant élite, in fostering a cooperative movement, in regenerating national and local syndicates in the 1950s, was both a response to the economic conjuncture, and an attempt to reshape the conditions and structures of agricultural progress.

For the historian, exploration of the paradoxes and contradictions of these movements provides fascinating insights into the structures of a rural society at a time of rapid social and economic change. It serves to emphasise that without looking first at individuals and their associations, the notion of modernisation, of agricultural progress, of economic rationalisation is stripped of real meaning. It is through the history of the local syndicate with its fertiliser turnovers, machinery sales, agricultural library, banal though they may be, that the nature of rural change can be seized. The records of the animal mutual, of the peasant farmer insuring first one, then two, then two more precious cattle, bring the same process to light. The conflict of priest and republican teacher, of small peasant and large landowner, of sharecropper and owner reveal, through concrete experience, the wider currents of social, political and economic change.

Such insights can, furthermore, shed light on current policies and preoccupations. What the widespread development of associations in the farming community emphasised was the desire of the profession itself (regardless of who were to be considered as representatives of that profession) to exercise some sort of collective control over their destiny. Unlike their industrial counterparts, agricultural unions have perforce focused not on the division between capital and labour, owner and worker, but on the conditions of production, processing and marketing which bear on their levels of remuneration. Such a focus has meant that agricultural groups, in particular the syndicate, have a privileged place in agricultural policy-making. The debates surrounding strategy are important, not simply in the light of the internal character of the movement, but equally in the light they shed on the relationship between the profession, their professional organisations and the state.

Current policy reflections, both within France and Europe, have stressed the problems of over-production. The transformation of the production process in farming, the increasing role of the food-processing sector, the uneven penetration of capitalism into farming, the place of the family farm, have acted to alter the way in which the farm economy should be analysed. In this process of profound agricultural restructuring, the place of agricultural associations will be crucial. It is these organisations, acting on national government, that provide the political context within which national and European decisions on farm policy will be made.

It is important that these various organisations – the syndicates, mutuals, cooperatives and banking organisations of rural France – be considered in the light of their history. The varied influences that shaped their origins – political, social or religious – have remained an important part of their heritage. Debates on the question of representativeness and syndical unity echo the conflicts of earlier periods. The nexus between the syndicate, mutual and cooperative, although in legal terms no longer as close as in earlier decades, has continued to influence the policies of a movement which has always sought to be more than purely *revendicatif* in character. The strength, diversity and rich traditions of association and organisation in rural France is testimony to the efforts of peasant and producer to shape their own destiny. If this book helps to encourage further analysis of the political context, leadership, geography and traditions of those diverse local and national associations whose influence has, and will continue to shape the fabric of farming life this century it will have more than served its purpose.

Notes

Introduction

1 R. Samuel (ed.), *Village life and labour* (London, 1975), p. xiii.

1 The transformation of rural France

1 The importance of this peasant influence is emphasised in F. Braudel, *L'Identité de la France* (3 vols., Paris, 1986), 2, pp. 9–13.
2 M. Bloch, *French rural history* (London, 1966); A. Fel, *Les hautes terres du Massif Central – tradition paysanne et économie agricole* (Paris, 1962); P. Flatrès, *Géographie rurale de quatre contrées celtiques: Irlande, Galles, Cornwall et Man* (Rennes, 1957); A. Meynier, *Les paysages agraires* (Paris, 1958); J.-R. Pitte, *Histoire du paysage français* (2 vols., Paris, 1983).
3 H. D. Clout, *Agriculture in France on the eve of the railway age* (London, 1980); H. D. Clout, *The land of France 1815–1914* (London, 1983).
4 G. Duby and A. Wallon (eds.), *Histoire de la France rurale* (4 vols., Paris, 1976); F. Braudel and A. Labrousse (eds.), *Histoire économique et sociale de la France* (4 vols., Paris, 1979–80), vols 1 and 2.
5 M. Agulhon, *The Republic in the village: the people of the Var from the French Revolution to the Second Republic* (Cambridge, 1982); P. Bois, *Paysans de l'ouest* (Paris, 1960); A. Corbin, *Archaisme et modernité en Limousin au XIXe siècle* (2 vols., Paris, 1975); G. Désert, *Une société rurale au XIXe siècle: les paysans du Calvados 1815–1895* (Paris, 1975); G. Garrier, *Paysans du Beaujolais et du Lyonnais 1800–1970* (2 vols., Grenoble, 1973); G. Gavignaud, *Propriétaires viticulteurs en Roussillon: structures, conjonctures, société 18è–20è siècles* (Paris, 1983); R. Hubscher, *L'Agriculture et la société rurale dans le département du Pas-de-Calais du milieu du XIXe siècle à 1914* (Paris, 1979); Y. Rinaudo, *Les Paysans du Var (fin XIXe siècle-début XXe siècle)* (Paris, 1982).
6 R. Hubscher, 'L'Histoire rurale: un bilan', paper presented at the Conference of Franco-British Rural studies, Oxford, March 1987, pp. 2–3.
7 E. Weber, *Peasants into Frenchmen: the modernization of rural France 1870–1914* (London, 1977).

8 Clout, *The land of France*, p. 142.

9 R. Price, *The modernization of rural France: communications networks and agricultural market structures in nineteenth-century France* (London, 1983).

10 P. M. Jones, *Politics and rural society – the southern Massif Central c. 1750–1880* (Cambridge, 1985); T. Judt, *Socialism in Provence 1871–1914* (Cambridge, 1979); R. Magraw, *France 1815–1914: the bourgeois century* (London, 1983), pp. 318–53; T. Zeldin, *France 1848–1945* (2 vols., Oxford, 1973/1977), 1, pp. 131–97.

11 R. Béteille, *La France du Vide* (Paris, 1981); R. Chapuis, *Les ruraux français* (Paris, 1986); B. Kayser, 'Subversion des villages français', *Etudes rurales*, 1 (1984), pp. 295–324; J. Klatzmann, *L'Agriculture française* (Paris, 1978); J. Klatzmann, *Géographie agricole de la France* (Paris, 1978); H. Mendras, *La Fin des paysans* (Paris, 1967); H. Mendras, *Sociétés paysannes* (Paris, 1976).

12 Quoted in G. Wright, *Rural revolution in France* (Stanford, 1964), p. 13.

13 Statistique agricole de la France, *Enquête décennale, 1892.*

14 Clout, *The land of France*, pp. 137–53.

15 *Ibid.*, p. 152.

16 Figure 1 aims to indicate only the broadest of regional divisions and does not attempt to reflect detailed nuances. It is based largely on Duby and Wallon (eds.) *Histoire*, 3, p. 65; Clout, *The land of France*, pp. 33, 37, 150.

17 Mendras, *Sociétés paysannes*, pp. 73–89.

18 Weber, *Peasants into Frenchmen*, p. 338. On the place of education in the transformation of peasant France see *inter alia:* F. Furet and J. Ozouf, *Lire et écrire* (Paris, 1977); R. Thabault, *Education and change in a village community* (London, 1971).

19 See *inter alia*: F. Boulard, *Problèmes missionaires de la France rurale* (2 vols., Paris, 1945); G. Le Bras, *Etudes de sociologie religieuse* (2 vols., Paris 1955); Le Bras, *L'Eglise et le village* (Paris, 1976); A. Coutrut and F. Dreyfus, *Les forces religieuses dans la société française* (Paris, 1965); F. Isambert and J.-P. Terrenoire, *Atlas de la pratique religieuse des catholiques en France* (Paris, 1980); P. M. Jones, 'La Vie religieuse dans la France villageoise au XIXème siècle', *Annales Economies, Sociétés, Civilisations*, 42 (1937), pp. 91–115.

20 R. Price, *A social history of nineteenth-century France* (London, 1987), p. 196.

21 E. Grenadou and A. Prévost, *Grenadou, paysan français* (Paris, 1966), pp. 63–139.

22 C. Dyer, *Population and society in twentieth-century France* (London 1978); R. Chapuis, *Les Ruraux français*, pp. 1–9.

23 P. E. Ogden, 'Migration, marriage and the collapse of traditional peasant society in France' in P. White and R. Woods (eds.), *The geographical impact of migration* (London, 1980), p. 154.

24 Béteille, *La France du Vide*, pp. 31–57.

25 Chapuis, *Les Ruraux français*, pp. 21–38.

26 Béteille, *La France du Vide*, pp. 135–65.

27 Bloch, *French rural history*, pp. 197–234.

28 A. Soboul, 'The French rural community in the eighteenth and nineteenth centuries', *Past and Present*, 10 (1956), 78–95.

29 P. Barral, *Les Agrariens français de Méline à Pisani* (Paris, 1968), pp. 41–66. On

the linkages between property, religion and politics see P. M. Jones, *Politics and rural society*, pp. 305–27 and the discussion by E. Berenson, 'Politics and the French peasantry: the debate continues', *Social History*, 12 (1987), 213–29.

30 Duby and Wallon (eds.), *Histoire*, pp. 154–8.

31 Weber, *Peasants into Frenchmen*, pp. 130–45.

32 P. Barral, *Les Sociétés rurales du XXe siècle* (Paris, 1978), p. 115; INSEE, *Annuaire Statistique*, 1986.

33 Ministère de l'Agriculture, *100 ans du Ministère de l'Agriculture* (Paris, 1981).

34 J. Chombart de Lauwe, *L'Aventure agricole de la France de 1945 à nos jours* (Paris, 1979), p. 18.

35 A. Gueslin, 'Agriculture et Crédit Agricole au XXème siècle', paper presented to the *Société française d'économie rurale*, Paris, September 1987.

36 Figure 2 is based largely on the maps produced for CNRS, *140 cartes sur la France rurale* (Paris, 1984), which provides an excellent overview of the agricultural and social structures of rural France in the early 1980s.

37 Duby and Wallon (eds.), *Histoire*, 3, pp. 409–13.

38 M. Augé-Laribé, *La Politique agricole de la France* (Paris, 1950), p. 438.

39 W. Ogburn and W. Jaffé, *Economic development of post-war France* (New York, 1929), pp. 474–84.

40 M. Bodiguel, *Le Rural en question* (Paris, 1986); J. Tuppen, *The economic geography of France* (London, 1983), pp. 28–119.

41 On the development of a political economy approach see: G. Cox, P. Lowe and M. Winter (eds.), *Agriculture: people and policies* (London, 1986); T. Marsden, J. Munton, S. Whatmore and J. Little, 'Towards a political economy of capitalist agriculture: a British perspective', *International journal of urban and regional research*, 10 (1986), 498–521.

42 An introduction to the theoretical debate is provided by: J. Ennew, P. Hirst and K. Tribe, 'Peasantry as an economic category', *Journal of peasant studies*, 4 (1977), 295–322; S. Mann and J. Dickinson, 'Obstacles to the development of a capitalist agriculture', *Journal of peasant studies*, 5 (1978), 466–81; K. Vergopoulos, 'Capitalism and peasant productivity', *Journal of peasant studies*, 5 (1978), 446–65; M. Winter, 'Agrarian class structure and family farming' in T. Bradley and P. Lowe (eds.), *Locality and rurality: economy and society in rural regions* (Norwich, 1984), pp. 115–45.

2 Individuals and associations in the farming community

1 See *inter alia* G. Dalton, 'Peasantries in anthropology and history', *Current anthropology*, 13 (1972), 385–415; S. Franklin, 'Systems of production – systems of appropriation', *Pacific viewpoint*, 6 (1965), 145–66; D. B. Grigg, *The dynamics of agricultural change* (London, 1982), pp. 93–100; T. Shanin (ed.), *Peasants and peasant societies* (Harmondsworth, 1971).

2 Bloch, *Rural history*, pp. 197–234.

3 Zeldin, *France*, 1, pp. 138–43.

4 Soboul, 'Rural community', pp. 78–95.

5 Gervais, 'Le Triomphe de l'exploitation familiale' in Duby and Wallon (eds.), *Histoire*, 4, pp. 193–224; see also R. Hubscher, 'La Petite exploitation en France:

reproduction et compétitivité (fin XIXè siècle – début XXè siècle)', *Annales economies, sociétés, civilisations*, 40 (1985), 3–34.

6 M. Dion-Salitot and M. Dion, *La Crise d'une société villageoise – les paysans du Jura français* (Paris, 1972), pp. 233–357; see also the section on communal life in A. Fel, *Les Hautes terres du Massif Central – tradition paysanne et économie agricole* (Paris, 1962), pp. 99–141.

7 A.-M. Brisebarre, *Bergers des Cévennes* (Paris, 1978), pp. 29–64; M. C. Cleary, 'Patterns of transhumance in Languedoc', *Geography*, 1 (1986), 25–33.

8 A. R. H. Baker, 'Ideological change and settlement continuity: the development of agricultural syndicalism in Loir-et-Cher during the late nineteenth century', *Journal of historical geography*, 6 (1980), 163–77; Baker, 'The infancy of France's first agricultural syndicate: the syndicat des agriculteurs de Loir-et-Cher 1881–1914', *Agricultural history review*, 34 (1986), 45–59.

9 M. Jollivet and H. Mendras, *Les collectivités rurales françaises* (2 vols., Paris 1971–4), 1, pp. 9–50.

10 Mendras, *Sociétés paysannes*, p. 80.

11 P. M. Jones, 'Parish, seigneurie and the community of inhabitants in southern Central France during the eighteenth and nineteenth centuries', *Past and present*, 91 (1981), 74–108.

12 Judt, *Socialism in Provence*, pp. 1–22.

13 M. Bodiguel, *Les Paysans face au progrès* (Paris, 1975).

14 P. Houée, *Les Étapes du développement rural* (2 vols., Paris, 1972), vol. 1, pp. 64–70.

15 Duby and Wallon (eds.), *Histoire*, 4, p. 117.

16 Archives départementales (henceforth AD) Aveyron: 7 M 53.

17 AD Aveyron: 7 M 53/7 M 54.

18 J. Jarriot, 'La société d'agriculture du département de l'Aveyron au début du XIX siècle', *Procès-Verbaux de la Société des Lettres, Sciences et Arts de l'Aveyron,* 42 (1977), 37.

19 Houée, *Les Étapes*, 1, p. 66.

20 Barral, *Les Agrariens,* p. 83.

21 J. Cloarec, 'Un exemple d'intervention de l'Etat: le financement public de l'agriculture', *Etudes rurales*, 69 (1978), 5–25; Ministère de l'Agriculture, *Cent ans de Ministère de l'Agriculture* (Paris, n.d.).

22 P. Barral, 'Les mouvements agrariens de l'érè industrielle (jusqu'à la 2 guerre mondiale)', *Revue historique*, 11 (1964), 299–330.

23 Barral, *Sociétés rurales*, p. 95.

24 P. Gratton, *Les Luttes de classe dans les campagnes* (Paris 1971); Gratton, *Les Paysans français contre l'agrarisme* (Paris, 1972).

25 G. Cox, P. Lowe and M. Winter, 'From state direction to self regulation: the historical development of corporatism in British agriculture', *Policy and politics*, 14 (1986), 475–6.

26 M. Augé-Laribé, *Syndicats et coopératives agricoles* (Paris, 1926), 23.

27 J. Fauvet and H. Mendras (eds.), *Les Paysans et la politique* (Paris, 1958), 232.

3 Agricultural associations before 1914

1 Duby and Wallon, *Histoire*, 3, pp. 116–18.

2 Barral, *Les Agrariens*, p. 107.

3 R. de Rocquigny, *Les Syndicats agricoles et leur oeuvre* (Paris, 1900); A. Toussaint, *L'Union Centrale des syndicats agricoles: ses idées directrices* (Paris, 1920). Both works typify the social paternalism of the conservative syndical movement.

4 A. Dansette, *Histoire religieuse de la France contemporaine sous la Troisième République* (Paris, 1951), pp. 180–215; H. Rollet, *Sur le chantier social – l'action sociale des catholiques en France 1870–1940* (Lyon, 1955); The conflict between church and state is examined in J. McManners, *Church and state in France, 1870–1914* (London, 1972); J.-M. Mayeur, *La Séparation de l'église et de l'état* (Paris, 1966); Mayeur, 'Géographie de la résistance aux Inventaires (fév–mars 1906)', *Annales. ESC,* 3 (1966), 1259–72.

5 Association Catholique de la Jeunesse Française, *Le Problème de la terre* (Paris, 1908); R. de Ponceau, *Petite histoire de l'ACJF* (Paris, 1929).

6 *Bulletin de l'Union Catholique Aveyronnaise,* 10, 1910.

7 Faure, *Les Paysans,* pp. 10–41.

8 P. Chalmin, *La Mutualité dans l'Adour,* unpub. man. (1983).

9 P. las Cases, *Petit manuel pratique rural* (Paris, 1931); A national history of the mutuality movement in rural France is currently being prepared by P. Chalmin and is due for publication in 1988.

10 E. Duport, *Les Engrais et les syndicats agricoles* (Lyon, 1889).

11 Barral, *Les Agrariens,* pp. 117–20.

12 A. Gueslin, *Histoire des crédits agricoles* (2 vols., Paris 1984); Gueslin, 'Pouvoir et conflits de pouvoir dans des structures de sociabilité organisée: le cas de la mutualité de crédit (fin XIXème, première moitié XXème)', in *Sociabilité, pouvoirs et société* (Rennes, 1987), pp. 265–76.

13 FNSEA, *100 ans de syndicalisme agricole* (Paris, 1984), 20–1.

14 The literature dealing with the Sud-Est is more substantial than for any other regional union of the time, reflecting its role as the leader of the rue d'Athènes. See in particular: H. de Gailhard-Bancel, *Le Syndicalisme agricole aux champs et au Parlement* (Paris, 1929); L. de Vogue, *Emile Duport, la leçon des ses oeuvres* (Lyon, 1909); C. Silvestre, *L'Union du Sud-Est des Syndicats Agricoles* (2 vols., Lyons, 1900).

15 G. Garrier, 'L'Union du Sud-Est des syndicats agricoles avant 1914', *Le Mouvement Social,* 67 (1969), 37.

16 R. Faucon, 'Les Origines du syndicalisme agricole dans la région du Nord', *Revue du Nord,* 48 (1966), 67–90; Hubscher, *L'Agriculture,* 2, pp. 614–35.

17 Hubscher, *L'Agriculture,* 2, p. 619.

18 S. Berger, *Peasants against politics: rural organisation in Brittany 1911–1967* (Cambridge, Mass., 1972), p. 32.

19 Y. Rinaudo, 'Le Syndicalisme agricole dans le Var', *Le Mouvement social,* 112 (1980), 79.

20 Y. Rinaudo, 'Les Paysans du Var (fin du XIX siècle – début du XX siècle)' Thèse de Doctorat, Université d'Aix en Provence (1978), p. 181.

21 Rinaudo, Les paysans, pp. 84–91.

22 Baker, 'Ideological change', pp. 163–77; Baker, 'The infancy', pp. 45–59.

23 R. Leveau, 'Le Syndicat de Chartres 1885–1914', *Le Mouvement Social,* 67 (1969), 61–78.

24 P. Barral, 'Mouvements paysans et traditions agricoles en France après la révolution Industrielle' in *Les Mouvements paysans dans le monde contemporain*

(Geneva, Istituto Italiano per la storia dei mouvimenti sociali e delle strutture sociali, 1973), pp. 150–63.

25 M. Augé-Laribé, *L'Évolution de la France agricole* (Paris, 1912), p. 221.

26 Gratton, *Luttes de classe*, p. 303.

27 On the question of class consciousness amongst the peasantry in France see the discussion in Judt, *Socialism in Provence*, pp. 254–80.

28 R. Braque, 'Aux origines du syndicalisme dans les milieux ruraux du centre de la France (Allier-Cher-Nièvre-Sud du Loiret)', *Le Mouvement social* (1963), pp. 79–116.

29 Barral, *Les Agrariens*, p. 146.

30 Barral, *Les Agrariens*, pp. 152–64.

31 E. Guillaumin, *La Vie d'un simple* (Paris, 1904). On the life and writings of Guillaumin see, R. Mathe, *Emile Guillaumin, l'homme et la terre et l'homme de lettres* (Paris, 1966).

32 D. Halévy, *Visites aux paysans du centre*, 3rd edn. (Paris, 1978), p. 63.

33 S. Sokoloff, 'Land tenure and political tendency in rural France: the case of sharecropping', *European studies review*, 10 (1980), 357–82.

34 Most mutual records give details of the property and animals insured by members and, since these include valuations, they provide membership information. It should be stressed, however, that their use as a surrogate for syndicate membership is limited. The poorer members of the community may not have appeared on insurance lists yet be members of the syndicate.

35 Garrier, 'L'Union', 31; M. C. Cleary, 'The Plough and the cross: peasant unions in south-western France', *Agricultural history review*, 30 (1982), p. 133; Cleary, 'Priest, squire and peasant: the development of agricultural syndicates in south-west France 1900–1914', *European history quarterly*, 17 (1987), 145–63.

36 Institut International d'Agriculture, *Enquête monographiques sur la coopération agricole dans quelques pays* (Rome, 1911), pp. 249–326.

37 de Gailhard-Bancel, *Le Syndicalisme*.

4 The heyday of the regional unions, 1918–30

1 Duby and Wallon, *Histoire*, 4, pp. 193–224.

2 Augé-Laribé, *La Politique agricole*, p. 442.

3 Augé-Laribé, *Syndicats et coopératives*, pp. 81–5.

4 Augé-Laribé, *Syndicats et coopératives*, p. 123.

5 M. Anglade, *Guide pratique pour la fondation d'une Mutuelle-Incendie* (Rodez, 1912).

6 AD Côtes-du-Nord, 7 M (Assurances Mutuelles Agricoles 1910–38; Caisses Locales 1898–1938); *Bulletin de l'Union Régionale des syndicats agricoles des Côtes-du-Nord*, Dec. 1923–June 1924.

7 Barral, *Les Agrariens*, p. 203.

8 Augé-Laribé, *Syndicats et coopératives*, pp. 106–23.

9 Barral, *Les Agrariens*, p. 203.

10 Documentation française, *Les Chambres d'agriculture* (Paris, 1965); 'Cinquantenaire des chambres d'agriculture 1924–1974', unpub. man., APCA, Paris.

11 C. Mora, 'Les Chambres d'agriculture: représentation et défense des intérêts agricoles 1924–1940', Thèse de Doctorat, Université de Bordeaux, Fac. des Lettres et Sciences Humaines, 1967, pp. 36–41, 43.

12 APCA, *Mémoires de Joseph Faure 1875–1944* (Paris, 175), pp. 24–35.
13 Mora, Les Chambres d'agriculture, pp. 187–95.
14 Documentation française, *Les Chambres*, p. 29.
15 Duby and Wallon, *Histoire*, 3, 531–44.
16 Barral, *Les Agrariens*, p. 202.
17 Houée, *Les Étapes*, 1, 104–5.
18 Houée, *Les Étapes*, 1, 105.
19 F. Julien-Labruyère, *Paysans charentais: histoire des campagnes d'Aunis, Saintonge et bas Angoumois* (La Rochelle, 1982, 2 vols.) 1, pp. 355–426; L. Papy, *Atlas et géographie de la France moderne – Le Midi – Acquitain* (Paris, 1978), pp. 102–3.
20 G. Reverseau, 'Les Industries laitières dans les Charentes', *Annales de géographie*, 34 (1925), 211.
21 Reverseau, 'Les Industries', pp. 212.
22 AD Charente, 5 M 91; 6 M 600.
23 AD Charente, 7 M 49; 7 M 51; *Monographie Agricole-Charente* (n.p., 1930).
24 R. Béteille, *La Vie quotidienne en Rouergue avant 1914* (Paris, 1974); R. Béteille, *Les Aveyronnais – essai géographique sur l'espace humain* (Poitiers, 1974); R. Calmès, *Les Campagnes des Ségalas et du Lévezou* (Rodez, 1980); A. Durand, *La Vie rurale dans les Massifs volcaniques des Dores, du Cézallier, du Cantal et de l'Aubrac* (Aurillac, 1946); H. Enjalbert (ed.), *Histoire du Rouergue* (Toulouse, 1979).
25 M. C. Cleary, 'Agricultural Syndicates in Aveyron (S-W France 1880–1960)', Ph.D. thesis, University of Cambridge, 1983, pp. 138–91.
26 R. Béteille, *Rouergue, terre d'exode* (Paris, 1978), pp. 103–68.
27 AD Aveyron 35 M 3; 35 M 4; *Livre d'Or de la Société d'encouragement aux institutions rurales du Plateau central* (Rodez, 1912).
28 Archives de l'Evêché (Rodez), Fonds Bonnafé.
29 AD Aveyron 35 M 3 (1); 35 M 3 (5).
30 AD Aveyron 35 M 5; data on the RAGT was regularly published in the syndical journal, *L'Echo du Plateau central* (fortnightly, 1919–29) and *le SOC* (fortnightly 1930–41).
31 AD Aveyron 35 M 3 (1).
32 AD Aveyron 35 M 3 (2).
33 AD Aveyron 35 M 3 (2).
34 Archives de l'Evêché (Rodez), Fonds Bonnafé; M. Anglade, *Le Plateau central à la Semaine sociale de Metz* (Rodez, 1919); Anglade, *Rôle de la profession agricole organisée contre l'injustice dans les relations économiques* (Rodez, 1921).
35 AGM, *Coopérative RAGT* (Rodez, 1926; 1929); AD Aveyron 34 M 1.
36 AD Aveyron 35 M 3 (7).
37 AD Aveyron 35 M 3 (1).
38 A. Meynier, *Ségalas, Lévezou, Chataîgneraie* (Aurillac, 1931), p. 164.
39 *La Fête paysanne – les associations agricoles de Gabriac* (Rodez, 1931); M. Colrat, 'Le Syndicat de Gabriac', *L'Opinion*, 1/3/19.
40 AD Aveyron 35 M 3 (6); *L'Ami de Vezins*, 1916–22; 1925–9.
41 P. Barral, 'Note historique sur l'emploi du terme paysan', *Etudes rurales,* 4 (1966), 72–80.
42 *Livre d'or*, 1912.

43 Union centrale des syndicats agricoles des agriculteurs de France, *XI Congrès National* (Paris, 1922).
44 AD Aveyron 35 M 6; Calmès, *Les Campagnes*, pp. 136–46; H. Enjalbert, *A travers le Ségala* (Rodez, 1950).
45 A chi-square test between rates of depopulation and percentage membership of syndicates indicated a possible relationship. The higher syndicalised cantons had lower rates of depopulation but the results were significant only at a low level of confidence and can be considered inconclusive.
46 Such sources, as was noted in chapter 3, do pose problems of interpretation but, in the absence of any other data, can be useful.
47 P. Arque, *Géographie du Midi – Acquitain* (Paris, 1939), pp. 52–99; J. Cailluyer, *Regards sur l'histoire sociale des Landes* (Toulouse, 1983); Centre National de la Recherche Scientifique, *La Grande Lande – histoire naturelle et géographie historique* (Paris, 1981).
48 On sharecropping see Sokoloff, 'Land tenure and political tendency'.
49 *Recensement Agricole-Landes 1929*, part 3 – Economie rurale.
50 AD Landes 10 M 110.
51 P. Bonnault-Cornu, 'Métayeurs, propriétaires: un rapport social complexe (le cas de St Martin-de-Seignaux dans le Bas-Adour), Thèse 3ème cycle, Université de Provence, Sociologie (1984), 174.
52 J. Cailluyer, *Regards*, pp. 146–80; P. Gratton, *Les Luttes*, pp. 115–32.
53 J. Cailluyer, *Regards*, p. 201.
54 P. Bonnault-Cornu, 'Metayeurs', 201.
55 AD Landes 10 M 111.
56 AD Landes 1 M 174; 10 M 113.
57 AD Landes 10 M 109.
58 AD Landes 10 M 97/98.
59 AD Landes 10 M 111.
60 AD Landes 10 M 111.
61 AD Landes 10 M 111.
62 Gratton, *Les Luttes*, p. 350.
63 AD Landes 1 M 166.

5 The economic crisis and the rise of corporatism, 1930–40

1 Wright, *Rural revolution*, p. 40.
2 Barral, *Les Agrariens*, p. 217.
3 Wright, *Rural revolution*, p. 41.
4 Braudel and Labrousse, *Histoire économique*, 4 vols., vol. 2, pp. 834–6.
5 Braudel and Labrousse, *Histoire économique*, 4 vols., vol. 2, p. 837.
6 Barral, *Les Agrariens*, p. 222.
7 Augé-Laribé, *La Politique agricole*, p. 430.
8 Gueslin, *Les Origines*.
9 M. Anglade, *La Situation du cheptel aveyronnais* (Rodez, 1941); *L'Echo du Plateau central* 1925–9; *le SOC* 1930–3.
10 Braudel and Labrousse, *Histoire économique*, 4 vols., vol. 2, pp. 836–7.
11 *Courrier de l'Aveyron* 1/1/33–10/9/33; quote from 23 April 1933.
12 AD Aveyron 35 M 5; *La Terre Rouergate*, Jan. 1934.

13 Gueslin, *Le Crédit Mutuel*, pp. 199–222.

14 UNSA, *Vers la Corporation Agricole* (Paris, 1934).

15 UNSA, *Congrès Syndical Paysan – Caen 1937* (Paris, 1937).

16 Berger, *Peasants against politics*, pp. 78–90.

17 Béteille, *Les Aveyronnais*, pp. 377–433; J. Ayrignac, 'Parmi les Monts Joie: un jalon – numero 100, *Revue de la Solidarité*, 100 (1978), 253–6.

18 *Revue de la Solidarité*, Jan.–Sept. 1938; interview with Dr J. Ayrignac; interview with Dr G. Puech.

19 *Revue de la Solidarité*, June 1938; *le SOC*, Jan. 1936–Sept. 1937; *L'Effort Paysan*, 1936/7.

20 *Bulletin de liaison entre l'Union régionale du Plateau central et les présidents des Syndicats affiliés*, July 1938; *L'Effort paysan*, 1938.

21 *Revue de la solidarité*, Sept.–Oct. 1936.

22 Interview with Dr J. Ayrignac.

23 AD Aveyron 7 M 34.

24 P. Barral, 'Les Syndicats bretons de cultivateurs-cultivants', *Le Mouvement Social*, 67 (1969), 147–61.

25 AD Aisne 11.403; 5186 (2); 5187; 18.000.

26 O. Petit, 'La Naissance et le développement du syndicalisme et de la mutualité agricole dans le département de l'Aisne entre les deux guerres', Thèse de Doctorat, University of Paris VI, Sorbonne (1986); M. de Saars, *Soixante ans de syndicalisme agricole dans le département de l'Aisne* (Laon, 1952); APCA, *Hommage*, pp. 41–79.

27 A. Toussaint, 'La Nouvelle bourgeoisie paysanne', *Revue des deux mondes* (1928), 925–41.

28 H.-Noilhan, *La République des paysans* (Aurillac, 1932); Wright, *Rural revolution*, pp. 49–51.

29 H. Dorgères, *Haut les fourches!* (Paris, 1935); H. Dorgères, *Au XXe siècle – 10 ans de jacquerie paysanne* (Paris, 1959); P. Ory, 'Le Dorgérisme: institution et discours d'une colère paysanne (1929–1939)', *Revue d'histoire moderne et contemporaine*, XXII (1975), 168–90.

30 Houée, *Les Étapes*, p. 141.

31 *Le SOC*, June–July 1935.

32 *La Croix de l'Aveyron*, 30 June 1935; *Courrier de l'Aveyron*, 16 June 1935, 30 June 1935.

33 Duby and Wallon, *Histoire*, 4, p. 436, gives a figure of 400,000. The lower figure of 40,000 is from Ory, p. 184.

34 Berger, *Peasants against politics*, p. 111.

35 Duby and Wallon, *Histoire*, 4, p. 409.

36 P. Gratton, 'Le Mouvement ouvrier et la question agraire de 1870 à 1947' in Y. Tavernier, M. Gervais, C. Servolin (eds.), *L'Univers politique des paysans dans la France contemporaine* (Paris, 1972), pp. 163–96.

37 Gratton, 'Le Mouvement', p. 183.

38 Barral, *Les Agrariens*, pp. 244–5.

39 AD Landes 10 M 114.

40 AD Landes 1 M 174.

41 AD Landes 10 M 115.

42 AD Landes 10 M 99–105.

43 AD 10 M 100; J. Tucoo-Chala, 'Introduction à l'histoire du mouvement syndical des gemmeurs: l'action de Charles Prat', *Bulletin de la Société de Bordas*, 394 (1984), 375–95.
44 AD Landes 10 M 115.
45 AD Landes 10 M 114; *Le Travailleur Landais: Hebdomadaire de la Fédération Socialiste SFIO des Landes*, 1936–9.
46 Gratton, *Les Luttes*, pp. 77–9.
47 Gratton, *Les Luttes*, p. 78.
48 AD Aisne 11. 404.
49 de Saar, *Soixante ans*, pp. 80–1; AD Aisne 11. 403.
50 F. Goguel, *Géographie des élections françaises sous la Troisième et Quatrième République* (Paris, 1970) pp. 92–7.
51 Duby and Wallon, *Histoire*, 4, pp. 558–62.
52 Wright, *Rural revolution*, p. 62.
53 Gratton in Tavernier, *L'Univers politique*, p. 188, gives the figure of 29; Barral, *Les Agrariens*, p. 245, gives the figure of 30.
54 Barral, *Les Agrariens*, p. 246.
55 Barral, *Les Agrariens*, p. 253.
56 *Ar vro goz – organe hebdomadaire de l'Union des syndicats agricoles du Finistère et des Côtes-du-Nord*, 20 Sept. 1936.
57 A. Durand, 'La Coopérative Blé de l'Aveyron' (1978).
58 *La Terre rouergate*, 12 Nov. 1938; 10 Dec. 1938.
59 Mora, 'Les Chambres', pp. 180–230.
60 Mora, 'Les Chambres', p. 222.
61 Mora, 'Les Chambres', p. 473.
62 M.-J. Durupt, *Les Mouvements d'Action Catholique – facteur d'évolution du monde rural* (Paris, 1973); *JAC-MRJC 1929–1979* (Paris, n.d.). Jeunesse Agricole Catholique and Jeunesse Agricole Chrétienne are often used interchangeably. The former is preferred here to reinforce the confessional nature of the movement which was always imbued with a specifically Catholic ethos.
63 *Manuel de la JAC* (Lyon, 1941).
64 *JAC-MRJC 1929–79*, p. 18.
65 *JAC–MRJC 1929–79*, pp. 20–1.

6 Agricultural associations under Vichy, 1940–44

1 P. Barral, 'Agrarisme de gauche et agrarisme de droite sous la Troisième République' in Tavernier *et al.* (eds.), *L'Univers politique*, p. 252.
2 Braudel and Labrousse, *Histoire économique*, 4 vols., vol. 2, 848.
3 M. Cépède, *Agriculture et alimentation en France durant la IIème guerre mondiale* (Paris, 1961), pp. 346–70.
4 R. Milward, *The new order and the French economy* (Oxford, 1970), p. 259.
5 Cépède, *Agriculture et alimentation*, p. 308; Houée, *Les Étapes*, 1, p. 159.
6 Barral, *Les Agrariens*, pp. 265–6.
7 Duby and Wallon, *Histoire*, 4, 97–9.
8 Cépède, *Agriculture et alimentation*, p. 449.
9 Barral, *Les Agrariens*, pp. 271–2.
10 I. Boussard, *Vichy et la Corporation paysanne* (Paris, 1980), pp. 23–50.

11 Louis Salleron provides a series of accounts of the creation and ideology of the Corporation. See *inter alia*: L. Salleron, *Naissance de l'Etat Corporatif: dix ans de syndicalisme paysan* (Paris, 1942); Salleron, *La Charte paysanne* (Le Mans, 1943); Salleron, *La Corporation paysanne* (Paris, 1943).

12 Barral, *Les Agrariens*, p. 276.

13 Salleron, *La Charte paysanne*, p. 7

14 Salleron, *La Charte paysanne*, pp. 4–6.

15 L. Prault, *Mort et résurrection des Chambres d'Agriculture 1940–1952* (Paris, 1978).

16 Boussard, *Vichy et la Corporation paysanne*, pp. 186–203.

17 Wright, *Rural revolution*, pp. 81–5.

18 Salleron, *Naissance de l'Etat*, p. 235.

19 Salleron, *La Charte paysanne*, p. 16.

20 Cépède, *Agriculture et alimentation*, p. 76.

21 Boussard, *Vichy et la Corporation paysanne*, pp. 106–10.

22 *Bulletin de la Solidarité Aveyronnaise*, Jan. 1938.

23 AD Aveyron 7 M 36.

24 *Revue de la Solidarité*, July 1940.

25 AD Aveyron 35 M 3 (6); *Revue de la Solidarité*, Feb. 1941.

26 *Revue de la Solidarité*, Nov.–Dec. 1941; *Rouergue-paysan – Organe officiel de la Corporation Paysanne du Rouergue*, April 1942–July 1944 (monthly).

27 *Rouergue-paysan*, April 1942.

28 *Revue de la Solidarité*, Nov.–Dec. 1941.

29 *Circulaire aux militants Corporatifs-Paysans du Rouergue*, 9, 25 May 1942.

30 AD Aveyron 36 M 1 (4); *Circulaire aux militants*, Feb. 1942; interview with Dr Ayrignac.

31 I. Boussard, 'Les Arguments économiques en faveur du retour à la terre dans le discours agrarien', paper presented to the *Société française d'économie rurale*, Paris, September 1987.

32 P. Caziot, *La Terre à la famille paysanne* (Paris, 1919).

33 I. Boussard, 'Les Arguments économiques', p. 11.

34 R. Mallet, *Nécessité d'un retour à la terre. Etude d'économie comparée* (Paris, 1941), pp. 1–2.

35 J. Gazave, *La Terre ne ment pas – introduction à une physiocratie nouvelle* (Villefranche-de-Rouergue, 1940), p. 26.

36 AD Aveyron 36 M 1 (4).

37 Duby and Wallon, *Histoire*, 4, p. 566.

38 *Rouergue-paysan*, 31 Oct. 1943.

39 *Rouergue-paysan*, 23 June 1944.

40 de Sars, *Soixante ans*, p. 120.

41 AD Aisne 5.650; 11.403; 14.547; 14.548; 14.549.

42 *Ar vro goz – organe de l'Union régionale corporative agricole du Finistère et des Côtes-du-Nord*, 12 Nov. 1942–27 Dec. 1942.

43 Gueslin, *Le Crédit mutuel*, pp. 224–44.

44 Gueslin, *Le Crédit mutuel*, p. 236.

45 Boussard, *Vichy et la Corporation paysanne*, p. 370.

46 Duby and Wallon, *Histoire*, 4, p. 446; Houée, *Les Étapes*, p. 158.

47 Wright, *Rural revolution*, pp. 90–2.

7 A rural revolution? Syndicates and cooperatives, 1944–65

1 Duby and Wallon, *Histoire*, 4, pp. 576–7.
2 FNSEA, *Cent ans*, pp. 67–8.
3 Barral, *Les Agrariens*, pp. 290–1.
4 Wright, *Rural revolution*, p. 104.
5 AD Aveyron 35 M 3 (6); *La Volonté paysanne*, March 1946.
6 E. Forget, *Le Serment de l'unité paysanne* (Paris, 1982), p. 126.
7 APCA, *Hommage*, pp. 42–4.
8 Houée, *Les Étapes*, 1, pp. 166–8, 2, pp. 174–7.
9 Prault, *Mort et résurrection*, pp. 12–16; Documentation française, *Les Chambres*, 22–3.
10 Houée, *Les Étapes*, 1, p. 167.
11 Prault, *Mort et résurrection*, p. 15.
12 C. Mora, 'Les Chambres d'Agriculture et l'unité paysanne' in Tavernier *et al*, *L'Univers politique*, p. 518.
13 Prault, *Mort et résurrection*, p. 16.
14 Y. Tavernier, *Le syndicalisme Paysan* (Paris, 1969), pp. 17–21; H. Mendras, 'Les Organisations agricoles' in J. Fauvet and H. Mendras (eds.), *Les Paysans et la politique* (Paris, 1958), pp. 231–51.
15 Duby and Wallon, *Histoire*, 4, pp. 461–2.
16 Barral, *Les Agrariens*, pp. 308–9.
17 FNSEA, *Cent ans*, p. 84.
18 Y. Tavernier, 'Le Mouvement de défense des exploitants familiaux' in Tavernier *et al., L'Univers politique*, pp. 469–71.
19 Y. Tavernier, *Le syndicalisme paysan*, p. 26.
20 de Saars, *Soixante ans*, p. 127.
21 J. T. Keeler, 'The politics of official unionism in French agriculture 1958–1976: a study of the corporatist bases of FNSEA hegemony' (unpublished Ph.D., Harvard University, Dept of Government, 1978), 292.
22 Keeler, 'The politics', 268.
23 *Bulletin de l'Union des syndicats agricoles de l'Aisne*, fortnightly, 1950–3; AD Aisne 15.260/1.
24 *Bulletin de l'Union des syndicats agricoles de L'Aisne*, 24/2/51, 8/9/51.
25 M. C. Cleary, 'The changing character of agricultural syndicates in Aveyron 1944–60', *Sociologia ruralis*, 25 (1985), 118–29.
26 *La Volonté paysanne*, April 1950.
27 *Le Rouergat*, 7/3/48; interview with M. Landes.
28 S. Maresca, *Les Dirigeants paysans* (Paris, 1983), pp. 154–75.
29 Journées sociales rurales, *Le Chrétien et les nouvelles institutions du monde rural* (Lyon, 1942).
30 JAC-MRJC, *50 ans d'animation*, p. 35.
31 Forget, *Le Serment*, pp. 103–5.
32 P. Bion, 'Enquête sur la JAC', unpub. man. (1942); interview with M. Laur.
33 *Manuel de la JAC*.
34 *L'Enquête à la JAC* (Rennes, 1940), p. 7.
35 JAC-MRJC, *50 ans d'animation*, pp. 41–7.

36 *Le Rouergat*, 14 July 1949.
37 *Jeunesse du rouergue*, Sept.–Oct. 1948, Aug.–Sept. 1949, June 1952.
38 National data and Figure 17 are based on: Durupt, *Les Mouvements*, maps 29–32; M. Faure, 'Action Catholique en milieu rural' in Fauvet and Mendras (eds.), *Les Paysans et la politique*, pp. 345–60; B. Hervieu and A. Vial, 'L'Eglise Catholique et les paysans' in Tavernier *et al.*, *L'Univers politique*, pp. 292–315.
39 JAC-MRJC, *50 ans d'animation*, pp. 56–8.
40 P. Bion, 'Notes doctrinales sur l'organisation professionelle', unpub. man. (1956); F. Romatif, *L'Engagement des Chrétiens dans les institutions du monde rural* (Paris 1952), p. 32.
41 S. Maresca, 'Ebauche d'une analyse sociologique des élites paysannes – cinq biographies de dirigeants paysans', *Etudes rurales*, 76 (1979), 50–82.
42 P. Bion, 'Histoire de la paysannerie aveyronnaise', unpub. man. (1962).
43 Interview with M. Cazals.
44 Interview with M. Laur.
45 Y. Lambert, 'Développement agricole et Action Catholique', *Sociologia Ruralis*, 18 (1978), 245–54.
46 JAC-MRJC, *50 ans d'animation*, p. 58.
47 This influential and controversial paper is included in R. Colson, *Un paysan face à l'avenir rural – la JAC et la modernisation de l'agriculture* (Paris, 1976), pp. 167–309.
48 P. Bion, 'L'Eglise et ses militants devant l'évolution du milieu rural', unpub. man. (1958).
49 R. Colson, *Un paysan*, p. 41.
50 L. Lauga, *CNJA – le pari des jeunes agriculteurs* (Paris, 1971), p. 98.
51 Duby and Wallon, *Histoire*, 4, p. 468.
52 B. Hervieu, 'L'Action Catholique Rurale' in 'Le Monde Paysan', *Cahiers français*, 187 (1978), 60.
53 Interview with M. Laur.
54 R. Lajoie-Mazenc, *Marcel Bruel et le défi agricole* (Villefranche-de-Rouergue, 1976), p. 69.
55 G. Wright, *Rural revolution*, p. 160.
56 M. Debatisse, *Le Projet paysan* (Paris, 1983), pp. 57–60.
57 M. Debatisse, *La Révolution silencieuse – le combat des paysans* (Paris, 1962).
58 Debatisse, *Le Projet paysan*, p. 18.
59 Maresca, 'Ebauche d'une analyse', p. 66.
60 Maresca, 'Ebauche d'une analyse', p. 65.
61 B. Lambert, *Les Paysans dans la lutte des classes* (Paris, 1970), p. 108.
62 Maresca, *Les Dirigeants*, pp. 30–50.
63 Duby and Wallon, *Histoire*, 4, p. 463.
64 Barral, *Les Agrariens*, pp. 322–3.
65 Duby and Wallon, *Histoire*, 4, p. 581.
66 Lauga, *CNJA*, p. 99.
67 Duby and Wallon, *Histoire*, 4, p. 589.
68 FNSEA, *Cent ans*, pp. 87–90.

69 J. Chombart de Lauwe, *L'Aventure agricole de la France* (Paris, 1979), pp. 216–56.

70 S. Quiers-Valette, 'Les Causes économiques du mécontentement des agriculteurs français en 1961', *Revue française de Science Politique*, 3 (1962), pp. 555–98; Y. Tavernier, 'Syndicalisme paysan et la politique agricole du gouvernement 1958–1962', *Revue française de Science Politique*, 3 (1962), 599–646.

71 *L'Agriculteur de l'Aisne*, 20 August 1960.

72 P. Houée, *Coopération et organisations agricoles françaises* (2 vols., Paris, 1969) provides a valuable review of cooperatives in rural France.

73 Houée, *Les Étapes*, 2, pp. 123–46.

74 Houée, *Les Étapes*, 2, pp. 50–3.

75 J. Chombart de Lauwe, 'Aspects économiques de l'utilisation en commun du matériel agricole', *Bulletin de la Société française d'économie rurale* (1952), 122–86.

76 Houée, *Les Étapes*, 2, p. 128.

77 P. Dorner, *Cooperative and commune* (Wisconsin, 1977).

78 P. Daucé and Y. Leon, 'L'Evolution de l'agriculture Bretonne depuis 1850', *Sciences Agronomiques* 2 (Rennes, 1982).

79 P. Flatrès, 'La deuxième "Révolution Agricole" en Finistère', *Etudes rurales*, 8 (1963), pp. 5–55.

80 J. Ardagh, *France in the 1980s* (Harmondsworth, 1982), pp. 137–9, 210–11; A. Baudoin and L.-R. Dautriat, *Alexis Gourvennec, paysan-directeur-général* (Paris, 1977); 'Alexis Gourvennec – 25 ans d'action', *Sociétés Bretonnes*, pp. 9–10, 197–240.

81 E. Morin, *Plodémet – report from a French village* (London, 1971), pp. 101–9.

82 J. Peyon, 'L'Essor des coopératives agro-alimentaires dans les années soixante-soixante-dix en France', paper presented to the *Société Française d'Économie Rurale*, Paris, September 1987, p. 3.

83 Lambert, 'Développement agricole', pp. 249–50.

84 *La Volonté paysanne*, September 1947.

85 *La Volonté paysanne*, 1–15 July 1958.

86 A. Durand, 'CALA – La Ruthenoise' unpub. man. (1978); *Entre-Nous – groupement interprofessionel des producteurs et transformateurs de lait de vache* (1958–9).

87 *La Volonté paysanne*, 1–15 September 1957.

88 A chi-square test at the cantonal scale in Aveyron showed a significant relationship between CUMA density and syndical membership at the 99 per cent significance level.

89 Wright, *Rural revolution*, p. 182.

8 The deceptions of progress, 1965–85

1 J. Cuisenier, 'Fonctions économiques des organisations et administrations agricoles en France', *Etudes rurales*, 11 (1966), pp. 5–71.

2 Debatisse, *Le Projet paysan*.

3 Tavernier, *Le Syndicalisme paysan*; Chombart de Lauwe, *L'Aventure agricole*, p. 143.

4 FNSEA, *30e Congrès Fédéral* (1976); FNSEA, *40e Congrès Fédéral (1986)*, *Rapport Moral*.

5 FNSEA, *Cent ans*, p. 111.
6 Chombart de Lauwe, *L'Aventure agricole*, p. 139.
7 J. Keeler, 'Corporatism and official union hegemony: the case of French agricultural syndicalism' in S. Berger, A. Hirschman, C. Maier (eds.), *Organising interests in western Europe: pluralism, corporatism and the transformation of politics* (Cambridge, 1981), p. 186.
8 Keeler, 'Corporatism and official union hegemony', p. 196.
9 This threefold division of the farming community forms the basis for the examination of syndicalism in Duby and Wallon, *Histoire*, 4, pp. 479–511.
10 H. Delorme, 'Le Rôle des forces paysannes dans l'élaboration de la politique agricole commune', *Revue française de Science Politique*, 19 (1969), 356–91; H. Delorme and Y. Tavernier, *Les Paysans français et l'Europe* (Paris, 1969); H. Delorme and L. Tubiana, 'L'Élargissement vers le sud du Marché commun agricole', *Revue française de Science Politique*, 28 (1978), pp. 698–716.
11 I. Boussard, 'Elections aux chambres d'agriculture et municipales: le vote des agriculteurs', *Revue politique et parlementaire*, 85 (1983), pp. 79–94.
12 Keeler, 'The politics of official unionism', pp. 280–96.
13 Keeler, 'The politics', p. 294.
14 E. Naylor, *Socio-structural policy in French agriculture*, O'Dell Memorial Monograph, 18 (University of Aberdeen, 1985), pp. 44–59.
15 A. Burguière, *Bretons de Plozévet* (Paris, 1977), pp. 172–206; S. Mallet, 'A propos du syndicalisme agricole Finistérien', *Etudes rurales*, 8 (1963), 56–61.
16 *La Volonté paysanne*, 1972–7 (monthly).
17 Interview with M. Cazals.
18 A. Durand, 'Coopératives agricoles', unpub. man. (1978).
19 *Statistiques Agricoles 1978*, Rodez, Chambre d'agriculture.
20 Béteille, *La France du Vide*, covers the national scene with numerous examples from Aveyron.
21 The opposition to the planned expansion of the military camp on the Larzac in the south of the department was in part a reflection of the fear of continued rural depopulation although support for the loose coalition of environmental, student and socialist groups amongst the farming population was by no means total. The planned expansion was abandoned by the incoming socialist government in 1981. See: Y. Hardy and E. Gabey, *Dossier L comme Larzac* (Paris, 1974); W. Holohan, 'Jacquerie sur la forteresse, le mouvement paysan du Larzac' in D. Fabre and J. Lacroix (eds.), *Communautés du Sud*, 1 (Paris, 1975), pp. 362–432.
22 *L'Information agricole,* Jan. 1987.
23 Debatisse, *Le Projet paysan*, p. 20.
24 FNSEA, *40e Congrès Fédéral*.
25 It is interesting that there is no mention of any dissident syndical movements in the official history of the FNSEA.
26 Barral, *Les Agrariens*, pp. 308–9.
27 Y. Tavernier, 'Le Mouvement de coordination et de défense des exploitations familiales', *Revue française de Science Politique*, 18 (1968), 542–63; F. Tello, 'Données sur l'origine et l'implantation du MODEF', *Cahiers d'histoire de l'Institut Maurice Thorez*, 28 (1978), pp. 39–80.
28 Tavernier, 'Le Mouvement', p. 543.
29 Chombart de Lauwe, *L'Aventure agricole*, p. 152.

30 Tello, 'Données', p. 76.
31 *L'Exploitant familial*, 1978–86 (monthly).
32 MODEF, *Le Livre vert ou comment Ruiner l'Agriculture française* (Angoulême, 1986).
33 Duby and Wallon, *Histoire*, 4, pp. 501–10.
34 Lambert, *Les Paysans*, pp. 68–75.
35 J. F. Nallet, 'La Fédération régionale des syndicats d'exploitants agricoles de l'Ouest' in Tavernier *et al.*, *L'Univers politique*, pp. 415–44.
36 *Le Travailleur-paysan des Côtes-du-Nord*, April 1985.
37 *Le Travailleur-paysan des Côtes-du-Nord*, Dec. 1983, Sept. 1985.
38 Boussard, 'Elections', p. 83.
39 J. Paris, 'Les Chambres d'Agriculture' (Thèse 3 cycle, Faculté de Droit, Poitiers, 1973).
40 APCA, *Les Chambres d'Agriculture* (Paris, 1984), p. 2.
41 L. Perrin, 'L'APCA', *Chambres d'Agriculture* (1980).
42 L'APCA (Paris, 1984), pp. 6–7.
43 L'APCA, pp. 11–12.
44 *Cinquantenaire des Chambres d'Agriculture 1924–1974* (Paris, 1974).
45 These activities are critically examined in F. Clavaud *et al.*, *Quelle agriculture pour la France?* (Paris, 1974), pp. 92–102; Lambert, *Les Paysans*, pp. 76–84.
46 Klatzmann, *L'Agriculture française*, pp. 50–71.
47 J. Peyon, *La Coopération agricole en France – Étude géographique des grands organismes coopératifs* (Paris, 1983).
48 CNRS, *140 cartes sur la France rurale* (Paris, 1984), carte 11.
49 Peyon, 'L'Essor des coopératives', pp. 2–3.
50 Klatzmann, *L'Agriculture française*, pp. 69–70.
51 Debatisse, *Le projet paysan*, p. 33.
52 Naylor, *Socio-structural policy*, p. 115.
53 A. Gueslin, 'Agriculture et Crédit Agricole au XX siècle', paper presented to the *Société Française d'Économie Rurale*, Paris, September 1987, pp. 5–6.
54 Gueslin, 'Agriculture et Crédit Agricole', pp. 22–3.
55 INSEE, *Annuaire des statistiques* (1986).
56 Naylor, *Socio-structural policy*, p. 124.
57 Naylor, *Socio-structural policy*, p. 161.
58 Gueslin, *Le Crédit mutuel*, p. 300.
59 Gueslin, *Le Crédit mutuel*, p. 325.

9 Representing the community

1 Duby and Wallon, *Histoire*, 4, pp. 194–6.
2 Chapuis, *Les ruraux français*, p. 168.
3 See chapter 1, notes 41 and 42.
4 *Congrès national des syndicats agricoles* (Lyon, 1894), p. 26.
5 de Rocquigny, *Les Syndicats agricoles*, p. 26.
6 Gailhard-Bancel, *Le Syndicalisme agricole*, p. 49.
7 Gratton, 'Le Mouvement ouvrier' in Tavernier *et al.*, *L'Univers politique*, pp. 163–80.
8 See chapter 3, note 25.

9 Gratton, *Les Paysans français*, pp. 76–80.

10 Duby and Wallon, *Histoire*, 4, p. 59.

11 Barral, *Les Agrariens*, p. 134.

12 Barral, *Les Agrariens*, p. 249.

13 Salleron, *La Charte paysanne*, pp. 10–16.

14 AD Aveyron 7 M 36; *Ar vro goz – organe de l'Union corporative agricole du Finistère et des Côtes-du-Nord*, 27 Dec. 1942.

15 L. Prugnaud, *Les Étapes du syndicalisme agricole en France* (Paris, 1963).

16 Duby and Wallon, *Histoire*, 4, pp. 275–87.

17 F. Bourquelot, 'Les Salariés agricoles et leurs organisations' in Tavernier *et al.*, *L'Univers politique*, pp. 545–57; J. Pasquier and F. Bourquelot, 'Chez les salariés agricoles: une singulière flexibilité' in P. Maclouf (ed.), *La Pauvreté dans le monde rural* (Paris, 1986), pp. 231–8.

18 Klatzmann, *L'Agriculture française*, p. 53.

19 See *inter alia*, Franklin, *European peasantry*, pp. 1–20; Mendras, *Sociétés paysannes*, pp. 39–72.

20 M. Segalen, *Love and power in the peasant family* (Oxford, 1983).

21 A. Frémont, *L'Élevage en basse Normandie: étude géographique* (Caen, 1967), pp. 145–6.

22 D. Fabre and J. Lacroix, *La Vie quotidienne des paysans du Languedoc au XIX siècle* (Paris, 1973), pp. 178–96.

23 L. Roubin, 'Male space and female space within the Provençal community' in R. Forster and O. Ranum (eds.), *Rural society in France* (Baltimore, 1977), p. 156.

24 Quoted in A. Audibert, 'Parler des femmes', *Mondes paysans – Sociétés Bretonnes*, 9 (n.d.), pp. 59–75.

25 Segalen, *Love and power*, p. 141.

26 M. Jollivet and H. Mendras (eds.), *Les Collectivités rurales françaises*, 1 (Paris, 1971), p. 85.

27 Jollivet and Mendras, *Les Collectivités*, p. 57.

28 Jollivet and Mendras, *Les Collectivités*, p. 155.

29 Audibert, 'Parler des femmes', pp. 68–9.

30 R.-M. Lagrave, 'Bilan critique des recherches sur les agricultrices en France', *Etudes rurales*, 92 (1983), 9.

31 Segalen, *Love and power*, pp. 175–8.

32 M. Moscovici, 'Le changement social en milieu rural et le rôle des femmes', *Revue française de sociologie*, 1 (1960), pp. 314–22.

33 Morin, *Plodémet*, pp. 147–64.

34 Quoted in Lagrave, 'Bilan critique', p. 23.

35 P. E. Ogden and M.-M. Huss, 'Demography and pronatalism in France in the nineteenth and twentieth centuries', *Journal of historical geography*, 8 (1982), pp. 293–4.

36 AD Aveyron 7 M 38.

37 J. Caniou, 'L'Enseignement agricole féminine', *Etudes rurales*, 92 (1983), pp. 41–56.

38 Caniou, 'L'Enseignement agricole', pp. 47–8.

39 *L'Echo du Plateau Central* 1919–30; *le SOC* 1930–40.

40 A major survey on the place of women in the organisations of the agricultural world entitled 'Crises in rural society and the women's movement in agriculture'

is currently being completed under the direction of R.-M. Lagrave at the Ecole des Hautes Etudes en Sciences Sociales, Paris. Some of the themes underpinning the work are sketched out in 'Femme et terre', *Pénélope. Pour l'histoire des femmes*, 7 (1982).

41 Achard, *La JACF*, p. 46.
42 Durupt, *Les mouvements*.
43 Interview with Mme. Cazals.
44 Interview with Mme. Laur.
45 Lagrave, 'Bilan critique', pp. 27–31.
46 E. Weber, 'Le travail hors de l'usine. Bricolage et double activité', *Cahiers d'Economie et Sociologie Rurale*, 3 (1986), 14.
47 Y. Rinaudo, 'Un travail en plus: les paysans d'un métier à l'autre', *Annales ESC*, 2 (1987), 283–302.
48 H. Mendras, *La Fin des paysans. Suivi d'une reflexion sur La fin des paysans vingt ans après* (Paris, 1984), p. 330.
49 Segalen, *Love and power*.
50 Mendras, *La Fin . . . Suivi*, p. 328.
51 FNSEA, *Cent ans*, p. 111.
52 Lagrave, 'Bilan critique', p. 29.
53 A.-M. Crolais, *L'Agricultrice* (Paris, 1982), p. 48.
54 Crolais, *L'Agricultrice*, p. 25.
55 M. Berlan, 'Farmers' wives in protest; a theatre of contradictions', *Sociologia ruralis*, 26 (1986), pp. 285–302.
56 Berlan, 'Farmers' wives in protest', p. 300.
57 Maresca, *Les Dirigeants*, pp. 29–50.

Bibliography

MANUSCRIPT SOURCES

Archives nationales, Paris
F(10) 2718/2722 Enseignement agricole
F(12) 4664 Grèves 1880–90
F(12) 4701/4704 Syndicats agricoles dissous (1884–1907)

Archives Départementales de l'Aisne, Laon

Series M
5.053 Agriculture-divers 1945–50
5.186 (2) Associations agricoles 1919–29
5.187 Crédit Agricole 1936–42
5.650 (2) Syndicats agricoles cantonaux 1941–6
7.371 Syndicats corporatifs agricoles 1932–9
9.786 Comité départementale des céreales 1936–5
9.788 (2) Correspondance 1948–54
9.856 (2) Communiqués 1950–3
11.403 Caisses Agricoles/Syndicats agricoles 1934–43
11.404 (1) Agriculture: grèves agricoles 1936–42
11.849 Syndicats agricoles cantonaux 1945
11.892 Chambre d'Agriculture – associations 1938
14.547 Agriculture – associations 1942–4
14.548 Agriculture – Soissons 1944/1945
17.996–998 Coopératives agricoles 1950–64
14.549 Agriculture – Soissons 1945–50
18.000 Etude sur la coopération agricole
18.041 Caisse Régionale de Crédit Agricole

Archives Départementales de l'Aveyron, Rodez

Series M
23 M 5 (1) Police 1869–1935

33 M 3 Etat de récoltes 1903
33 M 5 Généralités – cultures diverses
33 M 6 Elevage et Bétail
33 M 1 (5–16) Enseignement et formation agricole 1883–1939
34 M 2 (32–34) Comices Agricoles 1840–1920
35 M 1 (1) Sociétés d'Agriculture
35 M 1 (3) Société Centrale d'Agriculture
35 M 2 Chambre d'Agriculture
35 M 2 (5) Elections 1933–9
35 M 2 (6) Elections – associations 1933–9
35 M 2 (7) Délégués des associations 1935–9
35 M 3 (1) Syndicats agricoles – formation 1886–1913
35 M 3 (2) *Ibid* 1914–29
35 M 3 (3) *Ibid* 1930–5
35 M 3 (5) Syndicats des éleveurs de brebis
35 M 3 (6) Syndicats corporatifs paysans 1940–4
35 M 3 (7) Syndicats agricoles 1945–8 – Millau
35 M 3 (8) *Ibid* – Rodez
35 M 3 (9/11) Syndicats – communes 1945
35 m 4 (1) Mutuelles Agricoles – générale
35 M 4 (2) Caisses locales 1904–18
35 M 4 (3) Plateau central 1906–14
35 M 4 (4) Subventions 1904–12
35 M 4 (5) *Ibid* 1912
35 M 4 (6) *Ibid* 1913–14
35 M 4 (7) *Ibid* 1915–26
35 M 4 (8) Mutuelles par arrondissement 1920–2
35 M 5 (1) Sociétés coopératives 1917–19
35 M 6 (1) Crédit Agricole – création 1893–1910
35 M 6 (2) Caisses locales 1932
36 M 1 (4) Retour à la Terre 1874–1945
35 M 1 (5) Améliorations agricoles 1907–13
36 M 2 (21) Comités d'Action agricole 1941–5
The series is currently being reclassified as 7 M 25 – 7 M 56.

Series N
3 N Procès-Verbaux-Conseil Général
4 N 1 Rapports des chefs de service et du Préfet

Series P
15 P 1 Matrices Générales
21 P 1 Matrices Cadastrales 1811–1914

Series V
3 V 10 Congrès Catholique 1904–6

Archives Départementales de la Charente, Angoulême

Series M
5 M 91 Santé Publique – Laiteries

5 M 92 Laiteries; Beurreries 1836–1936
5 M 93 *Ibid*
6 M 600 Laiteries et fromageries 1916–22
6 M 674/5 Statistique agricole communaux 1918
6 M 681 *Ibid* 1938
7 M 42 Documents sur les sociétés, syndicats agricoles et viticoles 1910–15
7 M 43 *Ibid* 1916–37
7 M 48 Sections communales de l'Entente Paysanne 1926–33
7 M 49 Fédération des associations agricoles de la Charente 1919–23
7 M 50 Fédération des associations agricoles du Centre-Ouest 1920
7 M 51 Comité et syndicat du lait de la Charente 1939
7 M 52 Coopératives agricoles 1902–38
7 M 53 *Ibid* 1909–32
7 M 54 Crédit Agricole 1894–1934
7 M 58 Syndicats d'élevage: union Charentaise
7 M 101 Sociétés d'assurances mutuelles agricoles 1858–1931

Archives Départementales des Côtes-du-Nord, St Brieuc

Series M
7 M Sociétés d'Agriculture – généralités
7 M Associations, sociétés et syndicats locaux agricoles 1848–1939
7 M Assurances mutuelles agricoles – circulaires, caisse centrale 1910–38
7 M Assurances mutuelles agricoles – Caisses locales 1898–1938 (1–5)
7 M Associations, sociétés départementaux 1890–1936

Series W
Syndicats corporatifs locaux

Archives Départementales des Landes, Mont-de-Marsan

Series M
1 M 61 Police – gemmeurs 1938–40
1 M 117 Résiniers 1927
1 M 174 Conseil Paysan 1926–9
1 M 175 Syndicats agricoles 1926–39
6 M 684/685 Statistiques Agricoles 1929
7 M 38/40 Chambre d'Agriculture – élections 1927–8
7 M 41 *Ibid* 1929
7 M 42 *Ibid* 1938
7 M 83 Syndicats agricoles 1869–1939
7 M 86 Syndicats d'élevage 1913–35
7 M 88 Fédération des syndicats agricoles et viticoles du Sud-Ouest 1927
7 M 113 Crédit Agricole dans les Landes 1879–1939
7 M 128 Main d'Oeuvre Agricole – salariés 1930
7 M 508 Vente des résines – prix 1928–30
10 M 94 Situation des résiniers 1912–26
10 M 95 Grèves 1916–18

10 M 96 Enquête 1919
10 M 96 Grèves 1919–26
10 M 98 Grèves 1920
10 M 99 Crise des Résineux 1927–35
10 M 100 Fédération des Gemmeurs du Sud-Ouest 1925–40
10 M 101 Situation 1931–5
10 M 103 Commission de la résine 1934
10 M 105 Démission des conseils municipaux – correspondance 1934–9
10 M 106 *Ibid* 1934–5
10 M 107 Enquête 1936
10 M 108 *Ibid* 1937
10 M 109 Dossier Viro
10 M 110 Conditions du métayage 1919–20
10 M 111 Grève des métayers 1919–20
10 M 112 Commission 1920
10 M 113 Action syndicaliste agraire 1920–21
10 M 114 Mouvement agraire 1926–7
10 M 115 Menées communistes – Front Paysan 1930–5

Archives Départementales de la Lozère, Mende

Series M
4058 Associations agricoles – assurances 1908–32
4447 Usagers locaux 1936–8
6526 Agriculture – affaires diverses 1946–63
6743 Usagers locaux 1936–8
7586 Organisation professionelle 1945–66
12374 Retour à la Terre 1922–4

Archives Départementales de la Vendée, La Roche-sur-Yon

Series M
6 M 1141 Agriculture-associations, Sables d'Olonne
6 M 1143 *Ibid* Chaillé
6 M 1152 *Ibid* Lucon
7 M 41 Syndicats agricoles – communaux 1900–30

Archives de l'Evêché de Rodez (Aveyron)
Fonds Bion – documents, lettres, articles 1940–65
Fonds Bonnafé – 1900–14
Fonds Challiol – 1930–40
Dossier Dubois – 1948–54
Fonds Menard – 1950–60
Visites Diocésaines 1908–14
Visites Pastorales 1950–9

Press sources
Only where a continuous series has been consulted is a listing given.
Bulletin de l'Union Catholique Aveyronnaise (1906–12, Rodez)

Bulletin de l'Union des Syndicats Agricoles de l'Aisne (1950–63, Laon)
Bulletin de l'Union Régionale des Syndicats Agricoles des Côtes-du-Nord (1920–8, St Brieuc)
Chambres d'Agriculture (1954–69; 1976–86, Paris)
Courrier de l'Aveyron (1933–8, Rodez)
L'Exploitant familial (1974–86, Angoulême)
Jeunesse du Rouergue (1948–57, Rodez)
Jeunes forces rurales (1948–60, Paris)
L'Echo du Plateau Central (1919–29, Rodez)
L'Effort paysan (1936–9, Albi)
L'Information agricole (1955–60; 1974–82, Paris)
Revue de la Solidarité (1932–44, Rodez)
Rouergue-paysan (1942–4, Rodez)
La Terre (1937–9; 1963–8, Paris)
Le Travailleur Landais (1936–9, Mont-de-Marsan)
Le Travailleur-paysan des Côtes-du-Nord (1983–6, St Brieuc)
Ar vro goz – organe hebdomadaire de l'Union des Syndicats Agricoles du Finistère et des Côtes-du-Nord (1934–6; 1942–4, St Brieuc)
La Volonté paysanne (1947–82, Rodez)

SECONDARY SOURCES

Abel, W., *Crises agraires en Europe XIII–XX siècle,* Paris, 1974
Achard, A., *La JACF,* Paris, 1954
Ackerman, E. B., *Village on the Seine: tradition and change in Bonnières 1815–1914,* Ithaca, NY, 1978
Agulhon, M., *The republic in the village: the people of the Var from the French Revolution to the Second Republic,* Cambridge, 1982
Allauzen, M., *La paysanne française aujourd'hui,* Paris, 1967
Anglade, M., *Guide pratique pour la fondation d'une Mutuelle Incendie,* Rodez, 1912
   Le Plateau Central à la semaine sociale de Metz, Rodez, 1919
   Rôle de la profession agricole organisée contre l'injustice dans les rélations économiques, Rodez, 1921
   La situation du cheptel aveyronnais, Rodez, 1941
Ardagh, J., *France in the 1980s,* Harmondsworth, 1982
Arque, P., *Géographie du Midi–Acquitain,* Paris, 1939
APCA, *Hommage à Joseph Faure, Abel Maumont, René Blondelle,* Paris, 1974
   Mémoires de Joseph Faure, Paris, 1975
   Cinquantenaire des Chambres d'Agriculture 1924–1974, Paris, n.d.
   Les Chambres d'Agriculture, Paris, 1984
Association Catholique de la Jeunesse Française, *Le problème de la terre,* Paris, 1908
Audibert, A., 'Parler des femmes', *Mondes Paysans – Sociétés Bretonnes,* 9, 59–75
Augé-Laribé, M., *L'Evolution de la France agricole,* Paris, 1912
   Le paysan français après la guerre, Paris, 1923
   Syndicats et coopératives agricoles, Paris, 1926
   La politique agricole de la France, Paris, 1950
   La Révolution agricole, Paris, 1955

Ayrignac, J., 'Parmi les Monts Joie: un jalon–numéro 100, *Revue de la Solidarité*, 100 (1978) pp 253–6

Baker, A. R. H., 'On the historical geography of France', *Journal of historical geography*, 6 (1980), pp. 69–76

'Ideological change and settlement continuity in the French countryside: the development of syndicalism in Loir-et-Cher', *Journal of historical geography*, 6 (1980), 163–78

'The infancy of France's first agricultural syndicate: the Syndicat des Agriculteurs de Loir-et-Cher 1881–1914', *Agricultural history review*, 34 (1986), pp 45–59

Barral, P., *Le département de l'Isère sous la Troisième République*, Paris, 1962

'Les mouvements agrariens de l'érè industrielle', *Revue historique*, 11 (1964), pp. 299–330

'Note historique sur l'emploi du terme paysan', *Etudes Rurales*, 4 (1966), pp. 72–80

Les Agrariens français de Méline à Pisani, Paris, 1968

'Les syndicats bretons de cultivateurs-cultivants', *Le Mouvement social*, 67 (1969), pp. 147–61

'Mouvements paysans et traditions agricoles en France après la Révolution Industrielle' in *Les mouvements paysans dans le Monde contemporain*, Geneva, 1973, pp. 150–63

Les sociétés rurales du XXème siècle, Paris, 1978

'Aspects régionaux de l'agrarisme français avant 1930', *Le Mouvement Social*, 67 (1969)

Baudoin, A. and Dautriat, L-R., *Alexis Gourvennec, paysan-directeur-général*, Paris, 1977

Berenson, E., 'Politics and the French peasantry: the debate continues', *Social history*, 12 (1987) pp. 213–29

Berger, S., *Peasants against politics: rural organisation in Brittany*, Cambridge, Mass. 1972

Berger, S., *(ed.), Organizing interests in western Europe: pluralism, corporatism and the transformation of politics*, Cambridge, 1981

Bernard, M., *Le syndicalisme paysan dans l'Allier*, Paris, 1910

Béteille, R., *La vie quotidienne en Rouergue avant 1914*, Paris, 1973

Les Aveyronnais – essai géographique sur l'espace humaine, Poitiers, 1974

Rouergue – terre d'exode, Paris, 1978

La France du Vide, Paris, 1981

La population et le social en France, Paris, 1986

Blanc, M., *Les Paysanneries françaises*, Paris, 1967

Bloch, M., *French rural history (translation of Les caractères originaux de l'histoire rurale française)*, London, 1966

Blum, J., *The end of the old order in rural Europe*, Princeton, 1978

Bodiguel, M., *Les paysans face au progrès*, Paris, 1975

Le rural en question, Paris, 1986

Bois, P., *Paysans de l'Ouest. Des structures économiques et sociales aux options politiques depuis l'époque révolutionnaire*, Paris, 1960

Boisseau, P., 'La participation des agriculteurs français aux programmes de développement économiques', *Sociologia Ruralis*, 14 (1974), 108–20

Bombal, J. and Chalmin, P., *L'Agro-Alimentaire*, Paris, 1980

Bonnault-Cornu, P., 'Metayeurs, propriétaires: un rapport social complexe (le cas de St Martin-de-Seignaux dans le Bas-Adour)', Thèse 3ème cycle, Faculté des Lettres, Université de Provence, 1984

Boulard, F., *Problèmes missionaires de la France rurale*, 2 vols., Paris, 1945

Boussard, I., *Vichy et la Corporation Paysanne*, Paris, 1980

  'Elections aux chambres d'agriculture et municipales: le vote des agriculteurs', *Revue Politique et Parlementaire*, 85 (1983), 79–94

  'Les arguments économiques en faveur du retour à la terre dans le discours agrarien', paper presented to the *Société française d'économie rurale*, Paris, September 1987

Bovet, E., 'Le syndicalisme agricole et la société industrielle', *Sociologia Ruralis*, VIII (1968), 142–60

Braque, R., 'Aux origines du syndicalisme dans les milieux ruraux du centre de la France,' *Le Mouvement Social*, 45 (1963), 79–116

Bras, G. le, *Etudes de sociologie religieuse*, 2 vols., (Paris, 1955)

  'L'Eglise et le village, (Paris, 1976)

Braudel, F. and Labrousse, E. (eds), *Histoire économique et sociale de la France*, 4, tomes 1 and 2, Paris, 1979–80

Braudel, F., *L'Identité de la France*, 3 vols., Paris, 1986

Burguière, A., *Bretons de Plozévet*, Paris, 1977

Cailluyer, J., *Regards sur l'histoire sociale des Landes*, Toulouse, 1983

Calmès, R., *Les campagnes des Ségalas et du Lévezou*, Rodez, 1980

Caniou, J., 'L'Enseignement agricole féminine', *Etudes rurales*, 92 (1983), 41–56

Caralp-Landon, R., *Les chemins de fer dans le Massif Central*, Paris, 1956

Caziot, P., *La Terre à la famille paysanne*, Paris, 1919

Centre National de la Recherche Scientifique, *L'Aubrac – étude éthnologique, linguistique, agronomique et économique d'un établissement humain*, 7 vols., Paris, 1971–9

Centre National de la Recherche Scientifique, *La Grande Lande – histoire naturelle et géographie historique*, Paris, 1981

Centre National de la Recherche Scientifique, *140 cartes sur la France rurale*, Paris, 1984

Cépède, M., *Agriculture et alimentation durant la IIème guerre mondiale*, Paris, 1961

Cépède, M., 'Le monde paysan dans la société française', *Sociologia Ruralis*, XII (1972) pp. 42–54

Chalmin, P., 'La mutualité dans l'Adour', unpub. man., 1983

Chapuis, R., *Les ruraux français*, Paris, 1986

Chayanov, A., *The theory of peasant economy*, Homewood, Illinois, 1966

Chevalier, L., *Les Paysans*, Paris, 1947

Chiva, I. and Rambaud, P., *Les Etudes rurales en France*, Paris, 1972

Cholvy, G., *Géographie religieuse de l'Hérault contemporaine*, Paris, 1968

Chombart de Lauwe, J., *Pour une agriculture organisée: Danemark et Bretagne*, Paris, 1949

  'Aspects économiques de l'Utilisation en Commun du materiel agricole', *Bulletin de la Société Française d'Economie Rurale*, 4 (1952), 122–86

  L'Aventure agricole de la France, Paris, 1979

Clavaud, F., Flavien, J., Lajoinie, A., Perceval, L., *Quelle agriculture pour la France?*, Paris, 1974

Cleary, M. C., 'Le premier syndicalisme agricole aveyronnais', *Revue du Rouergue*, 33 (1979), pp. 44–54

'The Plough and the Cross: peasant unions in south-west France', *Agricultural history review*, 30 (1982), pp. 129–36

'Agricultural syndicates in Aveyron (s.w. France) 1880–1960', Ph.D. thesis, Faculty of Geography and Geology, University of Cambridge, 1983

'The changing character of agricultural syndicates in Aveyron 1944–60', *Sociologia ruralis*, 25 (1985), 118–29

'Patterns of transhumance in Languedoc', *Geography*, 71 (1986), pp. 25–33

'Priest, squire and peasant: the development of agricultural syndicates in southwest France 1900–1914', *European history quarterly*, 17 (1987), 145–63

Cloarec, J., 'Un exemple d'intervention de l'Etat: le financement public de l'agriculture', *Etudes rurales*, 69 (1978) pp. 5–25

Clout, H. D., *The geography of post-war France*, London, 1972

Agriculture in France on the eve of the Railway Age, London, 1980

The land of France 1815–1914, London, 1983

Clout, H. D. (ed.), *Themes in the historical geography of France*, London, 1977

Cobban, A., *A history of modern France*, 3 vols., Harmondsworth, 1961

Colson, R., *Un paysan face à l'avenir rural – la JAC et la modernisation de l'agriculture*, Paris, 1976

Corbin, A., *Archaisme et modernité en Limousin au XIX siècle*, 2 vols., Paris, 1974

Courtin, A., *Les étapes d'une organisation professionnelle – les Congrès nationaux des syndicats agricoles*, Paris, 1920

Coutrut, E., and Dreyfus, F., *Les Forces religieuses dans la société française*, Paris, 1965

Cox, G., Lowe, P., Winter, M., 'From state direction to self-regulation: the historical development of corporatism in British agriculture', *Policy and politics*, 14 (1986), pp. 475–90

Cox, G., Lowe, P., Winter, M. (eds.), *Agriculture: people and policies*, London, 1986.

Crolais, A-M., *L'Agricultrice*, Paris, 1982

Cuisenier, J., 'Fonctions économiques des organisations et des administrations agricoles en France', *Etudes rurales*, 11 (1966) pp. 5–71

Dalton, G., 'Peasantries in anthropology and history', *Current anthropology*, 13 (1972), 385–415

Dansette, A., *Histoire religieuse de la France contemporaine sous la Troisième République*, Paris, 1951

Daucé, P. and Léon, Y., 'L'Evolution de l'agriculture Bretonne depuis 1850', *Sciences Agronomiques-Rennes 2*, (1982)

Dauzat, A., *Le Village et le paysan en France*, Paris, 1941

Debatisse, M., *La Révolution silencieuse: le combat des paysans*, Paris, 1962

Debatisse, M., *Le Projet paysan*, Paris, 1983

Delorme, M. and Tavernier, Y., *Les Paysans français et l'Europe*, Paris, 1969

Delorme, H., 'Le Rôle des forces paysannes dans l'élaboration de la politique agricole commune', *Revue française de science politique*, 19 (1969), pp. 356–91

Delorme, H. and Tubiana, L., 'L'Elargissement vers le sud du Marché Commun Agricole', *Revue française de science politique*, 28 (1978), pp. 698–716

Désert, G. *Une société rurale au XIXème siècle: les paysans du Calvados 1815–1895*, Paris, 1975

Dion-Salitot, M. and Dion, M., *La Crise d'une société villageoise – les paysans du Jura français*, Paris, 1972

Documentation Française, *Les Chambres d'Agriculture*, Paris, 1965

Dorgères, H., *Haut les fourches!*, Paris, 1935

Au XXème siècle – 10 ans de jacquerie paysanne, Paris, 1959

Dorner, P., *Cooperative and commune*, Wisconsin, 1977

Dovring, F., *Land and labour in the 20th century*, The Hague, 1965

'The transformation of European agriculture' in *Cambridge economic history of Europe*, 6, pt II, Cambridge, 1965

Duby, G. and Wallon, A. (eds.), *Histoire de la France rurale*, 4 vols., Paris, 1976

Dugrand, A., *Villes et campagnes en Bas-Languedoc*, Paris, 1963

Dumont, R., *Nouveaux voyages dans les campagnes françaises*, Paris, 1977

Dupeux, G., *French society 1789–1970*, London, 1976

Duport, E., *Les engrais et les syndicats agricoles*, Lyon, 1889

Durand, A., *La vie rurale dans les Massifs volcaniques des Dores, du Cézallier, du Cantal et de l'Aubrac*, Aurillac, 1946

Durupt, M-J., *Les mouvements d'Action Catholique – facteur d'évolution du monde rural*, Paris, 1973

Dyer, C., *Population and society in twentieth-century France*, London, 1978

Enjalbert, H., *A travers le Ségala*, Rodez, 1950

Ainsi naquit Baraqueville, Rodez, 1975

Enjalbert, H., (ed.), *Histoire du Rouergue*, Toulouse, 1979

Ennew, J., Hirst, P. and Tribe, K., 'Peasantry as an economic category', Journal of peasant studies, 4 (1977), pp. 295–322

Fabre, D. and Lacroix, J., *La Vie quotidienne des paysans du Languedoc au 19 ème siècle*, Paris, 1973

Fabre, D. and Lacroix, J., *Communautés du Sud*, 2 vols., Paris, 1975

Faucon, R., 'Les Origines du syndicalisme agricole dans la région du Nord', *Revue du Nord*, 48 (1966), pp. 67–90

Faure, M., 'La Formation de promotion, l'exemple de l'institut de formation pour les cadres paysans, *Sociologia ruralis*, 3 (1962), pp. 360–8

Les Paysans dans la société française, Paris, 1966

Fauvet, J. and Mendras, H. (eds.), *Les paysans et la politique dans la France contemporaine*, Paris, 1958

FNSEA, *Cent ans de syndicalisme agricole*, Paris, 1984

Fel, A., *Les Hautes terres du Massif Central – tradition paysanne et économie agricole*, Paris, 1962

Flatrès, P., *Géographie rurale de quatre contrées celtiques: Irlande, Galles, Cornwall et Man*, Rennes, 1957

'La deuxième Révolution Agricole en Finistère', *Etudes rurales*, 8 (1963), pp. 5–55

Forget, E., *Le serment de l'unité paysanne*, Paris, 1982

Forster, O. and Ranum, O. (eds), *Rural society in France*, Baltimore, 1977

Franklin, S. H., 'Reflections on the peasantry', *Pacific Viewpoint*, 3 (1962), pp. 1–26
'Systems of production – systems of appropriation', *Pacific viewpoint*, 6 (1965), pp. 145–66
The European peasantry: the final phase, London, 1969
Rural societies, London, 1971
Frémont, A., *L'élevage en basse Normandie, étude géographique*, 2 vols., Caen, 1967
Friedmann. G., (ed.), *Villes et campagnes. Civilisation urbaine et civilisation rurale en France*, Paris, 1953
Furet, F. and Ozouf, J., *Lire et ecrire*, Paris, 1977
Gailhard-Bancel, H. de, *Le Syndicalisme agricole aux champs et au parlement*, Paris, 1929
Garrier, G., 'L'Union du Sud-Est des syndicats agricoles avant 1914', *Le mouvement social*, 67 (1969), 17–38
Paysans du Beaujolais et du Lyonnais 1800–1970, 2 vols., Grenoble, 1973
Gavignaud, G., *Propriétaires viticulteurs en Roussillon: structures, conjonctures, société 18–20 siècles*, Paris, 1983
Gazave, J., *La Terre ne ment pas – introduction à une physiocratie nouvelle*, Villefranche-de-Rouergue, 1940
George, P., *La Campagne – le fait rural à travers le monde*, Paris, 1956
Gerault, L., *Petit catechisme corporatif paysan*, Paris, 1943
Gervais, M., Servolin, C. and Weil, J., *Une France sans paysans*, Paris, 1966
Goguel, F., *Géographie des élections françaises sous la Troisième et Quatrième République*, Paris, 1970
Golob, E., *The Méline tarrif: French agriculture and nationalist economic policy*, New York, 1944
Grantham, J., 'The diffusion of the new husbandry in northern France', *Journal of economic history* (1978), pp. 311–37
Gratton, P., *Les luttes de classes dans les campagnes, 1870–1921*, Paris, 1971
Les paysans françaises contre les agrariens, Paris, 1972
Grenadou, E. and Prévost, A., *Grenadou, paysan français*, Paris, 1966
Grigg, D. B., *The dynamics of agricultural change*, London, 1982
Groupe de Sociologie Rurale, *Atlas de la France rurale*, Paris, 1968
Gueslin, A., *Les Origines du Crédit Agricole 1840–1914*, Paris, 1978
Le Crédit Mutuel. De la caisse rurale à la banque sociale, Strasbourg, 1982
Histoire des Crédits Agricoles, 2 vols., Paris, 1984
'Pouvoir et conflits de pouvoir dans des structures de sociabilité organisée: le cas de la mutualité de crédit (fin XIX-première moitie XX)', *Sociabilité, pouvoirs et société*, Rennes 1987, pp. 265–76
Guillaume, F., *Le Pain de la liberté*, Paris, 1983
Guillaumin, E., *La Vie d'un simple*, Paris, 1904
Halévy, D., *Visites aux paysans du centre*, 3rd edn, Paris, 1978
Hanley, D., Kerr, A. and Waites, N., *Contemporary France – politics and society since 1945*, London, 1979
Hardy, Y. and Gabey, E., *Dossier L comme Larzac*, Paris, 1974
Higgonet, P., *Pont-de-Montvert*, Cambridge, Mass., 1971
Houée, P., *Coopération et organisations agricoles françaises*, 2 vols., Paris, 1969
Les Etapes du développement rural, 2 vols., Paris, 1972
Quel avenir pour les ruraux?, Paris, 1974

'L'animation du développement en milieu rural: un nouveau pouvoir?', *Etudes rurales*, 65 (1977), pp. 129–37

House, J., *France: an applied geography*, London, 1978

Hubscher, R., *L'Agriculture et la société rurale dans le département du Pas-de-Calais du milieu du XIX siècle à 1914*, Paris, 1979

'La Petite exploitation en France: reproduction et compétitivité (fin XIX siècle – début XX siècle)', *Annales economies, sociétés, civilisations*, 40 (1985), 3–34

Institut International d'Agriculture, *Enquête monographiques sur la coopération agricole dans quelques pays*, Rome, 1911

Isambert, F. A. and Terrenoire, J-P., *Atlas de la pratique religieuse des catholiques en France d'après les enquêtes diocésaines et urbaines suscitées et rassemblées par F. Boulard*, Paris, 1980

Jarriot, J., 'La Société d'Agriculture du département de l'Aveyron au début du XIX siècle', *Procès-Verbaux de la Société des Lettres Sciences et Arts de l'Aveyron*, 42 (1977), pp. 26–38

JAC – MRJC, *50 ans d'animation rurale* (n.d., n.p.)

Jollivet, M., *Sociétés paysannes ou luttes de classes au village*, Paris, 1974

Jollivet, M. and Mendras, H. (eds.) *Les Collectivités rurales françaises*, Paris, 1971

Jones, P. M., 'Parish, Seigneurie and the community of inhabitants in southern central France during the eighteenth and nineteenth centuries', *Past and present*, 91 (1981), pp. 74–108

Politics and rural society – the southern Massif Central c. 1750–1880, Cambridge, 1985

'La vie religieuse dans la France villageoise au XIX siècle', *Annales economies, sociétés, civilisations*, 42 (1987), pp. 91–115

Jouve, P., *Un mouvement d'organisation professionel – le Plateau Central*, Aurillac, 1921

Judt, T., *Socialism in Provence 1871–1914*, Cambridge, 1979

Juillard, E., *La vie rurale dans la plaine de Basse Alsace*, Paris, 1953

Julien-Labruyère, F., *Paysans charentais: histoire des campagnes d'Aunis, Saintonge et bas-Angoumois*, 2 vols., La Rochelle, 1982

Kayser, B., 'Subversion des villages français', *Etudes rurales*, 93–4 (1984), pp. 295–324

Kedward, H. R., *Resistance in Vichy France*, Oxford, 1978

Keeler, J. T., 'The politics of official unionism in French agriculture 1958–1976: a study of the corporatist bases of FNSEA hegemony', Ph.D. thesis, Dept of Government, University of Harvard, 1978

'Corporatism and official union hegemony: the case of French agricultural syndicalism' in Berger, S., *Organising interests*, pp. 185–208

Kemp, T., *Economic forces in French history*, London, 1971

The French economy, 1913–1939, London, 1972

Keranguéven, Y., *Les Paysans – idéologies et sociétés*, Paris, 1977

Kindleberger, C., *Economic growth in France and Britain 1851–1950*, Cambridge, Mass., 1964

The world in depression, 1929–1939, London, 1973

Klatzmann, J., L'Agriculture française, Paris, 1978

Géographie agricole de la France, Paris, 1979

Ladurie, le Roy, *Les Paysans du Languedoc*, 2 vols., Paris, 1966

Lagrave, R-M., 'Le travail agraire dans le roman français contemporain', *Sociologia Ruralis*, 16 (1976), pp. 85–102

'Bilan critique des recherches sur les agricultrices en France', *Etudes Rurales*, 92 (1983), pp. 9–40

Lajoie-Mazenc, R., *Marcel Bruel et le défi agricole*, Villefranche-de-Rouergue, 1976

Lambert, B., *Les Paysans dans la lutte des classes*, Paris, 1971

Lambert, Y., 'Développement agricole et Action Catholique', *Sociologia Ruralis*, 18 (1978), pp. 245–54

Landsberger, H. (ed.), *Rural protest: peasant movements and social change*, London, 1974

Lanneau, G., 'Aspects de la mutation psycho-sociologique des paysans français', *Sociologia ruralis*, 10 (1970), pp. 120–42

Las Cases, P. de, *Petit manuel pratique rural*, Paris, 1931

Ce n'est rien, rien qu'une vie, Mende, 1961

Lauga, L., *CNJA – le pari des jeunes agriculteurs*, Paris, 1971

Lenco, M., 'Une nouvelle classification des exploitations agricoles françaises', *Etudes rurales*, 57 (1975) pp. 7–34

Leveau, R., 'Le Syndicat de Chartres 1885–1914', *Le mouvement social*, 67 (1969), pp. 61–78

Livet, R., *Habitat rural et structures agraires en Basse-Provence*, Aix-en-Provence, 1962

Livre d'Or de la Société d'Encouragement aux Institutions Rurales du Plateau Central, Rodez, 1912

Maclouf, P., (ed.), *La Pauvrété dans le monde rural*, Paris, 1986

Magraw, R., *France 1815–1914 – the bourgeois century*, Oxford, 1983

Maho, J., 'Modernisation technique en milieu rural', *Etudes rurales*, 16 (1965), pp. 66–78

Maître, J., 'Les prêtres Catholiques devant l'évolution économique des campagnes françaises', *Sociologia ruralis*, 8 (1968), pp. 58–78

Mallet, R., *Nécessité d'un retour à la terre. Etude d'économie comparée*, Paris, 1941

Mallet, S., *Les paysans contre le passé*, Paris, 1962

'A propos de syndicalisme agricole Finistérien', *Etudes rurales*, 8 (1963), pp. 56–61

Mann, S. and Dickinson, J., 'Obstacles to the development of a capitalist agriculture', *Journal of peasant studies*, 5 (1978), pp. 466–81

Maresca, S., 'Ebauche d'une analyse sociologique des élites paysannes – cinq biographies de dirigéants paysans', *Etudes rurales*, 76 (1979), pp. 51–81

Maresca, S., *Les Dirigeants paysans*, Paris, 1983

Marres, P., *Les Grands causses*, 2 vols. (Tours, 1936)

Marsden, T., Munton, J., Whatmore, S., Little, J., 'Towards a political economy of capitalist agriculture: a British perspective', *International journal of urban and regional research*, 10 (1986), pp. 498–521

Maspetiol, R., *L'Ordre éternel des champs – essai sur l'histoire, l'économie et les valeurs de la paysannerie*, Paris, 1946

Mathe, R., *Emile Guillaumin, l'homme et la terre et l'homme des lettres*, Paris, 1966

Mayeur, J-M., 'Géographie de la résistance aux inventaires (fév-mars 1906)', *Annales economies, sociétés, civilisations*, 20 (1966), pp. 1259–72

Mayeur, J-M., *La Séparation de l'Eglise et de l'Etat*, Paris, 1966
McManners, J., *Church and State in France, 1870–1914*, London, 1972
Mendras, H., *Etude de sociologie rurale: Novis et Virgin*, Paris, 1953
  'Les organisations agricoles et la politique', *Revue française de Science Politique*, 5 (1955), 736–60
  Les Paysans et la modernisation de l'Agriculture, Paris, 1958
  La Fin des paysans, Paris, 1967
  Sociologie de la campagne française, Paris, 1971
  Sociétés Paysannes, Paris, 1976
  La Fin des paysans. Suivi d'une reflexion sur La Fin des Paysans vingt ans après, Paris, 1984
Mendras, H. and Tavernier, Y., 'Les Manifestations de juin 1961', *Revue française de Science Politique*, 12 (1962), 647–71
Mendras, H. and Tavernier, Y. (eds.), *Terre, paysans et politique*, 2 vols., Paris, 1969
Merlin, P., *L'Exode rural*, Paris, 1971
Mesliand, C., 'Le Syndicat agricole Vauclusien 1887–1939', *Le Mouvement social*, 17 (1969), pp. 39–60
Meynaud, J., *La Révolte paysanne*, Paris, 1963
Meynier, A., *Ségalas, Lévezou, Chataîgneraie*, Aurillac, 1931
  Les Paysages agraires, Paris, 1958
Milward, A., *The new order and the French economy*, Oxford, 1970
Ministère de l'Agriculture, *Cent ans de Ministère de l'Agriculture*, Paris, n.d.
Montbron, H. de, *L'Action Syndicale dans l'Agriculture*, Paris, 1965
Mora, C., 'Les Chambres d'Agriculture: représentation et défense des intérêts agricoles 1924–1940', Thèse de Doctorat, Université de Bordeaux, 1967
Morin, E., *Plodémet – report from a French village*, London, 1971
Moscovici, M., 'Le changement social en milieu rural et le rôle des femmes', *Revue française de sociologie*, 1 (1960), pp. 314–22
MODEF, *Le Livre vert ou comment ruiner l'agriculture française*, Angoulême, 1986
Muller, P., 'Comment les idées deviennent-ils politiques? La naissance d'une nouvelle idéologie paysanne en France 1945–1965', *Revue française de Science Politique*, 32 (1982), pp. 90–108
Naylor, E. L., 'Les réformes sociales et structurales de l'agriculture dans le Finistère – l'activité de FASASA 1962–1973', *Etudes rurales*, 62 (1976), pp. 89–111
  Socio-structural policy in French agriculture, O'Dell Memorial Monograph 18, University of Aberdeen, 1985
Newell, W. H., 'The agricultural revolution in 19th century France', *Journal of economic history*, 33 (1973), pp. 697–731
Noilhan, H., *La République des paysans*, Aurillac, 1932
Ogburn, W. and Jaffé, W., *The economic development of post-war France*, New York, 1929
Ogden, P. E., 'Migration, marriage and the collapse of traditional peasant society in France' in White, P. and Woods, R. (eds.), *The geographical impact of migration*, London, 1980, pp. 145–60
Ogden, P. E. and Huss, M.-M., 'Demography and pronatalism in France in the nineteenth and twentieth centuries', *Journal of historical geography*, 8 (1982), pp. 283–98

Orry, P., 'Le Dorgèrisme. Institution et discours d'une colère paysanne', *Revue d'histoire moderne et contemporaine*, (1975), pp. 168–90

Painvin, R.-M., *Un métier . . . Agricultrice*, Paris, 1970

Papy, L., *Atlas et géographie de la France moderne – le Midi–Acquitain*, Paris, 1978

Parodi, M., *L'Economie et la société française depuis 1945*, Paris, 1981

Pautard, J., *Les Disparités régionales dans la croissance de l'agriculture française*, Paris, 1965

Paysans, 'La Coopération 1976–1980 – ses chances et ses atouts', pp. 115–16 (1975/1976)

Pénélope, Pour l'histoire des femmes, 'Numéro spécial – femme et terre', 7 (1982)

Perrin, L., 'L'APCA', *Chambres d'Agriculture* (1980)

Petit, O., 'La naissance et le développement du syndicalisme et de la mutualité dans le département de l'Aisne entre les deux guerres', Thèse de Doctorat, University of Paris, 6, 1986

Peyon, J., 'L'Essor des coopératives agro-alimentaires dans les années soixante-soixante-dix en France', Paper presented to the *Société française d'économie rurale*, Paris, September 1987

  La Coopération agricole en France – étude géographique des grands organismes coopératifs, Paris, 1983

Pinchemel, P., *Structures sociales et dépopulation rurale dans les campagnes picardes de 1836 à 1936*, Paris, 1957

  France: a geographical survey, London, 1969

Pingaud, M.-C., *Paysans en Bourgogne – les gens de Minot*, Paris, 1978

Pitaud, H., *Le Pain de la terre*, Paris, 1982

Pitié, J., *Exode rurale et migrations internes en France – l'exemple de la Vienne et du Poitou-Charentes*, Paris, 1976

Ponceau, R. de, *Petite histoire de l'ACJF*, Paris, 1929

Pounds, N. J., *An historical geography of Europe 1800–1914*, Cambridge, 1985

Prault, L., *Mort et Résurrection des Chambres d'Agriculture 1940–1952*, Paris, 1978

Price, R., *The modernization of rural France: communications networks and agricultural market structures in nineteenth-century France*, London, 1983

  A social history of nineteenth-century France, London, 1987

Prugnaud, L., *Les Etapes du syndicalisme agricole en France*, Paris, 1963

Quiers-Valette, S., 'Les Causes économiques du mécontentement des agriculteurs français en 1961', *Revue française de Science Politique*, 3 (1962), pp. 555–98.

Rambaud, P. 'Révoltes et révolution paysanne dans la France contemporaine', *Sociologia ruralis*, 4 (1963), 101–15

  Sociologie rurale, Paris, 1976

  'Crise économique, initiative collective et développement', *Sociologia ruralis*, 17 (1977), 124–40

Redfield, R., *Peasant society and culture; an anthropological approach to civilisation*, Chicago, 1956

Rinaudo, Y., 'Les paysans du Var (fin du XIX siècle – début XX siècle)' Thèse de doctorat, University of Aix-en-Provence, 1978

  'Le Syndicalisme agricole dans le Var', *Le mouvement social*, 112 (1980), pp. 79–95

  'Un travail en plus: les paysans d'un métier à l'autre', *Annales, economies, sociétés civilisations*, 42 (1987), pp. 283–302

Rocquigny, H. de, *Les Syndicats agricoles et leur oeuvre*, Paris, 1900

Rollet, H. *Sur le chantier social – l'action sociale des Catholiques en France 1870–1940*, Lyon, 1955

L'Action sociale des Catholiques en France, 1871–1901, Paris, 1958

Romatif, F., *L'Engagement des Chrétiens dans les institutions du monde rural*, Paris, 1952

Roy, P. le, *L'Avenir de l'Agriculture Française*, Paris, 1975

Saars, M. de, *Soixante ans de syndicalisme agricole dans le département de l'Aisne*, Laon, 1952

Salleron, L., *Naissance de l'Etat corporatif: dix ans du syndicalisme paysan*, Paris, 1942

La Charte paysanne, Le Mans, 1943

La Corporation paysanne, Paris, 1943

Samuel, R. (ed.), *Village life and labour*, London, 1975

Sauvy, A., *Histoire économique de la France entre les deux guerres*, 3 vols., Paris, 1965–73

Ségalen, M., *Love and power in the peasant family (trans. of Mari et femme dans la société paysanne)*, Oxford, 1983

Shanin, T., (ed.), *Peasants and peasant societies*, Harmondsworth, 1971

Silvestre, C., *L'Union du Sud-Est des Syndicats Agricoles*, 2 vols., Lyon, 1900

Soboul, A., 'The French rural community in the 18th and 19th centuries', *Past and present*, 10 (1956), pp. 78–95

Sokoloff, S., 'Land tenure and political tendency in rural France: the case of sharecropping', *European studies review*, 10 (1980), 357–82

Tavernier, Y., 'Le Syndicalisme paysan et la politique agricole du gouvernement (juin 1958–avril 1962), *Revue française de Science Politique*, 12 (1962), pp. 599–646

'Le Syndicalisme paysan et la V République (1962–1965)', *Revue française de Science Politique*, XVI (1965), pp. 839–912

La FNSEA, Paris, 1965

'Le Mouvement de coordination et de défense des exploitations agricoles familiales', *Revue française de Science Politique*, 18 (1968), pp. 542–63

Le Syndicalisme paysan, Paris, 1969

Tavernier, Y., Gervais, M. and Servolin, C., (eds.), *L'Univers politique des paysans dans la France contemporaine*, Paris, 1972

Tello, F., 'Données sur l'origine et l'implantation du MODEF', *Cahiers d'histoire de l'Institut Maurice Thorez* (1978), pp. 39–82

Thabault, R., *Education and change in a village community*, London, 1971

Tilly, C., *The Vendée*, Cambridge, Mass., 1964

The rebellious century 1830–1930, London, 1974

Toulat, P., Bougeard, A., and Templier, J., *Les Chrétiens dans le monde rural*, Paris, 1962

Tour du Pin, R. de, *Vers un ordre social chrétien*, Paris, 1907

Toussaint, A., *L'Union Centrale des Syndicats Agricoles – Ses idées directrices*, Paris, 1920

Toussaint, A., 'La Nouvelle bourgeoisie paysanne', *Revue des deux mondes*, 1928, pp. 925–41

Tucoo-Chala, J., 'Introduction à l'histoire du mouvement syndical des gemmeurs: l'action de Charles Prat', *Bulletin de la Société de Bordas*, 394 (1984), pp. 375–95

Tuppen, J. N., *The economic geography of France*, London, 1983

Union Centrale des Syndicats Agricoles des Agriculteurs de France, *XI Congrès National-Rodez*, Paris, 1922

Union Nationale des Syndicats Agricoles, *Vers la Corporation Agricole*, Paris, 1934 *Congrès Syndical Paysan – Caen 1937*, Paris, 1937

Vergopoulos, K., 'Capitalism and peasant productivity', *Journal of peasant studies*, 5 (1978), 446–65

Vial, A., *La foi d'un paysan. L'impasse de l'ACJF*, Paris, 1967

Vidalenc, J., *Les Peuples des campagnes*, Paris, 1971

Virieu, H. de, *La Fin d'une agriculture*, Paris, 1965

Vogue, L. de, *Emile Duport, la leçon de ses oeuvres*, Lyon, 1909

Walter, G., *Histoire des paysans de France*, Paris, 1963

Warner, G., *The winegrowers of France and the government since 1875*, New York, 1960

Warriner, D., *The economics of peasant farming*, Oxford, 1939

Weber, E., *Peasants into Frenchmen: the modernization of rural France 1870–1914*, London, 1977

Weber, E., 'Le Travail hors de l'usine. Bricolage et double activité', *Cahiers d'Economie et Sociologie Rurale*, 3 (1986)

Wolf, E. R., *Peasants*, Englewood Cliffs, NJ, 1966

Winter, M., 'Agrarian class structure and family farming' in Bradley, T. and Lowe, P. (eds.), *Locality and rurality: economy and society in rural regions*, Norwich, 1984, pp. 115–45

Wright, G., *Rural revolution in France*, Stanford, 1964

Wylie, L., *Village in the Vaucluse*, Cambridge, Mass., 1974

Zeldin, T. *France 1848–1945*, 2 vols., Oxford, 1973–8.

Index